John H. Thompson

HOOKED ON WORLD HISTORY!

101 Ready-to-Use Puzzle Activities Based on Civilizations From Prehistoric Times to the Present

THE CENTER FOR APPLIED RESEARCH IN EDUCATION
West Nyack, New York 10994

Library of Congress Cataloging-in-Publication Data

Thompson, John H.
Hooked on world history: 101 ready-to-use puzzle activities based on world history from prehistoric times to the present/John H. Thompson.
p. cm.
ISBN 0-87628-417-9 (paper).—ISBN 0-87628-414-4 (spiral)
1. History—Miscellanea. 2. Crossword puzzles. I. Title.
D23.T46 1996
909—dc20 95-51550
CIP

Many of the illustrations are reproductions from the Dover Clip Art and Dover Pictorial Series.

Printed in the United States of America

10 9 8 7 6 5 4 3 2 1

ISBN 0-87628-414-4(S) ISBN 0-87628-417-9(P)

THE CENTER FOR APPLIED RESEARCH IN EDUCATION
West Nyack, NY 10994
A Simon & Schuster Company

On the World Wide Web at http://www.phdirect.com

Prentice-Hall International (UK) Limited, *London*
Prentice-Hall of Australia Pty. Limited, *Sydney*
Prentice-Hall Canada Inc., *Toronto*
Prentice-Hall Hispanoamericana, S.A., *Mexico*
Prentice-Hall of India Private Limited, *New Delhi*
Prentice-Hall of Japan, Inc., *Tokyo*
Simon & Schuster Asia Pte. Ltd., *Singapore*
Editora Prentice-Hall do Brasil, Ltda., *Rio de Janeiro*

About This Resource

This resource can help you meet one of the daily challenges that faces any teacher today—the ability to create interest in lessons that are informative and exciting for your students, but not time-consuming for you to prepare. World history trivia is a unique way to grab students' interest in the history of the world and all the important events that occurred from prehistoric times to the present. Students love to learn these unusual facts about world history and geography. Specifically, the goals of *Hooked on World History!* are:

- to save the instructor valuable time in lesson preparation
- to provide information and ideas that challenge all students
- to enliven historical facts with activities that are enjoyable and meaningful to students
- to encourage correct spelling and vocabulary mastery

With this collection of ready-to-use puzzle activities, you can spark involvement in students of varying abilities while shortening your lesson planning time by hours!

Included are numerous reproducible puzzle activities appropriate for students in grades 7–12. The puzzles cover information about countries and cultures around the globe from the prehistoric period to the 1990s—the great civilizations and empires, key shifts in world power, wars and revolutions, and turning points in science and philosophy. The puzzles also cover the people who shaped world history—the great explorers and scientists, rulers and statesmen, writers, artists, and composers, and religious leaders—from British kings and queens to African nationalists and Japanese shoguns.

For quick access and easy use, the puzzles are presented in chronological order and numbered consecutively. Each puzzle is ready to be photocopied as many times as you need it for use with individual students, small groups, or an entire class. Moreover, complete answer keys are provided at the end of the book. You may want to keep these at your desk, or photocopy and place them at a central location if you wish to permit students to check their own work.

You'll find the activities in this teaching resource have many possible uses. For example, they may serve as homework assignments, extra-credit activities, make-up tests, emergency or daily lesson plans, textbook reviews, or individual workbooks. Few students can resist the challenge of solving puzzles; they motivate unexcited and less capable students and provide excellent reinforcement for more advanced students who finish other class assignments ahead of schedule. They also offer a great break in the daily routine.

I have found the most productive uses of these activities are to arouse students' interest at the beginning of a history unit and to review information at the end of a lesson. Students learn while having fun. Historical people and events take on new life and meaning when they become part of a puzzle!

John H. Thompson

About the Author

John Thompson received his B.A. in English and History from East Tennessee State University in Johnson City. He has been a teacher in the public schools of Tennessee, Arizona, and Virginia for over 20 years and has taught English, American Government, Economics, Geography, International Relations, World History, and United States History. His students have been diverse also, ranging in level from remedial eighth graders to adults and coming from many ethnic groups. He is a member of the National and Virginia Councils for the Social Studies.

Mr. Thompson is also the author of *Hooked on American History!—101 Crossword Puzzle Activities Based on U.S. History from Pre-exploration to the 1990's, Hooked on Presidents!—75 Ready-to-Use Puzzle Activities Based on American Presidents from 1789 to 1994,* and *State Smart!—Over 130 Ready-to-Use Puzzle Activities Based on the Geography & History of the 50 United States,* all published by The Center.

Contents

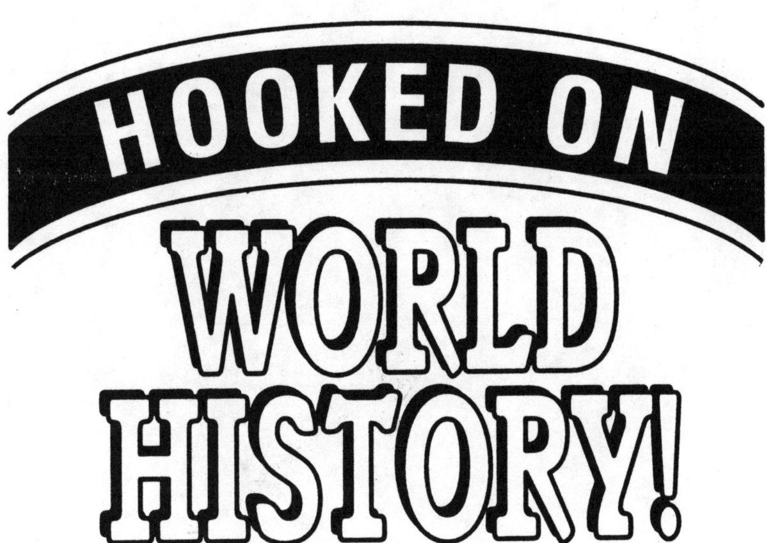
HOOKED ON
WORLD
HISTORY!

Name ______________________________ Date ____________________

1. PREHISTORIC CULTURES

ACROSS:

1. The scientific name for "thinking man" or "modern man"
2. Method of dating ancient remains
3. Scientific name for the Old Stone Age
4. The period before written records
5. A network of people who interact with one another
6. Common name for the Neolithic Age
7. Common name for the Paleolithic Age
8. Probably the first animals to be domesticated
9. The remains left by ancient peoples
10. The scientific name for the New Stone Age
11. Tools and the skills to use them
12. The glacial period of history
13. The way of life that a group of people develop and pass on to their children
14. Scientists who study the remains of ancient peoples
15. Location of some ancient cave paintings in Spain
16. The transition from Paleolithic Age to Neolithic Age was caused by this
17. Scientists who study the behavior of ancient peoples
18. The belief in many gods
19. People who move in search of food

2. CIVILIZATION IN SOUTHWEST ASIA

ACROSS: ______

1. King of the Persians
2. Ancient form of writing using wedge-shaped symbols
3. An agreement between man and God
4. River in Mesopotamia
5. The builders of Babylon
6. Civilization that built the Royal Road
7. Sumerian temple
8. Another river in Mesopotamia
9. A form of trade without the use of money
10. A skilled worker who makes goods by hand
11. A symbol used in ancient writing
12. The science of the heavenly bodies
13. Ancient professional writers
14. Inventors of the alphabet
15. Nickname of Mesopotamia
16. A messenger sent to reveal God's will
17. Author of an ancient written law code
18. The belief in more than one god
19. King of the Chaldeans
20. The first monotheistic culture
21. The ability to read and write
22. An ancient Hebrew prophet
23. The belief in only one God
24. The builders of the world's largest library in 650 B.C.
25. An ancient Persian prophet
26. Mesopotamia today
27. The world's first civilization

Name ______________________ Date ______________________

2. Civilization in Southwest Asia

1 C
2 I
3 V
4 I
5 L
6 I
7 Z
8 A
9 T
10 I
11 O
12 N

13 I
14 N

15 S
16 O
17 U
18 T
19 H
20 W
21 E
22 S
23 T

24 A
25 S
26 I
27 A

3. THE ANCIENT EGYPTIANS

ACROSS:

1. British archaeologist who discovered King Tut's tomb
2. Frenchman who deciphered hieroglyphics
3. The best example of hieroglyphics
4. Rapids on the Nile River
5. A series of rulers from a single family
6. A decorated casket designed by the ancient Egyptians
7. The ancient Egyptian method of preserving the body for the afterlife
8. A female pharaoh of ancient Egypt
9. Peninsula east of Egypt
10. A sacred symbol of ancient Egypt
11. The last great pharaoh of ancient Egypt
12. The system of writing designed by the ancient Egyptians
13. The source of paper used by the ancient Egyptians
14. Immense structures built by the ancient Egyptians as tombs for the pharaohs
15. The capital of ancient Egypt
16. Egypt's river
17. Another sacred symbol of ancient Egypt
18. A famous child pharaoh of ancient Egypt
19. The ancient Egyptian god of the dead

Name ______________________________ Date ______________________

3. The Ancient Egyptians

Clue	Letter
1	T
2	H
3	E
4	A
5	N
6	C
7	I
8	E
9	N
10	T
11	E
12	G
13	Y
14	P
15	T
16	I
17	A
18	N
19	S

4. ANCIENT INDIA AND CHINA

ACROSS:

1. Rulers of ancient India
2. System of writing designed in ancient India
3. Rebirth of the soul into another life form
4. River in northwest India
5. Nickname of the Yellow River in China
6. Holy river of the Hindus in India
7. Rigid social groups determined by birth in India
8. Major desert in China
9. Seasonal winds bringing rain or dryness in India
10. Siddhartha Gautama
11. Buddha's word for release from pain and selfishness
12. Route through the mountains in northwest India
13. Highest group in Indian society
14. Ancient method used to predict the future
15. Mountains in northwest India
16. Philosopher of ancient China
17. Major desert in India
18. Major religion in India
19. Northeastern area of China
20. Mountains separating India from the rest of Asia

Name ________________________ Date ________________

4. Ancient India and China

1 A
2 N
3 C
4 I
5 E
6 N
7 T

8 I
9 N
10 D
11 I
12 A

13 A
14 N
15 D

16 C
17 H
18 I
19 N
20 A

5. THE MEDITERRANEAN WORLD OF GREECE—I

ACROSS:

1. Mythical monster that was half human and half bull
2. Author of the Greek dramas *Oedipus* and *Antigone*
3. Island south of Greece
4. A sacred site where the Greeks held athletic contests every four years
5. Greek god of the underworld
6. Greek historian, author of *History of the Peloponnesian Wars*
7. Famous epic poem by Homer
8. Famous student of Plato
9. Greek city-state defeated by Sparta
10. Trojan prince who kidnapped Helen, wife of the king of Sparta
11. Famous philosopher of ancient Greece
12. Greek who conquered Asia Minor and the Persian Empire
13. Name for the southern area of Greece
14. Greek god of the sea
15. Philosopher who set up the Academy, a school in Athens
16. Greek temple built for the goddess Athena
17. Famous statue of a Greek athlete
18. A fortified hilltop at the heart of a Greek city-state
19. The largest Greek city-state
20. Greek slaves or peasants forced to stay on the land they worked
21. Another famous epic poem by Homer
22. Greek word for outsiders or uncivilized people
23. Comic play written by Aristophanes
24. Sea between Greece and Asia Minor
25. Scene of a decisive victory of Athens over Persia
26. Greek goddess of wisdom
27. A play that portrays a heroic character whose very strength leads to his downfall
28. A long poem that tells the story of a historical or legendary hero
29. Famous poet of ancient Greece

Name ______________________________ Date ______________________

5. The Mediterranean World of Greece—I

6. THE MEDITERRANEAN WORLD OF GREECE—II

ACROSS: ____

1. Greek goddess of the hearth
2. Greek mathematician
3. The chief Greek god
4. Greek scientist who discovered the principle of the lever and invented the double pulley and a catapult
5. Greek goddess of marriage
6. Greek sculptor of a huge statue of the goddess Athena
7. Athenian general during the Peloponnesian Wars
8. Famous pupil of Socrates, author of *The Republic*
9. Greek god of war
10. Another Greek historian, author of *History of the Persian Wars*
11. Greek goddess of love
12. The first Greek philosopher
13. A massive formation of heavily armed Greek foot soldiers
14. A school established in Athens by Aristotle, the world's first scientific institute
15. Author of the first Athenian law code
16. Name for the northern area of Greece
17. Play written by Euripides, expressing sympathy for women and the oppressed
18. Famous Greek physician
19. Greek philosopher who taught that the greatest good was being happy
20. Greek mathematician who advanced the study of geometry, author of *The Elements*
21. Athenian runner who spread the news of the victory over the Persians at Marathon
22. Greek god of the sun
23. Socrates' motto as a code of conduct for human behavior
24. Famous Greek drama by Sophocles
25. Officials of ancient Greece
26. Greek goddess of victory
27. Athenian poet who created the world's first drama, or play
28. The father of Greek tragedy
29. Greek poems honoring special occasions

Name ______________________ Date ______________

6. The Mediterranean World of Greece—II

1 T
2 H
3 E
4 M
5 E
6 D
7 I
8 T
9 E
10 R
11 R
12 A
13 N
14 E
15 A
16 N
17 W
18 O
19 R
20 L
21 D
22 O
23 F
24 G
25 R
26 E
27 E
28 C
29 E

7. ANCIENT ROME

The answers to the following clues are hidden in the puzzle. Circle the answer in the puzzle and write the answer next to the correct number. Answers can be found horizontally, vertically, diagonally, and backward.

1. One of the mythical founders of Rome
2. Vast outdoor arena in Rome where chariot races took place
3. Roman clothing
4. Roman marketplace
5. Roman enemy in the Punic Wars
6. Roman language
7. Roman leader assassinated on March 15, 44 B.C.
8. Roman goddess of the hearth
9. Trained fighters who battled in the Colosseum
10. River in central Italy near Rome
11. Large Roman plantations
12. Roman official who registered the population for tax and voting purposes
13. Caesar's calendar, used in Europe until 1582 A.D.
14. Roman senator who stated, "Carthage must be destroyed!"
15. Roman commoners, including farmers, merchants, and artisans
16. Nickname of Rome
17. Island south of Italy
18. Roman poet
19. Roman god of war
20. Mountains in Italy
21. Roman officials elected from the plebeians to speak for their interests
22. Date when Caesar was killed as he entered the Senate
23. Roman law code
24. Roman port at the mouth of the Tiber River
25. Roman leader who formed an alliance with Cleopatra, queen of Egypt
26. Island west of Italy
27. Leader of Carthage in the First Punic War
28. Another mythical founder of Rome
29. Roman judges who ruled in all legal matters
30. River in northern Italy
31. Roman god of beginnings
32. Latin word for "I forbid"
33. Ancient name for France, conquered by the Roman Empire
34. Roman tribune who was murdered in 133 B.C., along with 300 of his followers
35. Chief Roman god
36. Military road connecting Rome to other Italian cities
37. One of the assassins of Julius Caesar
38. Wealthy Roman landowners
39. Leader of Carthage in the Second Punic War
40. River that separated Italy and Gaul
41. Roman military groups made up of about 6,000 soldiers
42. Another island west of Italy
43. Forced payment to the Romans from conquered areas, usually in the form of grain
44. Epic Roman poem
45. Roman counting board used to solve problems in mathematics
46. Mountains in northern Italy, crossed by Hannibal in the Second Punic War
47. Officials chosen to administer the laws of Rome
48. Roman tribune who was murdered in 123 B.C., along with 3,000 of his supporters
49. Roman goddess of love
50. Roman ruler who committed suicide in 68 A.D.
51. The first Roman emperor, "The Exalted One"

Name ______________________________ Date ____________________

7. Ancient Rome

I O E E A A Y T I C L A N R E T E E H T G E A

S R O M U L U S A U G U S T U S A L A A T S S

M R G M I L N O C I B U R O C M Y L U V N C J

F C A C A R T H A G E R O R T A J L D A C A I

T M I M C L C T P T S J T E W R E B I T G A C

A S U R S A I T S O R N E N E W J L A T I N P

N R S V C B T L U G A V A N L A U A T B Y N C

S E G F E U U O H A M I R I V J P T S U N A J

E M R R O S S S C I P W P T E T I I E V O M A

N U A O N R T M C P A B S A T B T N V P T C S

U S C O B J U A A A T S P L A L E G I O N B M

B T C S A C S M R X R M L E B K R L F M A L P

I S H N E J L I G R I Z A T L R T O P A K S Z

R B U N M R U H S L C M J M E I R M L R R R I

T S S L S S N L U T I H U M S U I A E C A O E

N O U D U E A A I F A O U S M D B I L U M T R

R L G N C M G N R U N S U O J I U T A S U A V

A E E A A F O U E C S N K U N E N S T B A I Y

C V W R B T T R B R E C L N V N E O I R A D L

L I S N A G D O I V O I A W N E S R F U T A H

I S U C A B A E T R A H S E V A T T U T R L E

M A I N I D R A S N E T V E S T A O N U M G Y

A B A P E N N I N E S A T B Y A C A D S N T W

H R E S T H C R A M F O S E D I R V I R G I L

L Y B U O A U G H T T O S E H E B O A X F Y A

1. ____________
2. ____________
3. ____________
4. ____________
5. ____________
6. ____________
7. ____________
8. ____________
9. ____________
10. ____________
11. ____________
12. ____________
13. ____________
14. ____________
15. ____________
16. ____________
17. ____________
18. ____________
19. ____________
20. ____________
21. ____________
22. ____________
23. ____________
24. ____________
25. ____________
26. ____________
27. ____________
28. ____________
29. ____________
30. ____________
31. ____________
32. ____________
33. ____________
34. ____________
35. ____________
36. ____________
37. ____________
38. ____________
39. ____________
40. ____________
41. ____________
42. ____________
43. ____________
44. ____________
45. ____________
46. ____________
47. ____________
48. ____________
49. ____________
50. ____________
51. ____________

8. THE ROMAN HERITAGE

The answers to the following clues are hidden in the puzzle. Circle the answer in the puzzle and write the answer next to the correct number. Answers can be found horizontally, vertically, diagonally, and backward.

1. Canal-like structures to carry water to the cities
2. German invaders of the Roman Empire in 455 A.D.
3. German chief who captured Rome in 476 A.D. and proclaimed himself king of Italy
4. Roman method of execution
5. Ruler who divided the Roman Empire in half
6. German invaders of the Roman Empire in 410 A.D.
7. First Roman emperor to convert to Christianity
8. Roman emperor who persecuted Christians
9. Roman coins
10. The founder of Christianity
11. Asian invaders of the Roman Empire, stopped at the battle of Troyes in 451 A.D.
12. Italian city buried by a volcano in 79 A.D.
13. The official religion of the Roman Empire in 395 A.D.
14. German invaders of the Roman Empire
15. Roman author of essays on government, morality, and philosophy
16. Non-Christians in the Roman Empire
17. City where Jesus grew up
18. A roof formed by rounded arches, invented by the Romans
19. A savior chosen by God
20. Apostle of Jesus who traveled to Rome to convert people to Christianity
21. Volcano that erupted in 79 A.D., burning the city of Pompeii
22. Roman capital in 324 A.D., formerly Byzantium
23. Roman poet, famous for his odes praising the Pax Romana
24. Short stories with a simple moral lesson
25. Disciple of Jesus who helped spread Christianity in the Roman Empire for 30 years
26. Birthplace of Jesus
27. Leader of the Huns, the "Scourge of God"
28. Author of *Commentaries on the Gallic Wars*
29. Organization in which officials are arranged according to rank
30. Pictures formed of chips of colored stone
31. Roman official who condemned Jesus to die
32. "Father of the Church," the bishop of Rome
33. Author of the *Annals,* a history of Rome from the death of Augustus to 70 A.D.
34. Non-Jewish people in the Roman Empire
35. Author of *Natural History,* a 37-volume work of information on subjects ranging from astronomy to botany, geography, and medicine
36. People who suffer or die for their beliefs
37. The first four books of the New Testament of the Bible
38. Small farmers in the Roman Empire
39. Author of *History of Rome*
40. German invaders of the Roman Empire

Name ______________________________ Date ____________________

8. The Roman Heritage

S A E A T O L S P I K N A L E C K E T S
U L U A P U S N M R P E S L O U U P H O
W B E O A L U E E E C R P L I N Y R T I
T I G P A M H C T R I O O P O P E T S A
N I D D S E A E G L N N L P O T R R N A
V R N Y L O R R W I I I I O E M H H O O
W A P H D C G G T V N F V P N I P I I R
V N T O A E E N S Y Y O Y E D I T E X H
A E T E N N A R U N R F R A N K S R I S
B D S H T T A C I T U S O E T T I A F I
M A E I S S I L V L H O R A C E S R I E
R I L N E S P U U U M S N U H I T C C O
N E O A I E A Y S A S N U H T M C H U H
S C C P E T E R E P O P E S O A U Y R E
S C B A T N N A V N I S U S E J D A C S
D E H I H O R A C E P L A S D J E L I T
R L L R S T E G T S C I A S O M U S R O
A A I B I C E O V S C R Y T M B Q H I N
B G O V A S O R F S N P D P E L A T E P
M G D R Y R T O A D R O A O P I F O A E
O R O O E S A I N Z M G C U S O R G R T
L H G N M A T P A E A R Y S L J A I O E
D I O C L E T I A N T N E N E N N S R R
Y R O I Y V I R S N I M W U S A K I H O
O F V I N O L O C A C T E H M A S V N J
O Y S H B U A B B A S A Y M K D L D E T

1. ______________
2. ______________
3. ______________
4. ______________
5. ______________
6. ______________
7. ______________
8. ______________
9. ______________
10. ______________
11. ______________
12. ______________
13. ______________
14. ______________
15. ______________
16. ______________
17. ______________
18. ______________
19. ______________
20. ______________
21. ______________
22. ______________
23. ______________
24. ______________
25. ______________
26. ______________
27. ______________
28. ______________
29. ______________
30. ______________
31. ______________
32. ______________
33. ______________
34. ______________
35. ______________
36. ______________
37. ______________
38. ______________
39. ______________
40. ______________

9. THE BYZANTINE EMPIRE

The answers to the following clues are hidden in the puzzle. Circle the answer in the puzzle and write the answer next to the correct number. Answers can be found horizontally, vertically, diagonally, and backward.

1. Byzantine artform, pictures formed of chips of colored stone
2. The richest city in Europe in the 12th century, capital of the Byzantine Empire
3. Ruler of the Byzantine Empire from 527 to 565
4. Strait connecting the Sea of Marmara and the Black Sea
5. The bishop of Constantinople
6. The official language of the Byzantine Empire
7. Small art objects that depict Jesus, Mary, or a Christian saint
8. Turkish conquerors of Constantinople in 1453, ending the Byzantine Empire
9. Body of water between the Black Sea and the Aegean Sea
10. Strait connecting the Aegean Sea and the Sea of Marmara
11. The spacious harbor of Constantinople
12. Nickname of Constantinople
13. The original Greek town on Constantinople's site
14. Byzantine court historian, author of *Secret History*
15. Justinian's best general who conquered Italy and the northern coast of Africa
16. Justinian's wife
17. Another nickname of Constantinople
18. Constantinople's main street, the marketplace
19. The great cathedral of Constantinople
20. Constantinople's colosseum where sporting events and chariot races were held
21. A person whose ideas are incorrect, in the opinion of the Church
22. Name of the eastern branch of the Christian Church, from the Greek words meaning "correct belief"
23. The official religion of the Byzantine Empire
24. To cut off from the Christian Church

Name ______________________ Date ______________________

9. The Byzantine Empire

T H E H I R K O N W A M F N W R
D W S L A E H C S I J A I O U S
A K A P E G O L D E N H O R N E
S U I R A S I L E B M Y I N J P
T A G L N C M A E E I T N E U K
Y K A M O E P F S G X I A W S R
T Y E N N T W E E O E C C R T D
I E S E H A T R D M P E M O I E
C I T E R E H O O A R H L M N S
E W E A E G H S M M T T I E I S
H M A R C T A S H A E A T A A S
T N C H R I S T I A N I T Y N E
N S I O C C N C S H O S L S M L
O E N S M O O U N I T C A O U L
E A W G J N I S M A H L R C I E
M O H R S P C C R M E D F P T N
O F S T O I B O S P O R U S N A
R M B C A M D O A P D C B I A D
D A O S S O E T P E O A X N Z R
O R O C E H R I R M R M I E Y A
P M S H B I H I L E A L E J B D
P A T N A I N I T S U J E S A N
I R S R H A R B L E A K D A E R
H A C O N S T A N T I N O P L E
L H A T A M A L I O V E H O B F

1. ______________________
2. ______________________
3. ______________________
4. ______________________
5. ______________________
6. ______________________
7. ______________________
8. ______________________
9. ______________________
10. ______________________
11. ______________________
12. ______________________
13. ______________________
14. ______________________
15. ______________________
16. ______________________
17. ______________________
18. ______________________
19. ______________________
20. ______________________
21. ______________________
22. ______________________
23. ______________________
24. ______________________

10. THE RISE OF ISLAM

The answers to the following clues are hidden in the puzzle. Circle the answer in the puzzle and write the answer next to the correct number. Answers can be found horizontally, vertically, diagonally, and backward.

1. The largest peninsula in the world, birthplace of Islam
2. Arab holy men who worshipped only one god
3. Fertile areas in a desert with enough water to support trees and plants
4. Animal used by the Bedouin, "ship of the desert"
5. The Arabic word for God
6. The number of times Muslims are required to pray daily
7. Believers of Islam, the Arabic word for "the surrendering ones"
8. Islam's holy book
9. An Islamic holy war
10. The Islamic guidelines for right living
11. The official language of Islam
12. The holy city of Islam
13. One of the duties of Islam, a journey to the holy city
14. One who delivers divine messages from God
15. The body of water that separates Arabia from Africa
16. The sacred shrine of Islam, the Arabic word for "cube"
17. The Arabic word for a chapter in the Koran
18. A Muslim crier who summoned people to prayer each morning at dawn
19. The last of the orthodox caliphs, who was assassinated in 661
20. One of the duties of Islam, the belief in one God and Muhammad as His Prophet
21. The second caliph who became the leader of Muslims after the death of Muhammad, Islam's greatest conqueror
22. The founder of Islam who stated that the angel Gabriel had spoken to him, saying that God had chosen him to be his prophet
23. Nomads who lived on the Arabian desert
24. One of the duties of Islam, giving help to the needy
25. Islam's holy month, when Muslims were to eat nothing or drink nothing between sunrise and sunset
26. The escape of Muhammad from Mecca to Medina, the Arabic word for "flight"
27. A forbidden drink of Muslims
28. Battle where the Muslim armies were defeated in France in 732
29. Islamic physician who wrote more than 100 articles on medicine, the most famous on how to diagnose smallpox
30. Islamic scientists who tried to turn ordinary metals into gold
31. A forbidden food of Muslims
32. Religion founded by Muhammad, the Arabic word for "surrender to God"
33. Muhammad's wife
34. Islamic place of worship
35. The most sacred object of the Muslims
36. The number of wives a Muslim was allowed to marry, but only if he could support them all equally well
37. The town to which Muhammad fled in 622, known as the "City of the Prophet"
38. One of the duties of Islam, refusing to eat or drink from sunrise to sunset during the holy month
39. Islamic leaders after Muhammad's death, the Arabic word for "successors to the prophet"
40. The center of Muslim civilization during its golden age
41. One of the duties of Islam, required five times daily
42. Muslim leader who ordered the writing of the Koran, a collection of Muhammad's prayers and teachings

Name ______________________________ Date ____________________

10. The Rise of Islam

A	M	B	E	L	S	F	S	E	Z	A	H	R	R	J	A	C
A	C	C	E	M	I	U	A	L	M	S	B	K	C	P	O	B
I	A	M	F	V	A	L	R	D	I	U	R	U	O	F	L	S
E	A	H	E	G	I	R	A	A	S	A	S	R	B	M	L	B
C	A	C	O	D	R	H	E	F	L	W	K	L	A	A	A	H
M	U	E	Z	Z	I	N	I	N	A	R	O	K	I	O	K	R
F	O	N	W	J	D	N	O	D	M	L	P	B	H	M	I	R
I	N	I	S	S	A	A	A	A	Y	D	A	H	K	A	S	B
V	N	U	E	H	A	D	L	P	O	R	K	B	P	R	T	L
E	R	O	M	U	H	A	M	M	A	D	R	M	I	A	S	A
A	A	D	F	G	F	M	S	S	S	F	E	A	L	B	I	C
E	P	E	A	B	A	A	K	L	E	O	Y	L	G	I	M	K
M	R	B	I	U	S	R	E	D	S	E	A	S	R	C	E	S
N	O	D	T	W	T	R	U	O	F	H	R	I	I	E	H	T
R	P	S	H	P	I	L	A	C	M	U	P	S	M	P	C	O
O	H	T	Q	C	N	N	R	O	O	A	L	L	A	H	L	N
A	E	C	K	U	G	E	E	T	O	U	R	S	G	L	A	E
H	T	I	A	F	E	S	R	A	L	L	I	P	E	V	I	F

1. ____________________
2. ____________________
3. ____________________
4. ____________________
5. ____________________
6. ____________________
7. ____________________
8. ____________________
9. ____________________
10. ____________________
11. ____________________
12. ____________________
13. ____________________
14. ____________________
15. ____________________
16. ____________________
17. ____________________
18. ____________________
19. ____________________
20. ____________________
21. ____________________
22. ____________________
23. ____________________
24. ____________________
25. ____________________
26. ____________________
27. ____________________
28. ____________________
29. ____________________
30. ____________________
31. ____________________
32. ____________________
33. ____________________
34. ____________________
35. ____________________
36. ____________________
37. ____________________
38. ____________________
39. ____________________
40. ____________________
41. ____________________
42. ____________________

11. THE EARLY MIDDLE AGES

The answers to the following clues are hidden in the puzzle. Circle the answer in the puzzle and write the answer next to the correct number. Answers can be found horizontally, vertically, diagonally, and backward.

1. Name given to the Early Middle Ages because learning and civilization declined
2. A tax charged by the Church
3. Armored warriors who fought on horseback
4. King of the Franks from 768 to 814, "the Great"
5. The feudal ceremony in which a vassal received land from a lord
6. The leader of a monastery
7. The code of conduct developed by feudal nobles
8. Viking explorer who discovered and named Greenland
9. A piece of land given to a vassal by a lord
10. The first king ever to be anointed by a pope, "the Short"
11. Women who lived in convents and devoted their lives to prayer
12. Treaty that divided Charlemagne's empire into three kingdoms
13. A charge to cross a vassal's land or bridge
14. Viking name for Newfoundland
15. The head of the Catholic Church
16. Communities in which groups of Christian men gave up all their private possessions and lived very simply, devoting their lives to worship and prayer
17. A lord's estate, from which his family gained its livelihood
18. Invaders of Europe from Scandinavia
19. Frankish leader who defeated the Muslims in Spain at the Battle of Tours in 732
20. A political and military system based on the holding of land
21. Pope who crowned Charlemagne "Emperor of the Romans" in 800
22. Monk who established a strict set of rules for monastic life
23. Peasants bound to a manor
24. Decorating the first letter of a paragraph and the margins of a page with brilliant designs
25. Languages that evolved from Latin
26. Men who lived in monasteries
27. Viking explorer who reached America about the year 1000
28. A person who received land from a lord
29. Benedict's sister who established the rules for convents
30. Part of northern France conquered by the Vikings in 911, from the French word meaning "men from the north"

Name ______________________________ Date ____________________

11. The Early Middle Ages

F K N I G H T S A C I T S A L O H C S
E V E R D U N O S C I R E F I E L T E
U I T T N G P F E N U N S Y N A H V I
D N F L H E R E A L U N D S O G B A R
A L P O P E C N C C U N F E I F E S E
L A L I S R D R O N A M V N T A N S T
I N N L M I D A T M A X K A A F E A S
S D N S O C H A R L E M A G N E D L A
M V I K K T L O A K O A O L I I I Y N
S E P N N H N E J N A E N R M F C R O
G R E O Y E C L K A L G N F U R T L M
N D P M P R H S R B I L E M L O I A A
I U S F R E S T A B E I P S L N T V B
K N N A W D V K I O F Y A L I A H I B
I Z C S I N V E S T I T U R E M E H O
V A S S A L E T R A M S E L R A H C T

1. ______________________________
2. ______________________________
3. ______________________________
4. ______________________________
5. ______________________________
6. ______________________________
7. ______________________________
8. ______________________________
9. ______________________________
10. ______________________________
11. ______________________________
12. ______________________________
13. ______________________________
14. ______________________________
15. ______________________________
16. ______________________________
17. ______________________________
18. ______________________________
19. ______________________________
20. ______________________________
21. ______________________________
22. ______________________________
23. ______________________________
24. ______________________________
25. ______________________________
26. ______________________________
27. ______________________________
28. ______________________________
29. ______________________________
30. ______________________________

12. THE HIGH MIDDLE AGES

ACROSS:

1. Norman invader of England in 1066, "the Conqueror"
4. Medieval scientists who attempted to change worthless metals into gold
8. Famous medieval poet, author of *The Canterbury Tales*
10. Location of the headquarters of the Catholic Church
11. English scientist and philosopher, "the founder of experimental science"
12. Famous epic poem about medieval England
14. One of the most famous heroic poems of the Middle Ages, praising the courage of French soldiers
18. An association of people who work at the same occupation
19. Wandering poets who entertained at feudal castles
22. The strongest ruler of medieval Germany, "the Great"
23. A fee charged to cross a feudal lord's territory
27. A person who, after completing an apprenticeship, works at a craft for wages under the supervision of a master
28. English king in the Third Crusade, "the Lion-hearted"
30. In western Europe, the period from 1000 to 1300 is known as ______
33. University founded by English students during the Middle Ages
34. Something that people believed had once belonged to Jesus or one of the Christian saints
37. Members of a Roman Catholic religious order who took the same vows as a monk but traveled about preaching instead of living in a monastery
40. A young man who waited on a knight, helping him with his armor and weapons
44. The item made by a journeyman as the final step to being accepted into a guild
45. The bishop of Rome, head of the Roman Catholic Church
46. Notre ______
48. Skilled workers who made goods by hand
49. In medieval England, people who lived in towns rather than in rural areas
52. A league of towns and cities in northern Germany for protection and trade purposes
53. Short, humorous poems that mocked nobles, the clergy, and townspeople during the Middle Ages
55. A person whose ideas were incorrect in the opinion of the Church
56. Men who lived in monasteries and devoted their lives to prayer
57. Famous epic poem about medieval Spain
59. An order of friars who took their name from a Spanish priest who walked barefoot through southern France preaching against heresy
60. Armored warriors who fought on horseback

DOWN:

2. Italian merchant who traveled overland to China in the 1270's
3. The last Christian stronghold in the Holy Land, seized by Muslim forces in 1291
5. The estate from which a lord's family gained its livelihood
6. Peasants who were bound to a manor
7. Another university founded by English students during the Middle Ages
9. Formal combat between two mounted knights armed with lances
13. In medieval Germany, people who lived in a walled town rather than in rural areas
15. The leader of a monastery
16. French word meaning "oath," a group of people who answered questions about the facts of a case for a royal judge
17. The basic item for much of medieval trade
19. Payment to the Church of 10 percent of a person's income
20. In medieval France, people who lived in burghs or towns rather than in rural areas
21. The practice of lending money for interest
24. In the feudal system, the person who made a grant of land to another person
25. Medieval style of architecture, similar to the buildings in ancient Rome
26. Location of the Cathedral of Notre Dame
29. English king who was defeated at the Battle of Hastings in 1066
30. A tax assessed for the support of the clergy and the Church
31. The piece of land given to a vassal by a lord
32. Medieval scholar and author of *Suma Theologiae,* in which he attempted to answer philosophical questions about God and the universe
35. A Catholic worship service
36. A young nobleman who was sent to the castle of another lord where he waited on his hosts and learned manners, the first step in becoming a knight
38. City where the spiritual leader of Christendom ruled
39. Famous epic poem about medieval Germany
41. A person who is learning a trade or craft from a master and works without pay except for room and board
42. Workers who owed duties to the lord of a manor
43. In 1163, the tallest church in Christendom, 114 feet
47. Europe's largest city by the year 1200
50. The buying and selling of Church offices
51. Famous medieval poet, author of *Divine Comedy*
54. Pope who called for the First Crusade
56. A deep, wide, and usually water-filled trench around a castle, designed to discourage attempts at invasion
58. Women who lived in convents and devoted their lives to prayer

Name ______________________ Date ______________________

12. The High Middle Ages

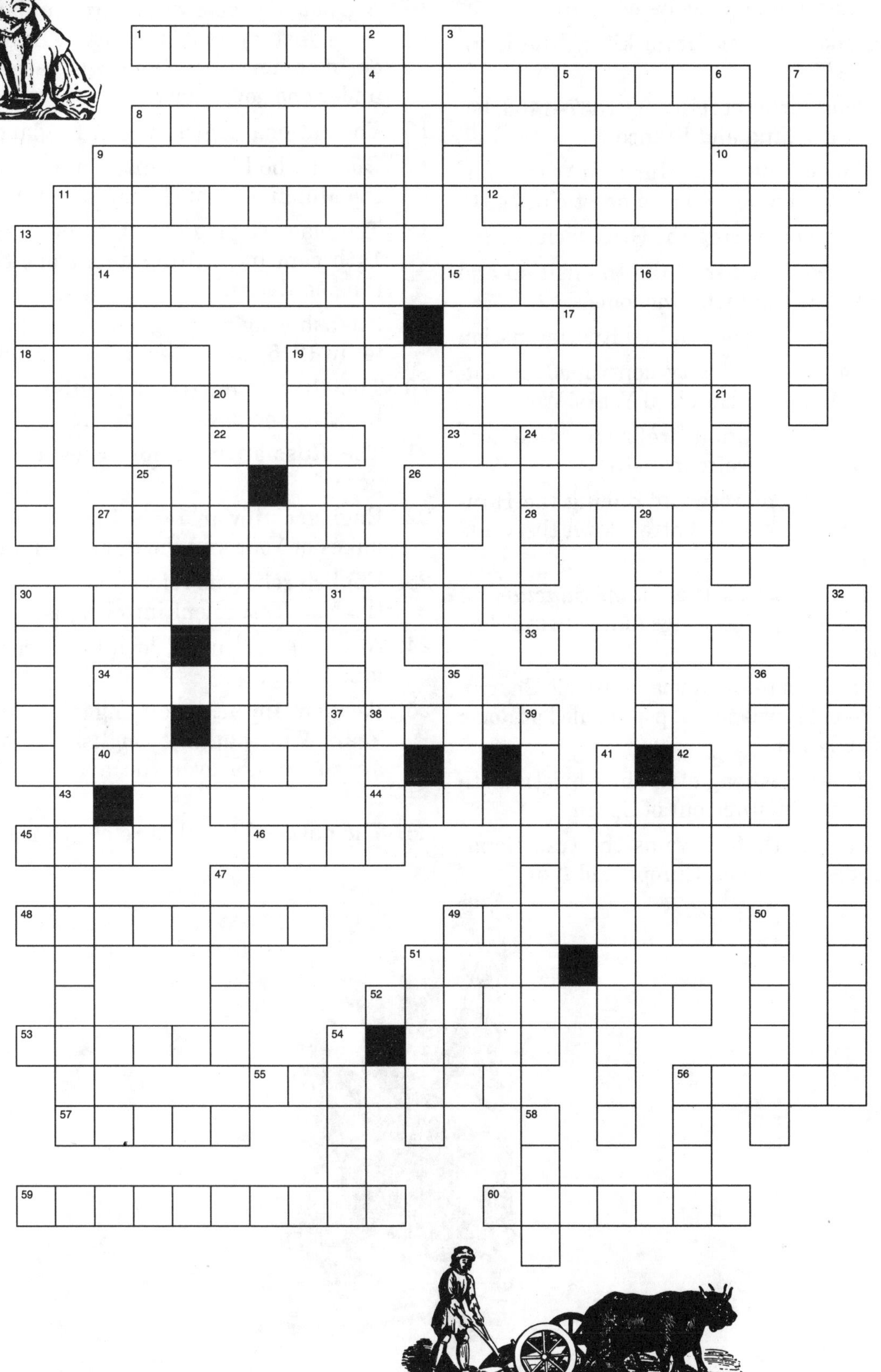

13. THE ORIGIN OF EUROPEAN NATIONS

ACROSS:

1. The national legislature of Spain
2. England's last medieval king, "the Lion-hearted"
3. The long series of fighting, 1337–1453, between England and France
4. French heroine in the Hundred Years' War, captured and burned as a heretic in 1431
5. Italian pope during the Great Schism
6. King who established the Inquisition and united the Spanish kingdoms
7. The first leader of a united Russian nation
8. The only French city controlled by England after the Hundred Years' War
9. Bohemian religious reformer who was burned as a heretic in 1415
10. Huge weapons invented during the Hundred Years' War to batter down the walls of castles
11. Pope who issued the *Unam Sanctam* in 1302, stating that kings must always obey popes
12. The division in the Roman Catholic Church, 1378–1417, when rival popes ruled at Rome and Avignon
13. The centuries-long effort by Christians to drive the Muslims out of Spain
14. Mountains that serve as the traditional boundary between Europe and Asia
15. A group of people who share similar traditions, history, and language, who occupy a definite territory, and who are united under one government
16. The national legislature of England
17. Queen who helped unite Spain and drive the Muslims from Granada in 1492
18. The massive plague in Europe during the 14th century, killing about one-third of the population
19. English king who signed the Great Charter in 1215, guaranteeing basic legal rights
20. The Great Charter of English liberties, limiting the power of the king
21. The Russian word for "caesar" or "emperor"
22. English civil war, 1455–1485, between the dukes of York and the dukes of Lancaster
23. English religious reformer who translated the New Testament into English
24. A strong feeling of loyalty to one's own land and people
25. Weapon invented during the Hundred Years' War that gave English foot soldiers an advantage over the armored French cavalry
26. The national legislature of France

Name ______________________________ Date ______________________

13. The Origin of European Nations

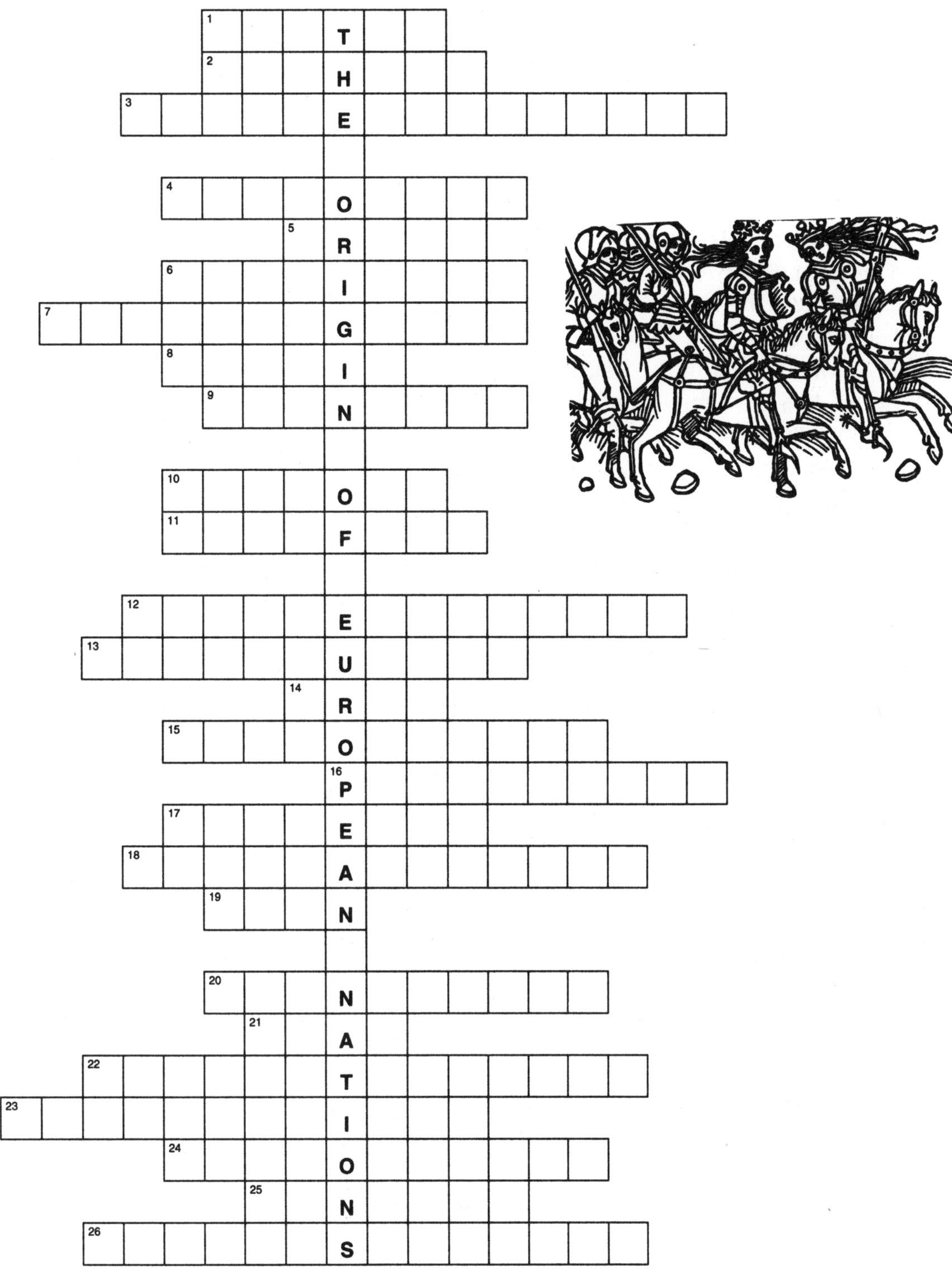

14. THE GOLDEN AGE OF CHINA

The answers to the following clues are hidden in the puzzle. Circle the answer in the puzzle and write the answer next to the correct number. Answers can be found horizontally, vertically, diagonally, and backward.

1. Trade route constructed to link China to the west
2. A major item of trade during China's golden age, a hard, shiny pottery
3. The most famous European to travel to China, serving the government of Kublai Khan from 1275 to 1292
4. The walled section of Peking that contained the royal palaces of the emperor of the Ming dynasty
5. A series of rulers from a single family
6. The ancient Chinese custom that affected women, which was considered beautiful and feminine, but painful and often crippling
7. The earliest known printed work, a Buddhist text produced in 868
8. Chinese dynasty, 618-906, one of China's greatest periods of literature and art
9. During the 1600's, the only Chinese port open to foreign merchants
10. China's only woman emperor, 690–705
11. River in northern China
12. Chinese invention during its golden age
13. The leader of a group of Mongols
14. Chinese dynasty, 960–1280, noted for its achievements in art and philosophy
15. Subject of Chinese painting during the Sung dynasty
16. One of the most hated emperors in China's history, strangled by his own servants in 618
17. Founder of the Mongol dynasty in China, ruling from 1260 to 1294
18. Monumental defensive barrier in northern China, extending approximately 1,500 miles
19. Capital of the Ming dynasty, now called Beijing
20. Chinese dynasty that printed the first paper money used in the world
21. The major agricultural crop of China during its golden age
22. Waterway constructed to link China's two great rivers, the Yellow River in the north to the Yangtze River in the south
23. River in southern China
24. Another Chinese invention during its golden age
25. In Chinese society, the social class of scholar-officials ranking below nobles but above common people
26. Chinese name for Kublai Khan's dynasty
27. China's major item of trade during its golden age
28. Chinese dynasty, 589–618, during which the Grand Canal was built
29. Another Chinese invention during its golden age
30. One of China's most celebrated poets during the 700's of the T'ang dynasty
31. The first Europeans to reach China by sea in 1513
32. The last ruling dynasty of truly Chinese origin, 1368–1644, noted for its scholarly and artistic achievements, especially porcelain

Name ______________________________ Date ____________________

14. The Golden Age of China

```
T M D L Y C G N U S R E D W O P N U G S
A Y S I U N A N U B G R E A T W A L L N
S T K I A L A N A C D N A R G M L K E A
M I P T N M G S J T A G I R R L Y S I H
R C E I C I O U A H N T E M E I T U G K
A N K H A N E N K I G A I N A P S N E I
O E I S N G G G D N T U B S T O A G N A
X D N S T D Y N A S T Y U K W R N G T L
A D G A O Y I Y I M U I Z U A C Y N R B
E I A P N B R L L A S T W B L E D I Y U
E B P M T Y K E N R T J R L L L K T E K
I R M O D R E P A C S D N A L A L N L U
N O O C O L Y L K O A U P I R I I I L H
O F D A R U A L L P H A I K M N S R O P
T I D I A L I P O O W U C H A O O P W N
A N C N N S U N G L W B Y A N G T Z E O
R E S E U G U T R O P U M N A E L C G D
```

1. ____________________ 17. ____________________
2. ____________________ 18. ____________________
3. ____________________ 19. ____________________
4. ____________________ 20. ____________________
5. ____________________ 21. ____________________
6. ____________________ 22. ____________________
7. ____________________ 23. ____________________
8. ____________________ 24. ____________________
9. ____________________ 25. ____________________
10. ____________________ 26. ____________________
11. ____________________ 27. ____________________
12. ____________________ 28. ____________________
13. ____________________ 29. ____________________
14. ____________________ 30. ____________________
15. ____________________ 31. ____________________
16. ____________________ 32. ____________________

15. THE GOLDEN AGE OF INDIA

ACROSS:

4. A member of the first of the four Hindu castes of India
8. One of the hereditary social classes into which Hindus are divided
9. Mountain range northwest of India
10. Turkish-Mughal conqueror of northern India in 1526, nicknamed "the tiger"
12. In Islam, the one supreme being
14. A mausoleum of white marble built, 1631–1645, by Shah Jahan; India's greatest monument
15. Site of a famous university on the Ganges River that attracted students of philosophy from faraway kingdoms
16. River in northwest India
17. A cotton cloth printed in a figured pattern of bright colors, named after the Indian city of Calicut, where it was first obtained
20. Nickname of Samudra Gupta, ruler also called "exterminator of all other kings"
23. Sea west of India
24. Oral records celebrating past events, meaning "so it was told"
25. An island south of India
26. The eight pure emotions recognized in Indian drama: laughter, sadness, pride, love, anger, fear, loathing and wonder
30. City conquered by the Turkish sultan Muhammad Ghuri in 1192, who also destroyed its famous university
32. A major religion in India, characterized by the worship of Brahma, the single supreme being, and by the observance of a now illegal caste system
34. Famous fifth-century Hindu poet and dramatist, whose genius has been compared to Shakespeare's
35. Taj ______
36. Hindu prince who was crowned king of the upper Ganges valley in 320, the first in a line of remarkable rulers who brought a golden age to India
38. Western Indian port seized by the Portuguese in 1510, that served as their headquarters for trade
40. High, slender towers attached to the Taj Mahal, surrounded by balconies from which leaders call Muslims to prayer
41. The sacrifice of a Hindu widow on the funeral pyre of her husband
44. Site of the Taj Mahal
46. Turkish-Mughal conqueror of northern India in 1398, who destroyed Delhi
48. The first Europeans to gain commercial privileges in India
50. The Muslim practice of keeping women in seclusion
52. The Muslim name for God
53. Empire established by Babur in 1526, another form of the name Mongol
54. A soft fabric made from the fine wool of goats, known by the name of the Indian region where it was woven

DOWN:

1. Mughal emperor, 1628–1658, who founded Delhi and built the Taj Mahal
2. Sea that is part of the Indian Ocean
3. A cloth with thick strands at intervals, giving it a checked effect, known by the name of the Indian city where it was woven
5. One of the three major gods of importance in Hinduism, "the Preserver"
6. The ruler of a Muslim territory
7. Wife of Mughal ruler Jahangir, probably the most powerful woman in India's history before modern times
11. The first European to reach India by sea in 1498
13. Members of a powerful and warlike Hindu caste, meaning "sons of kings"
18. Location of the most famous example of Mughal architecture
19. Mughal ruler from 1556 to 1605, whose name means "most great"
21. Island off India's west coast, site of towering sculptures of Hindu gods and caves that were cut into solid rock
22. Mountain range northeast of India
27. The Hindu god of destruction and reproduction
28. The heroine of a famous Sanskrit drama of the same name, one of the most famous plays in world literature
29. A major religion in India, characterized by the worship of Allah, the single supreme being, and Muhammad as his prophet
31. Capital established by Muslim rulers of India in 1206
33. Bay east of India
35. Wife of Shah Jahan, for whom the Taj Mahal was constructed as her tomb
37. A coarse cotton cloth used for work clothes, tents, sails, etc., known by the Indian section of Bombay where the sturdy blue denim was woven
39. Hinduism's second highest caste, meaning "warriors"
42. In Hinduism, a teacher or guide
43. River in India, flowing about 1,900 miles to the Arabian Sea
45. Dynasty that ruled a mighty empire in India for nearly 150 years, 320–467
47. The official name of Ceylon, adopted in 1972
49. River in northern India
51. A religious teacher

Name ______________________ Date ______________________

15. The Golden Age of India

16. THE GOLDEN AGE OF JAPAN

The answers to the following clues are hidden in the puzzle. Circle the answer in the puzzle and write the answer next to the correct number. Answers can be found horizontally, vertically, diagonally, and backward.

1. Under the Japanese feudal system, a member of the soldier class who fought for his lord; meaning "one who serves"
2. Japan's earliest religion, consisting chiefly in ancestor worship and nature worship; meaning "the way of the gods"
3. Any of the hereditary military dictators who ruled Japan until the 19th century and under whom the emperor was merely a figurehead
4. The largest island of Japan, 88,745 square miles
5. A great masterpiece of Japanese literature, one of the world's first novels
6. Japanese general who brought all of Japan under his control in the late 1500's, establishing the foundations for a united nation, and regarded as the greatest of the country's founding fathers
7. Port city on the northwest of Kyushu island, the only Japanese port open to outside trade from 1639 to the late 1800's
8. The code of the samurai, prescribing rigorous military training, severe self-discipline, personal honor, and loyalty to superiors; meaning "the way of the warrior"
9. A loose robe fastened with a wide sash, worn in Japan as an outer garment
10. A group of people who are descended from the same ancestor
11. Jesuit priest who led the first Christian mission to Japan, 1549–1551, baptizing hundreds of converts
12. Tokugawa capital, present-day Tokyo
13. About 400 A.D., the strongest clan in Japan, which established the first and only Japanese dynasty
14. The Japanese name for European newcomers; meaning "southern barbarians"
15. The earliest inhabitants of Japan, hunters and fishers who crossed to Japan from the Asian mainland
16. Japanese prince who converted to Buddhism and, in 607, sent a group to study Chinese civilization
17. In 1543, the first European visitors to Japan
18. The Japanese word for meditation; practiced by Buddhists
19. One of the four main islands of Japan
20. Site of the shogun's military headquarters during the 1200's
21. A chain of islands
22. Spirits that early Japanese believed controlled the forces of nature
23. A feudal lord in Japan who commanded a private army of samurai; meaning "great name"
24. A Japanese form of wrestling in which each of two contestants endeavors to force the other out of the ring or off his feet
25. The name *Japan* comes from these Chinese words that mean "origin of the sun"
26. According to legend, the sun goddess who created Japan
27. Samurai soldiers without lords
28. In 1192, the first Japanese shogun to gain political power away from the emperor
29. Another one of the four main islands of Japan
30. Japanese emperor who built a new capital city in 794 called Heian, present-day Kyoto
31. A ritual suicide, traditionally practiced by high-ranking Japanese when disgraced or in lieu of execution
32. Present-day name for the ancient Japanese capital of Heian, 794–1868
33. The first capital in Japanese history, 710–784; a magnificent square city on the island of Honshu modeled after the Chinese style of architecture during the T'ang dynasty
34. Japanese shogunate that ruled from 1603 to 1868
35. Another one of the four main islands of Japan
36. A short Japanese poem with 17 syllables that creates a mood or describes a scene
37. A simple script used by Japanese women who wrote diaries, essays, and novels during its golden age
38. Japanese capital built in 794, present-day Kyoto
39. The leading writer of Japan's golden age, author of *The Tale of Genji*
40. Japan's greatest artist during the late 1400's, painter of a silk scroll 55 feet long showing the four seasons of the year in shades of black, white, and gray

Name ______________________ Date ______________________

16. The Golden Age of Japan

```
A S K E A R M I H O U T I C A N E X I P
T H L A R U K A M A K K Y O R I T O M O
C O O I M A K E L J U D A U D O N N E R
S T M D S M B S C H A H M N J E E L T J
J O F A E R U E S U N I A I A Z P D O C
J K R S H O G U N E M D T A I S H D K T
S U A G L O Y G Z P B E O I K S I C U S
M A N R T K S U O T O Y K A A H J E G I
U O C N C U O T O Y K O U R S I U E A Y
H T I Z M H S R H O N S H U A K D S W M
S H S O E L I O T P A H B M G O E R A K
S K X I A N E P I R O I U A A K Y O T O
E D A I M Y O S E C R Y E S N U C N I S
S N V M T H E T A L E O F G E N J I N O
N W I S I P A E N A A A N A P M A N T I
O A E A P M A I A N R G K I M O N O G M
T E R U A H O K K A I D O T N A M A O T
C A K A T A D S N U O F Z S L U R W O F
N U W G T C R A M I K V R C S E M L K R
```

1. ______________
2. ______________
3. ______________
4. ______________
5. ______________
6. ______________
7. ______________
8. ______________
9. ______________
10. ______________
11. ______________
12. ______________
13. ______________
14. ______________
15. ______________
16. ______________
17. ______________
18. ______________
19. ______________
20. ______________
21. ______________
22. ______________
23. ______________
24. ______________
25. ______________
26. ______________
27. ______________
28. ______________
29. ______________
30. ______________
31. ______________
32. ______________
33. ______________
34. ______________
35. ______________
36. ______________
37. ______________
38. ______________
39. ______________
40. ______________

17. THE GOLDEN AGE OF SOUTHEAST ASIA

ACROSS:

1. The only country of Southeast Asia to be heavily influenced by China rather than India
2. Body of water east of Southeast Asia
3. The native inhabitants of Cambodia, who developed a great civilization that reached its height in the 9th to 14th centuries
4. Capital of the Khmer empire
5. Body of water between Southeast Asia and India
6. The southernmost peninsula of Asia
7. One of the major religions of Southeast Asia
8. A river in Southeast Asia, flowing 2,600 miles south to the China Sea
9. Capital of Vietnam
10. The greatest Khmer king, who came to the throne in 802
11. Invaders from China who sacked Vietnam's capital of Hanoi in 1257 and conquered Burma in 1287
12. The third largest island in the world, 286,969 square miles, between the Java and South China seas
13. A river in Southeast Asia
14. Body of water between the Malay Peninsula and Indochina
15. Another one of the major religions of Southeast Asia
16. The most famous of the Khmer buildings, a temple built to a Hindu god in the early 1100's
17. The modern country that was ruled by the Khmers from about 850 to about 1250
18. Body of water between the Malay Peninsula and Sumatra
19. Another one of the major religions of Southeast Asia
20. Another river in Southeast Asia
21. Invaders from China who captured Angkor in 1430, ending the Khmer empire
22. Former name of Thailand
23. An island of Indonesia south of the Malay Peninsula
24. Another river in Southeast Asia
25. The Hindu god for whom the temple complex of Angkor Wat was built
26. Country north of Southeast Asia
27. Former name of Kampuchea

Name ______________________________ Date ____________________

17. The Golden Age of Southeast Asia

18. EARLY AFRICAN EMPIRES

The answers to the following clues are hidden in the puzzle. Circle the answer in the puzzle and write the answer next to the correct number. Answers can be found horizontally, vertically, diagonally, and backward.

1. Capital of the Mali empire, famous for its university
2. An island in the Indian Ocean off the southeast coast of Africa
3. Places in a desert where underground water comes to the surface in a spring or well
4. Muslim ruler of the Mali empire from 1307 to 1332, who made a pilgrimage to Mecca in 1324
5. Previous name of the Zaire River, Africa's second longest river, flowing 2,900 miles to the Atlantic
6. The highest mountain in Africa, 19,565 feet
7. A language of East Africa, basically Bantu with a mixture of Arabic elements
8. African kingdom that developed along the upper Nile, 1000 B.C. – 150 A.D.
9. The largest lake in Africa, 26,828 square miles
10. Specially trained men and women who preserved the oral traditions of their people by memorizing the great deeds of past kings
11. West African kingdom that controlled the gold-salt trade, 1450 A.D. – 1600 A.D.
12. King of the Axum kingdom, who converted to Christianity in 324 A.D.
13. Powerful inland kingdom in southeast Africa, reaching its height in the 15th century
14. A lake in northwest central Africa, about 6,000 square miles
15. A blood-sucking insect that infects both people and animals with sleeping sickness
16. A river in southern Africa, flowing 1,000 miles to the Indian Ocean
17. Founder of the Songhai empire, "Always conqueror, never conquered"
18. One of the major items of trade in ancient Africa
19. Desert in southwest Africa
20. King of the Kush empire who conquered Egypt in 750 B.C.
21. A river in southern Africa, flowing 1,300 miles to the Atlantic
22. West African kingdom that controlled the gold-salt trade, 1200 A.D. – 1450 A.D.
23. A mountain group in northern Africa
24. A lake in eastern Africa, about 11,000 square miles
25. The world's largest desert area, about 3 million square miles
26. Another one of the major items of trade in ancient Africa, the chief substance of the tusks of elephants
27. The longest river in Africa, flowing 3,485 miles to the Mediterranean Sea
28. Yoruba state whose sculptors created striking bronze figures
29. A river in northwest Africa, flowing about 1,000 miles to the Atlantic
30. The longest and deepest (4,700 feet) lake in Africa
31. Mountain range in northwest Africa
32. Body of water between Egypt and Arabia, 1,450 miles long and about 170,000 square miles
33. East African language that fused with Arabic words to form Swahili
34. "Ships of the desert"
35. Desert between the Nile valley and the Red Sea
36. The southern tip of Africa
37. Another one of the major items of trade in ancient Africa
38. Ancient kingdom in what is now Ethiopia
39. Grassy plains with a few scattered trees
40. A salt-mining village deep in the Sahara Desert
41. Desert region in southern Africa
42. Another mountain group in northern Africa
43. Creators of some of the most famous African sculptures, a group of people in the rain forest of what is now Nigeria
44. Capital of the Kush empire, location of a large iron industry
45. A river in western Africa, flowing 2,600 miles to the Atlantic
46. A people who lived in what is today Nigeria
47. Another one of the major items of trade in ancient Africa, a hard, heavy wood, usually black
48. Wealthy West African kingdom, 800 A.D.–1000 A.D.
49. A river in southern Africa, flowing 1,650 miles to the Indian Ocean
50. Desert in western Egypt

Name ______________________________ Date ____________________

18. Early African Empires

```
A B E J E V O B S O N N I A L I S K E N D
S T O I R G G T I M B U K T U T N A B A I
L T M R N Y O G S B M C E S T Y Z N H I J
A Y R O V I L H M E R O E L A E I C I B O
C M C I R U D A S A T L A S A G M Y I U C
S A T G S A N N A V A S A S E R B M A N B
K D P N G S J A L N I L E R S T A F H D I
R A H E A E R N T T B E E F B N B H S R A
E G S M O Y I E A O E M O E L U W Y A B M
S A U H S F B N G M N A R Z Z Y E H K S I
M S K E A N G I S I I C E A C S A Y S A M
A C S I B A I O L R N L M N W L O G A U T
E A I L N O N L O O Y B I A A R U L X W A
O R X Y I G N T E D E C H K U S H A K D G
T R I U H M C Y C Z H I H B K E E G N H H
K K A A M I P I I I L O A A Z S H E A O A
A A I N V H L O L I H O P P D A S N V S Z
H R A G G A H A P O N I N E B O A E I W A
H A E I M E M O R O L M R T I B E S T I M
```

1. ____________
2. ____________
3. ____________
4. ____________
5. ____________
6. ____________
7. ____________
8. ____________
9. ____________
10. ____________
11. ____________
12. ____________
13. ____________
14. ____________
15. ____________
16. ____________
17. ____________
18. ____________
19. ____________
20. ____________
21. ____________
22. ____________
23. ____________
24. ____________
25. ____________
26. ____________
27. ____________
28. ____________
29. ____________
30. ____________
31. ____________
32. ____________
33. ____________
34. ____________
35. ____________
36. ____________
37. ____________
38. ____________
39. ____________
40. ____________
41. ____________
42. ____________
43. ____________
44. ____________
45. ____________
46. ____________
47. ____________
48. ____________
49. ____________
50. ____________

19. EARLY AMERICAN EMPIRES

ACROSS:

1. The last Aztec emperor of Mexico, who reigned from 1502 to 1520
2. An early civilization developing on the Pacific coast of South America about 1450 A.D., the last great empire in the Andes region
3. A mountain chain in central Mexico
4. The Aztec god of art and learning, sometimes represented as a snake
5. An early civilization developing in Central America and reaching its height between 300 A.D. and 900 A.D.
6. A river in South America, which carries more water than any other river in the world, flowing 3,300 miles from the Andes to the Atlantic
7. The first major American civilization, developing on Mexico's gulf coast around 1200 B.C.
8. An early civilization that conquered southern Mexico, establishing a capital on an island in the middle of Lake Texcoco in 1325
9. The major mountain system of western North America, extending from Alaska to Mexico
10. The capital of the ancient Aztec empire, on the site of Mexico City; "Place of the Prickly-Pear Cactus"
11. The capital of the ancient Inca empire in southern Peru
12. Peninsula of Central America where the Maya civilization flourished between 300 A.D. and 900 A.D.
13. The capital of the ancient Maya empire in Central America
14. The most important crop in the Americas, "the food of the gods"
15. The isthmus connecting North and South America
16. The Aztec sun god, who required human sacrifices
17. A device used by the Incas for keeping records, consisting of a series of knotted strings tied at one end to a thicker cord
18. A mountain range in eastern California
19. An early civilization developing in southern Mexico around 1000 A.D.
20. A mountain range in western South America, the world's longest mountain chain

Name ______________________________ Date ____________________

19. Early American Empires

1 E
2 A
3 R
4 L
5 Y

6 A
7 M
8 E
9 R
10 I
11 C
12 A
13 N

14 E
15 M
16 P
17 I
18 R
19 E
20 S

20. THE RENAISSANCE

ACROSS:

5. City in which Leonardo da Vinci spent his most productive years
7. River in central Italy, flowing 251 miles south to the Tyrrhenian Sea
9. A family of Florentine bankers and statesmen prominent in Italian Renaissance history
10. City in which Leonardo da Vinci produced one of the most famous paintings in history, the "Mona Lisa"
11. Site of the Vatican City
14. The celebrated wall painting of the meal of Jesus Christ and his disciples before the Crucifixion
16. London theater where many of Shakespeare's tragedies, comedies, and historical dramas were performed
17. Country in which the Renaissance began
18. Florentine statesman and writer on politics, who advised rulers that "the end justifies the means"
20. A handbook for rulers of the Italian city-states, which advised them to use a mixture of cunning, diplomacy, and ruthlessness
21. Italian poet, author of *The Divine Comedy*
22. City in northwestern Italy, noted for its leaning tower
24. Narrative poem dealing with the poet's imaginary journey through hell, purgatory, and paradise
25. A representation of the Virgin Mary, usually with the infant Jesus
27. Florentine painter, architect, and sculptor, whose acclaimed frescoes began a revolution in art
29. German printer, inventor of movable type
33. Italian painter, noted for his flattering portraits, including dozens of the Madonna
34. Italian poet and scholar who traveled about Europe in search of Greek and Roman manuscripts, considered the first humanist
36. The Pope, from 1503–1513, who asked Michelangelo to paint the ceiling of the Sistine Chapel in the Vatican
38. Portrait of a Florentine woman, one of the most famous works of art in the world, renowned for her haunting smile
39. The leading city of Renaissance Italy, the "City of Flowers"
42. French humorist and satirist, creator of the giant character Gargantua
43. Italian writer and poet, author of the *Decameron,* the first prose work written in Italian
44. Novel that satirizes the medieval ideals of chivalry

DOWN:

1. Michelangelo's mighty statue, which summed up the Renaissance belief in human dignity and greatness
2. Florentine painter, sculptor, and architect; pioneer in biology, geology, engineering, and military science
3. English translation of the French word "renaissance"
4. River in central Italy, flowing 150 miles west to the Gulf of Genoa
6. A port city in northeastern Italy
7. Nickname of Lorenzo de Medici, patron of the arts
8. A port city in northwestern Italy
12. French author of *Pantagruel,* in which he advised people to live by one rule: "Do as you wish"
13. Spanish novelist and dramatist, author of *Don Quixote*
15. English poet and dramatist, author of *Othello*
18. Italian sculptor, painter, architect, and poet
19. The principal chapel in the Vatican Palace, decorated with frescoes by Michelangelo
23. Another port city in northwestern Italy
26. Florentine sculptor, the first European since ancient times to make a large, free-standing human figure in the nude
28. One of the Renaissance scholars and writers who devoted themselves to the study of the subjects taught in ancient Greek and Roman schools
30. Dutch theologian, classical scholar, and humanist; author of *In Praise of Folly*
31. English poet, author of the *Canterbury Tales*
32. Flemish painter of scenes of everyday life, such as the "Peasant Wedding"
35. Location of Saint Peter's Cathedral, designed by Michelangelo
37. The pope's palace in Rome
40. "The Eternal City"
41. English statesman and scholar, author of *Utopia,* which described an ideal society where people lived at peace with one another

Name ______________________________ Date ____________________

20. The Renaissance

1 2 3 4 5 6 7 8 9 10 11 12 13 14 15 16 17 18 19 20 21 22 23 24 25 26 27 28 29 30 31 32 33 34 35 36 37 38 39 40 41 42 43 44

21. THE PROTESTANT REFORMATION

ACROSS:

1. German inventor of movable type, who printed a Bible around 1455
2. Swiss Reformation leader
3. French Protestants of the 16th and 17th centuries
4. A religious sect that rejected the practice of infant baptism, limiting church membership to adults baptized after a confession of faith
5. English king, 1509–1547, who asserted royal supremacy over the Catholic Church in England
6. Scottish Reformation leader
7. City in Germany where the Protestant Reformation originated
8. Pardons from the Church for certain sins in exchange for money
9. Dutch priest who criticized the Church for emphasizing pomp and ritual rather than the teachings of Jesus
10. German Reformation leader
11. French Reformation leader
12. A former nun who became the wife of Martin Luther in 1525
13. Name given to the followers of John Knox in Scotland
14. One who holds beliefs or opinions contrary to the established doctrines of his religion
15. A list of books the Roman Catholic Church condemned as dangerous to faith and morals and forbade its members to read
16. Famous book by Erasmus, in which he poked fun at greedy merchants, quarrelsome scholars, and pompous priests
17. Pope who excommunicated Martin Luther in 1520
18. English Protestants of the 16th and 17th centuries, who advocated simpler forms of creed and ritual in the Church of England
19. To be cut off by ecclesiastical authority from sharing in the sacraments, worship, privileges, or fellowship of a church
20. English queen, 1558–1603, who returned her kingdom to Protestantism
21. Calvin's doctrine that the salvation or damnation of men had been determined by God since the beginning of time
22. Another name for the Church of England
23. English humanist, author of *Utopia,* who was ordered beheaded by King Henry VIII
24. Reformation leader who translated the New Testament into German

Name ______________________________ Date ____________________

21. The Protestant Reformation

1	T
2	H
3	E
4	P
5	R
6	O
7	T
8	E
9	S
10	T
11	A
12	N
13	T
14	R
15	E
16	F
17	O
18	R
19	M
20	A
21	T
22	I
23	O
24	N

22. THE SCIENTIFIC REVOLUTION

ACROSS:

1. Homeland of Ambroise Pare
3. Author of *On the Structure of the Human Body*
9. Homeland of Sir Isaac Newton
11. Homeland of Paracelsus
15. Homeland of Anton van Leeuwenhoek
16. Physician who developed a technique for closing wounds with stitches
18. Dutch pioneer in microscopy
21. Author of *The Mathematical Principles of Natural Philosophy*
22. Homeland of Galileo Galilei and Evangelista Torricelli
23. The inventor of calculus, which he used to prove his theories
25. Astronomer who built one of the first observatories to study the planets and stars
28. Astronomer who created a mercury thermometer, which showed water freezing at 0 degrees and boiling at 100 degrees
29. Homeland of Tycho Brahe
31. Florentine astronomer and physicist, founder of the science of dynamics
33. Homeland of Nicolaus Copernicus
34. Homeland of William Harvey
35. Physician who discovered that blood circulates throughout the body rather than remaining stationary
36. Physician who made accurate drawings of the organisms of the human body, the founder of modern anatomy

DOWN:

2. Mathematician who discovered the law of gravity
4. Homeland of Anders Celsius
5. Dutch cloth merchant who constructed a primitive microscope, which he used to observe bacteria and describe red blood cells
6. Physician and alchemist who produced distilled liquids
7. Physician who discovered arteries and veins
8. Physicist who made the first thermometer using mercury, which showed water freezing at 32 degrees and boiling at 212 degrees
10. Astronomer who discovered that the planet Jupiter had four moons, which no one had seen before
12. Physicist who developed the first mercury barometer, a tool for measuring atmospheric pressure and predicting weather
13. Author of *On the Revolutions of the Heavenly Bodies*
14. Astronomer who first declared that the sun, not the earth, was the center of the universe, and that the earth was not stationary but turned on its axis once a day
17. Mathematician who discovered that the moon's gravity caused tides on the earth and the sun's gravity kept the planets within their orbits
19. Homeland of Christian Huygens
20. Astronomer who discovered that planets orbit the sun in an ellipse rather than a perfect circle
24. The first astronomer to study the night sky through a telescope, author of *Starry Messenger*
26. Homeland of Johannes Kepler and Gabriel Fahrenheit
27. Astronomer who built a clock using a pendulum
30. Astronomer who formulated the laws of planetary motion
32. One of the founders of modern surgery

Name ______________________________ Date ____________________

22. The Scientific Revolution

23. THE AGE OF EXPLORATION

ACROSS:

3. Spanish queen who sponsored Columbus's voyages
5. Lines on a map that show distances north and south of the equator
8. A state that conquers other lands and then rules them
9. Genoese explorer who discovered America for Spain, October 12, 1492
10. Venetian explorer in the service of England who discovered North America in 1497
11. A narrow piece of land extending into a body of water and connecting two larger land masses
15. The smallest of the three ships of Columbus on his first voyage to America
17. A region governed by a foreign power
18. A fleet of ships
22. An instrument that measured the positions of the stars, which enabled sailors to calculate a ship's latitude
25. A three-masted sailing vessel developed by the Portuguese
26. The first Asian country European explorers reached by water
27. Continent that Columbus hoped to reach by sailing west from Europe
28. An instrument for determining direction, consisting essentially of a freely suspended magnetic needle that points toward the magnetic north
32. Portuguese prince, patron of explorers and sea expeditions, known as "the Navigator"
33. European country that explored Central and South America
34. Country that led the way in the early voyages of exploration
35. Ocean discovered by Vasco de Balboa and first crossed by Ferdinand Magellan
36. Portuguese explorer in the service of Spain, whose crew first sailed around the world

DOWN:

1. The flagship of Columbus on his maiden voyage to America
2. English explorer for whom a river in New York and a bay in Canada are named
4. Mexican empire destroyed by Hernando Cortes in 1521
6. Italian explorer for whom America was named
7. Portuguese explorer who reached the southern tip of Africa in 1488, naming it the Cape of Storms
12. A narrow passage of water connecting two larger bodies of water
13. Lines on a map that show distances east or west of the prime meridian
14. Italian sea captain in the service of France who explored the coast of North America from what is today the Carolinas to Nova Scotia
16. Italian sea captain who sailed for England and explored the coast of North America from what is today Delaware to Newfoundland
19. Caribbean island explored by Columbus, present-day Haiti and the Dominican Republic
20. Portuguese explorer who rounded the southern tip of Africa and reached the Indian port of Calicut in 1498
21. European country that explored the eastern coast of North America
23. Pope who ordered the Line of Demarcation drawn from north to south through the Atlantic Ocean in 1493, dividing newly discovered lands between Spain and Portugal
24. Scandinavian adventurer who probably discovered North America about 1000
28. Portuguese explorer who claimed Brazil for Portugal in 1500
29. Portuguese king who renamed the southern tip of Africa the Cape of Good Hope
30. The isthmus connecting North and South America
31. European country that explored the Great Lakes and the Mississippi Valley

Name ______________________________ Date ______________________

23. The Age of Exploration

24. SPANISH EXPLORATION IN THE NEW WORLD

ACROSS: ______________________________

5. Spanish conquistador who conquered Mexico
6. Spanish explorer who discovered Florida in 1513 and searched for the legendary fountain of youth
11. Spanish explorer who discovered the Mississippi River in 1541
12. Flagship of Columbus on his maiden voyage to America
13. One of the three ships of Columbus on his maiden voyage to America
14. Mexican empire invaded by Hernando Cortes in 1519
15. Portuguese sailor in the service of Spain, whose crew was the first to sail around the world
18. Spanish conquerors of Mexico and Peru during the 16th century
19. Land of the Incas, controlled by the Spanish by 1535
20. One of the three ships of Columbus on his maiden voyage to America
22. Aztec emperor of Mexico who was dethroned by Cortes in 1520
25. South American area conquered by Pizarro
27. Islands of the New World first reached by Columbus in 1492
29. Spanish explorer who discovered the Grand Canyon in 1540
30. Spanish port from which Magellan embarked in 1519
31. Famous Spanish missionary in America
32. Name mistakenly given to the natives of America by Columbus
33. Spanish king who sent the first African slaves to the New World

DOWN: ______________________________

1. Spanish king who promoted the expeditions of Columbus and Vespucci
2. Children born to Spanish and Native American parents
3. South American empire invaded by Francisco Pizarro in 1532
4. The smallest ship of Columbus on his maiden voyage to America
7. The oldest permanent town in the United States, founded by Spain in 1565
8. Spanish conquistador who conquered Peru
9. Caribbean island explored by Columbus, present-day Haiti and the Dominican Republic
10. Aztec capital destroyed by Cortes in 1521
16. Inca capital captured by Pizarro in 1533
17. Italian explorer who discovered America for Spain, October 12, 1492
19. Islands where Magellan was killed during his quest to sail around the world
21. Italian explorer in the service of Spain for whom America was named
23. Spanish queen who sponsored the voyages of Columbus
24. Spanish explorer who discovered the Pacific Ocean in 1513
26. Spanish port from which Columbus embarked in 1492
28. Number of voyages Columbus made to the New World

Name ______________________ Date ______________

24. Spanish Exploration in the New World

25. FRENCH EXPLORATION IN THE NEW WORLD

ACROSS:

4. French name for the Mississippi Valley claimed by La Salle
5. Great Lake explored by Samuel de Champlain in 1614
9. French Jesuit missionary and explorer in North America
11. The basis of the French trade in North America
15. French trappers in North America
17. The largest of the Great Lakes explored by the French
18. The only Great Lake entirely within the United States
19. Items traded by Native Americans for French weapons, tools, and trinkets
21. French explorer who discovered the St. Lawrence River in 1535
26. French explorer who traveled all the way down the Mississippi River to the Gulf of Mexico in 1682
28. French explorer who founded Quebec in 1608, gaining the title "Father of New France"
29. River discovered by Jacques Cartier in 1535
30. French explorer who made three voyages to North America, discovering the Gulf of St. Lawrence and exploring as far as present-day Montreal

DOWN:

1. King for whom the French territory in America was named
2. The first permanent French settlement in the New World
3. The smallest and easternmost of the Great Lakes explored by the French
6. River explored by Marquette, Joliet, and La Salle
7. Lake along the boundary between present-day New York and Vermont, named in honor of a French explorer
8. French governor of New France
10. The second largest of the Great Lakes explored by the French
12. French missionaries who came to the New World
13. The southernmost of the Great Lakes explored by the French
14. Settlement founded by the French at the mouth of the Mississippi River
16. Italian sea captain who commanded the first French expedition to the New World in 1524, exploring the eastern coast of North America from what is now North Carolina to Newfoundland
19. French king who sent the first expedition to America in 1524
20. French explorer who named the Mississippi Valley "Louisiana" in honor of his king
22. French explorer of the Great Lakes and the upper Mississippi
23. The most popular fur traded by the French in America
24. Present-day state with a French name, which means "green mountain"
25. French settlement on the St. Lawrence River, formerly called Hochelaga
27. French name for a region in eastern Canada, including Nova Scotia and New Brunswick

Name ______________________________ Date ______________________

25. French Exploration in the New World

26. ENGLISH EXPLORATION IN THE NEW WORLD

The answers to the following clues are hidden in the puzzle. Circle the answer in the puzzle and write the answer next to the correct number. Answers can be found horizontally, vertically, diagonally, and backward.

1. The first Englishman to circumnavigate the globe in 1580
2. One of the three ships that brought the first English settlers to Jamestown in 1607
3. English colonist in charge of the colony of Roanoke Island, grandfather of Virginia Dare
4. English explorer for whom a bay in Canada was named
5. English leader of the colony of Jamestown
6. English colonist who married Pocahontas in 1614
7. English explorer who unsuccessfully attempted to establish a colony in North America in 1585
8. One of the three ships that brought the first English settlers to Jamestown in 1607
9. Nickname of English sea captains who attacked Spanish ships and raided Spanish coastal towns in the New World
10. Native American chief in Virginia, father of Pocahontas
11. English queen who attempted to colonize North America
12. Christian name taken by Pocahontas before she married John Rolfe
13. Italian sea captain who sailed for England in 1497, exploring the coast of North America from what is today Delaware to Newfoundland
14. The basic cash crop grown in Virginia during the early years of colonization
15. Name given to the area where Sir Walter Raleigh landed in North America, after Queen Elizabeth I, the virgin queen
16. Italian explorer in the service of England who named Newfoundland, lost at sea on his second voyage to America
17. The first child of English parents in the New World, born at Roanoke Island in 1587
18. English king for whom the first permanent English settlement in the New World was named
19. English explorer who searched for a northwest passage through North America to Asia in 1576
20. The only child of Pocahontas and John Rolfe
21. Site of the first English attempt to found a settlement in North America
22. English settler who introduced tobacco into the colony of Virginia
23. English explorer who reached Newfoundland in 1583, lost at sea on the return trip
24. Nickname of the unsuccessful English settlement at Roanoke Island in 1587
25. One of the three ships that brought the first English settlers to Jamestown in 1607
26. English king who sent the first expedition to America in 1497
27. Native American who married an English colonist in 1614, became a Christian, and went to England
28. Pirate ship of Sir Francis Drake
29. Site of the first permanent English settlement in America, founded in 1607 and named in honor of their king
30. English sea captain who led the defeat of the Spanish Armada in 1588

Name ______________________________ Date ____________________

26. English Exploration in the New World

S	Y	T	D	S	R	M	K	M	G	J	M	P	L	S	C	C	A	M	I
C	N	S	G	J	P	L	O	N	O	S	D	U	H	Y	R	N	E	H	T
F	M	E	I	T	J	D	R	H	H	P	P	P	B	H	V	N	V	S	B
B	L	M	A	R	T	I	N	F	R	O	B	I	S	H	E	R	I	B	D
E	J	A	H	K	F	C	T	S	W	G	E	U	F	R	M	R	R	C	N
P	O	J	J	G	A	R	E	H	M	J	S	T	E	F	H	B	G	A	A
A	H	W	C	B	C	E	A	S	A	A	A	M	K	U	K	R	I	P	L
F	N	L	O	J	S	T	J	N	N	C	B	A	M	R	L	L	N	J	S
F	R	T	J	A	A	R	H	C	C	V	H	P	G	B	S	J	I	E	I
M	O	H	E	N	R	Y	O	E	T	I	H	W	N	H	O	J	A	C	E
J	L	G	L	L	K	N	B	D	K	R	S	D	J	H	M	D	D	S	K
D	F	O	B	D	S	E	I	P	E	G	J	D	N	C	O	R	A	J	O
W	E	M	S	T	R	S	L	Y	E	I	O	S	R	G	Y	T	R	A	N
S	F	J	A	T	C	J	G	I	D	N	M	L	S	A	N	S	E	M	A
B	C	N	B	O	C	I	T	M	Z	I	O	P	D	O	K	S	D	E	O
S	T	G	V	N	L	O	D	I	T	A	F	C	H	E	A	E	T	S	R
T	D	E	R	B	W	R	L	H	P	R	B	A	C	M	N	C	J	T	C
V	R	D	E	E	P	S	D	O	G	C	C	E	O	A	G	H	O	O	L
Y	J	R	C	P	V	O	R	B	N	O	M	H	T	K	B	L	I	W	M
A	T	M	M	A	C	L	K	A	P	Y	T	A	E	H	I	O	U	N	Y
G	S	I	R	W	A	L	T	E	R	R	A	L	E	I	G	H	T	B	D

1. ______________________
2. ______________________
3. ______________________
4. ______________________
5. ______________________
6. ______________________
7. ______________________
8. ______________________
9. ______________________
10. ______________________
11. ______________________
12. ______________________
13. ______________________
14. ______________________
15. ______________________
16. ______________________
17. ______________________
18. ______________________
19. ______________________
20. ______________________
21. ______________________
22. ______________________
23. ______________________
24. ______________________
25. ______________________
26. ______________________
27. ______________________
28. ______________________
29. ______________________
30. ______________________

27. SHIFTS IN EUROPEAN POWER

ACROSS:

1. A fertile strip of land along the west bank of the Rhine River, taken by France in the Thirty Years' War
2. French cardinal and prime minister of Louis XIII who became the virtual ruler of France from 1624 to 1642
3. Queen mother of France, a Catholic, who approved of the massacre of Paris Protestants in 1572
4. Founder of the Dutch republic, assassinated in 1584, known as the "father of his country"
5. By 1650, the financial and commercial center of Europe
6. The Netherlands parliament
7. Catholic leader during the Thirty Years' War
8. The first Bourbon king of France
9. The long struggle between Protestants and Catholics in Europe, 1618–1648
10. A government under which citizens with the right to vote choose their leaders
11. Country that declared independence from Spain in 1581
12. An order granting religious freedom and political equality to the Huguenots, issued by Henry IV of France in 1598 and revoked by Louis XIV in 1685
13. Peace agreement signed by France, Sweden, and the Holy Roman Empire at the end of the Thirty Years' War in 1648
14. French humorist and satirist, author of *Gargantua* and *Pantagruel*
15. French writer who developed the essay, a short written work on a single topic, usually expressing the personal views of the writer
16. Dutch artist, famous for his group painting, "The Night Watch," which showed his mastery of light and shadow
17. An economic system characterized by the investment of money in business ventures with the goal of making a profit
18. An elected governor of a province of the Netherlands
19. The slaughter of the Huguenots in Paris on August 24, 1572
20. In 1600, the European country with the largest fleet in the entire world—10,000 ships
21. The founder of modern philosophy, author of *Discourse on Method,* who stated, "I think, therefore I am."

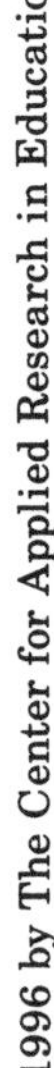

Name ______________________ Date ______________________

27. Shifts in European Power

28. THE ELIZABETHAN AGE

ACROSS:

1. Queen of Scots, Elizabeth's Catholic cousin, whom she ordered beheaded in 1587
2. English poet and dramatist, whom many people regard as the greatest writer of all time
3. Enterprising actor who built the first permanent playhouse just outside the walls of London in 1576, simply called "The Theater"
4. Ship of Francis Drake, aboard which Queen Elizabeth knighted him in 1580
5. One of Shakespeare's most famous plays
6. Men and women who demanded changes in the Church of England
7. The last and greatest ruler of the Tudor dynasty of England, reigning from 1558 to 1603
8. River in southern England, flowing 209 miles east through London to the North Sea
9. Famous tragedy written by William Shakespeare
10. Religion of Queen Elizabeth I
11. English playhouse built in 1599, where Shakespeare's most famous plays were first performed
12. Wife of William Shakespeare
13. Nickname of English sea captains who raided Spanish treasure fleets that sailed from the Americas
14. English sea captain and pirate, the first person since Magellan's crew to sail around the world
15. The grandest church of Elizabethan London
16. Nickname of Elizabeth I, who remained unmarried until her death
17. Another one of Shakespeare's most famous plays

Name ______________________________ Date ____________________

28. The Elizabethan Age

			1					T										
2								H										
					3			E										
				4				E										
					5			L										
					6			I										
					7			Z										
						8		A										
					9			B										
				10				E										
			11					T										
				12				H										
						13		A										
		14						N										
					15			A										
					16			G										
					17			E										

29. THE STUART KINGS

The answers to the following clues are hidden in the puzzle. Circle the answer in the puzzle and then write the answer next to the correct number. Answers can be found horizontally, vertically, diagonally, and backward.

1. The first Stuart king of England, 1603–1625
2. The greatest writer during the period of Stuart kings, author of *Paradise Lost*
3. The second Stuart king to rule England, 1625–1649
4. English Protestants who advocated simpler forms of creed and ritual in the Church of England, many of whom fled to America to escape persecution
5. Country also ruled by James I while he was the king of England
6. Name given to the bloodless overthrow of James II by William and Mary in 1688
7. The first English colony in North America
8. English architect who rebuilt St. Paul's Cathedral and many other churches after the great fire of London in 1666
9. Stuart king who supervised a new translation of the Bible, first printed in 1611
10. Document signed by Charles I in 1628, limiting his power to levy taxes, imprison people without cause, or house soldiers in private homes
11. Stuart king called "the merry monarch"
12. Stuart king called "the most learned fool in Christendom"
13. The legislature of England
14. English philosopher who believed that people had the gift of reason and the natural ability to govern their own affairs, author of *Treatises on Government*
15. Mother of James I, executed by Queen Elizabeth I 16 years before James took the throne
16. Englishmen who supported King Charles I during the English civil war
17. Oldest daughter of James II, married to Prince William of Orange
18. The second English colony in North America
19. Englishmen who supported King James II
20. Archbishop of Canterbury appointed by Charles I in 1633 and beheaded in 1645
21. Englishmen who supported Parliament during the English civil war
22. Law passed by Parliament in 1679, making it impossible for the monarch to hold someone in jail indefinitely without a trial
23. The lower division of the British Parliament, whose members are elected
24. The first English monarch to face a public trial and an official execution
25. River in southern England, flowing 200 miles east through London to the English Channel
26. English philosopher who believed an absolute monarchy was best, author of *Leviathan*
27. The theory that rulers receive their authority from God and are answerable only to God
28. Englishmen who opposed King James II
29. French king who secretly aided Charles II in hopes that he would become a Catholic
30. English general who led the Puritans against Charles I in the English civil war
31. Protestant daughter of James II, queen of England from 1689 to 1694
32. Famous epic poem written during the period of Stuart kings, an attempt to explain why life's suffering and pain are justified in God
33. The first permanent English settlement in the New World, founded in 1607 and named in honor of the king
34. Name given to the return of Charles II to the English throne in 1660 and the following period until 1685
35. The upper division of the British Parliament, in which nobles served for life
36. Parliament's military machine, led by Oliver Cromwell, that defeated the Cavaliers and captured Charles I in 1648
37. Religion of King James II
38. The first settlement in New England, founded by the Pilgrims in 1620 and named after the English port from which they sailed
39. Protestant prince of the Netherlands who became king of England in 1689 by invitation, ruling jointly with his wife, the daughter of James II
40. Title held by Oliver Cromwell as ruler of England from 1653 to 1658

Name ______________________________ Date ____________________

29. The Stuart Kings

N S E B B O H S A M O H T H A M E S C O T
O L T H A J M J A T S O L E S I D A R A P
T E H G L O A A P A R L I A M U T I S I A
L O G L Y R A M R I W H O X A H O N E W R
I D I O J S G E E Y I N W L O R O N S T L
M D R R O L R S P S L A M L K M L E O J I
N J F I H A L B C E L A I A M G I W A A A
H A O O N H J E M R I C S O R R T M O M M
O M N U L W A S W L A E C Z O Y E O I E E
J E O S O B H G L M M F A T C S G D T S N
D S I R C H R I S T O P H E R W R E N R T
I T T E K L W H G E F R G L O R I L A E Y
V O I V E M O W S S O E C G E J K A N I B
I W T O D L T U I V R E A R L T C R O L G
N N E L F E O P I C A I N M E H S M I A V
E K P U S H L U H S N M A T A V L Y T V A
R M P T T Y D A I I G N I R C R I O A A S
I F A I M H R T G S E W L B V T Y L R C N
G C G O S L A R O T C E T O R P D R O L A
H B U N E A I M A S S A C H U S E T T S T
T T B S I V A S E L R A H C D A L A S C I
H S D R O L F O E S U O H R G A D Q E N R
A H C S P S E I S D A E H D N U O R R B U
T H A B E A S C O R P U S D I V I N O S P

1. ____________
2. ____________
3. ____________
4. ____________
5. ____________
6. ____________
7. ____________
8. ____________
9. ____________
10. ____________
11. ____________
12. ____________
13. ____________
14. ____________
15. ____________
16. ____________
17. ____________
18. ____________
19. ____________
20. ____________
21. ____________
22. ____________
23. ____________
24. ____________
25. ____________
26. ____________
27. ____________
28. ____________
29. ____________
30. ____________
31. ____________
32. ____________
33. ____________
34. ____________
35. ____________
36. ____________
37. ____________
38. ____________
39. ____________
40. ____________

30. THE AGE OF ABSOLUTE MONARCHS

ACROSS: ____________________

1. Louis XIV's minister of finance, 1665–1683
2. Ruler of the Hapsburg lands from 1740 to 1780
3. The first king of Prussia, 1701–1713
4. Site of Louis XIV's grand palace
5. Czar of Russia, 1682–1725, who made Russia a major European power for the first time
6. Fighting between the countries of Europe, 1756–1763, with Austria, France, and Russia allied against Britain and Prussia
7. The family of Prussian kings
8. Famous room in Louis XIV's palace, where he held his most lavish receptions
9. The family of Russian czars
10. The family of German rulers
11. French dramatist who modeled his tragedies on the works of the ancient Greek playwrights
12. Religion of Louis XIV
13. Famous painting by Leonardo da Vinci that hung in Louis XIV's bedroom
14. The most powerful monarch in French history, 1643–1715
15. French composer and chief musician at Louis XIV's court
16. French dramatist and actor, stage name of Jean Baptiste Poquelin
17. Louis XIV's second wife who founded a boarding school for girls at St.-Cyr in 1686
18. French dramatist who modeled his tragedies on the works of Aeschylus and Sophocles
19. Mother of Louis XIV, regent for her son, 1643–1661
20. French cardinal and prime minister under Louis XIV, 1643–1661
21. The family of French rulers
22. King of Prussia, 1740–1786
23. The first Bourbon king of Spain, 1700–1746, grandson of Louis XIV of France
24. Nickname of Louis XIV

Name ______________________________ Date ______________________

30. The Age of Absolute Monarchs

31. THE ENLIGHTENMENT

The answers to the following clues are hidden in the puzzle. Circle the answer in the puzzle and then write the answer next to the correct number. Answers can be found horizontally, vertically, diagonally, and backward.

1. Pen name of the best-known French philosopher, who is credited with saying, "I do not agree with a word you say but I will defend to the death your right to say it."
2. Scottish professor who defended the idea of a free economy in his book *The Wealth of Nations*, published in 1776
3. The idea that government should give merchants a free hand to produce and sell their goods openly in the world market, the French phrase for "leave alone"
4. The most influential hostess of social gatherings in Voltaire's time, helping to shape the taste and manners of the Enlightenment
5. One of the most noted composers during the Enlightenment, considered by many to have been the greatest European composer of all time
6. French nobleman who advocated separation of powers in government, author of *On the Spirit of Laws,* published in 1748
7. Social gatherings at which writers, musicians, painters, and philosophers presented their works and exchanged ideas
8. One of the greatest German composers during the Enlightenment, best known for his religious music
9. Swiss philosopher, best known for his book on government, *The Social Contract,* published in 1762
10. A group of thinkers in the 1700's who believed in reason, liberty, natural law, progress, and human happiness
11. French philosopher who supervised the publication of a huge encyclopedia that summarized human knowledge during the Enlightenment
12. Name given to the music of the 1700's, which in French means "odd," noted for its drama and complexity
13. One of the greatest German composers during the Enlightenment, who eventually settled in England, where his operas became very popular
14. The cultural and intellectual capital of Europe during the 1700's
15. The most famous work written by Voltaire, a short, satiric novel published in 1758
16. One of the most noted composers during the Enlightenment, who wrote great operas such as *The Marriage of Figaro* and *The Magic Flute*
17. French prison where Voltaire was jailed by King Louis XV
18. French author and philosopher, famous throughout Europe for his letters, pamphlets, plays, and satires
19. One of the most noted composers during the Enlightenment, honored as the "father of the symphony"
20. French theorists who searched for natural laws to explain the economy

Name ______________________ Date ______________

31. The Enlightenment

T R L A C Y S U S T E V M A R M I C H E L M A R

T H E A L Y N C I N D L A R R T O P H Y L V A E

A R D E N I S D I D E R O T L E L I Z B I F A N

N A N R U A E S S U O R S E U Q C A J N A E J N

T H A F F R E I D A A R R J O N S A S N I T E A

J O H D A R N N E J A N E O T I B S B N I V E L

L Y K M A C A J U D L U C H R B A O A P O E R G

M B C A R M D N A V E R I A T L O V S H I L I D

C A I A P R S L C W A L P N O T E R T S E H A C

L R R A H R K M C O R A D N O C K E I A R N T S

T O E E Y P L O I P I E S S A J E O L C I H L U

R N D C S H H L A T N S D E E B A S L T A T O E

N D E N I I E P S S H E M B N E S T E A F T V E

N E R W O L F G A N G A M A D E U S M O Z A R T

O M F R C O F B O R L E V S R K S E E T E B A T

E O E U R S N A I V I G D T E I D R U S S A I T

Y N G O A O F R P H I S O I E I E X Q N S S O R

T T R H T P E O R W N A R A D I Z A O O I T N A

U E O N S H I Q D V E R S N I N T Y R H A I I L

L S E C R E E U S T M O A B R I A S A O L L T O

W Q G N J S L E E F E C R A S O J C B O U L H N

S U O N C I T V I R G B E C A C H N O R F E O L

N I R F F O E G E S E R E H T E I R A M C H T E

K E A S P E K E J O S E P H H A Y D N S U F I L

S U E O W I G H I S A B A R K M G K M J R F Y A

1. ______________________ 11. ______________________
2. ______________________ 12. ______________________
3. ______________________ 13. ______________________
4. ______________________ 14. ______________________
5. ______________________ 15. ______________________
6. ______________________ 16. ______________________
7. ______________________ 17. ______________________
8. ______________________ 18. ______________________
9. ______________________ 19. ______________________
10. ______________________ 20. ______________________

32. THE FRENCH AND INDIAN WAR

ACROSS: ____________________

1. Present-day city that got its name from the British fort that was captured from the French and renamed in honor of the British secretary of state
2. Colonial leader during the French and Indian War
3. Seaport at the mouth of the Mississippi River that Spain received from France as a result of the French and Indian War
4. Author of the Albany Plan of Union, an unsuccessful effort to join the 13 British colonies in America under a single government
5. British king during the French and Indian War
6. A French stronghold at the junction of the Allegheny and Monongahela rivers, captured by the British in 1758
7. Territory that Britain received from France as a result of the French and Indian War
8. Stockade built by Washington and his men, site of the opening battle of the French and Indian War in 1754
9. French commander who was killed at the battle of Quebec during the French and Indian War
10. British general who captured Louisbourg, the most important French Canadian fortress
11. Native Americans who allied with the French during the French and Indian War
12. British general who was killed in an attempt to seize Fort Duquesne during the French and Indian War
13. French king during the French and Indian War
14. Site of the final battle of the French and Indian War, captured by the British in 1760
15. Nickname of British soldiers during the French and Indian War
16. Native Americans who allied with the British during the French and Indian War
17. Site of the peace treaty that ended the French and Indian War in 1763
18. British general who captured and burned Fort Duquesne during the French and Indian War
19. British commander who was killed at the battle of Quebec during the French and Indian War
20. British secretary of state during the French and Indian War
21. Territory that Britain received from Spain as a result of the French and Indian War

Name ______________________ Date ______________________

32. The French and Indian War

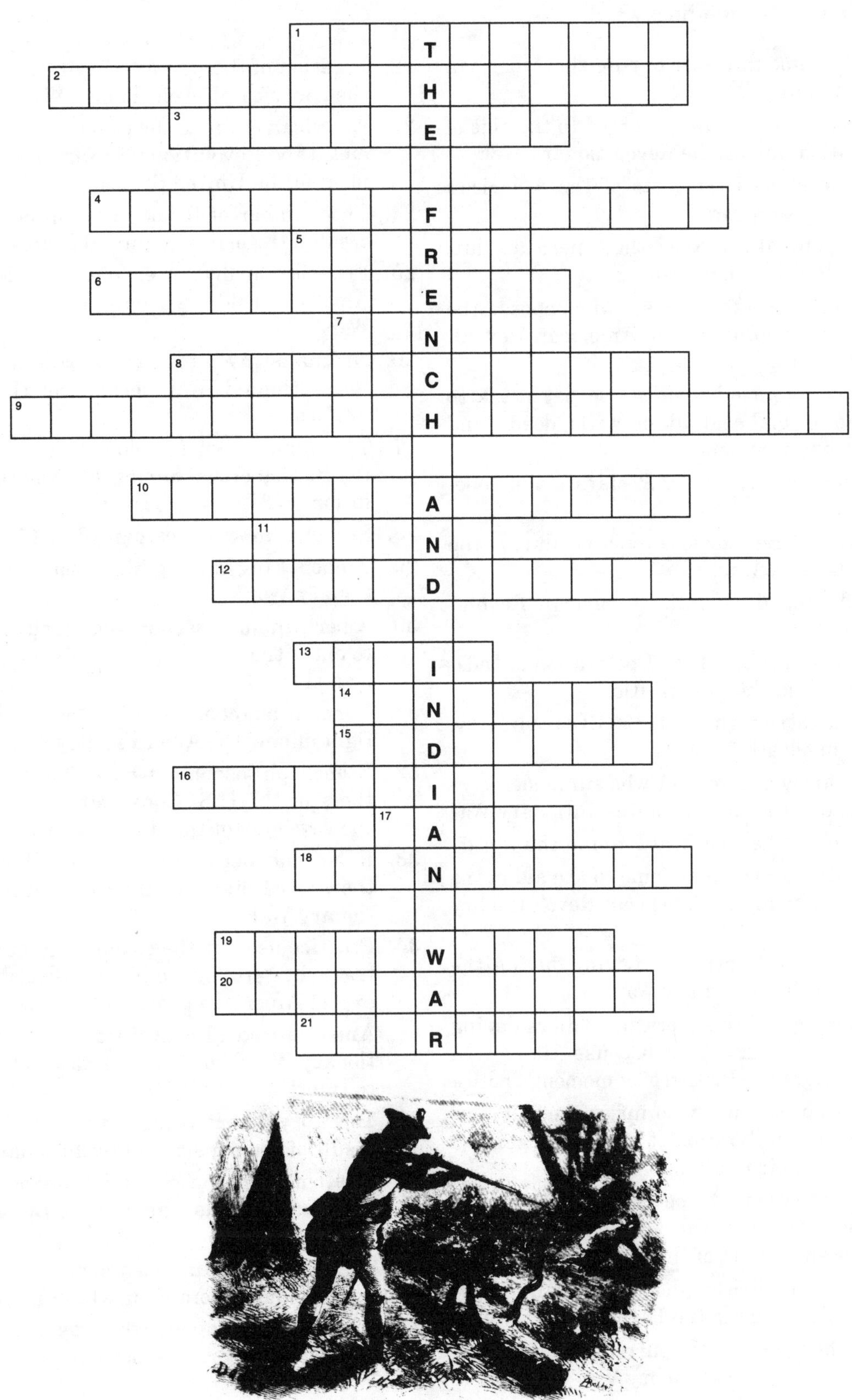

33. REVOLUTION IN COLONIAL AMERICA

The answers to the following clues are hidden in the puzzle. Circle the answer in the puzzle and then write the answer next to the correct number. Answers can be found horizontally, vertically, diagonally, and backward.

1. British prime minister during the American Revolutionary War
2. American general who deserted to the side of the British during the Revolutionary War
3. Site where the first shots of the American Revolution were fired
4. French general who aided the Americans during the Revolutionary War
5. The name given to colonists who opposed the British crown during the American Revolutionary War
6. Law that required colonists to pay a tax to have an official seal put on wills, deeds, and other legal documents
7. The prime author of the Declaration of Independence
8. Site of the first American victory during the Revolutionary War
9. British king during the American Revolutionary War
10. Site of the signing of the Declaration of Independence and the Constitution
11. Virginia patriot who stated, "Give me liberty, or give me death!"
12. British army commander who surrendered in 1781 to end the American Revolutionary War
13. Location of "the shot heard 'round the world"
14. European country that came to the aid of the colonists during the American Revolutionary War
15. Leader of the Continental Army during the American Revolutionary War
16. Nickname given to American soldiers during the Revolutionary War because they were ready to fight the British on a moment's notice
17. English philosopher who influenced the authors of the Declaration of Independence, who expressed their unalienable rights
18. American envoy to the peace treaty that ended the Revolutionary War, first chief justice of the Supreme Court of the United States
19. Polish cavalry officer who helped train American soldiers during the Revolutionary War
20. Site of the final British surrender that ended the American Revolutionary War
21. Author of *Common Sense* and *The Crisis,* encouraging the colonists to rebel against Britain
22. Location of the peace treaty talks that ended the American Revolutionary War
23. American envoy to the peace treaty talks that ended the Revolutionary War; first vice-president of the United States
24. The number of former British colonies that created the original United States
25. Prussian army veteran who helped train American soldiers during the Revolutionary War
26. Nickname given to British soldiers during the Revolutionary War because of their bright uniforms
27. The name given to colonists who supported the British crown during the American Revolutionary War
28. Site of a famous "tea party" in 1773
29. French king during the American Revolutionary War
30. American ambassador who persuaded France to enter the Revolutionary War on the American side
31. German mercenaries hired by the British to fight during the American Revolutionary War
32. French philosopher who influenced the authors of the U.S. Constitution, who divided the government into three separate branches
33. River that became the western boundary of the United States as the result of the Revolutionary War
34. Practice used by the colonists to hurt British trade, by refusing to import British goods or export American goods to Britain
35. American naval captain during the Revolutionary War who stated, "I have not yet begun to fight!"
36. Territory that Britain returned to Spain as a result of the American Revolutionary War
37. Chairman of the Second Continental Congress and famous signer of the Declaration of Independence
38. Site where the American army spent a bitter, hungry, and demoralizing winter in 1777–1778
39. British secret agent who was captured and hanged during the American Revolutionary War
40. American patriot who warned colonists, "The British are coming!"

Name ______________________ Date ______________________

33. Revolution in Colonial America

P H I L A D E L P H I A E B I P T G E O N A V S E S

S T A M A N I L K N A R F N I M A J N E B T H O T B

O H N G I F B O S T O B L E Z W A R U S E R E A O I

V O L E E F A D A B P A T R I O T S I C E N O Y F R

C M S I E O S Y B O K R A F T F V L N S A C C W P A

F A D P I T R C E G R O F Y E L L A V C D O C P C N

I S R P A A R G U T A N W E S A R O M E T O A R N O

L J D I P T X I E N T D I S W F O I R T Y U E L B A

T E S S S M R M H K M E L N C A N I S I L R N E E M

L F X S T M R I J T C M R P V U B I L R D N E N N E

J F R I E D R I C H V O N S T E U B E N W A S I E B

E E A S N C P E L K C N L E S O E V A O R T C A D J

A R R S F G K A O D H T M N L J E N T B A S J P I A

J S M I B L T C R F J E R A H R H K B M N B M S C J

S O L M K R B O D I N S N P E O R M P A J O S A T E

M N H D E C L N N W S Q D R J O J A I M G S P M A J

A L T N J B D C O H K U A P Y C C S Z T B T H O R B

D A T I H U Y O R E Y I B A S T S I L A Y O L H N D

A O R P G A N R T E G E O R G E W A S H I N G T O N

N S L N J L N D H L G U J A H T V N C F L A L S L C

H G A N M D A C R R K T X L A M S A L D E C O N D R

O I H M S S E N O J L U A P N H O J N Y P A U W V K

J O Y O K N M E A C A S I M I R P U L A S K I Z C A

J A I F H E G S B L K R K A G M R D E L T C S L J S

1. ______________________

2. ______________________

3. ______________________

4. ______________________

5. ______________________

6. ______________________

7. ______________________

8. ______________________

9. ______________________

10. ______________________

11. ______________________

12. ______________________

13. ______________________

14. ______________________

15. ______________________

16. ______________________

17. ______________________

18. ______________________

19. ______________________

20. ______________________

21. ______________________

22. ______________________

23. ______________________

24. ______________________

25. ______________________

26. ______________________

27. ______________________

28. ______________________

29. ______________________

30. ______________________

31. ______________________

32. ______________________

33. ______________________

34. ______________________

35. ______________________

36. ______________________

37. ______________________

38. ______________________

39. ______________________

40. ______________________

34. REVOLUTION IN FRANCE

ACROSS:

2. French legislators who sat on the right side of the meeting hall, those who opposed changes in government
5. French revolutionary leader who was executed on July 28, 1794
7. Month in which the French Revolution began
9. French legislators who sat on the left side of the meeting hall, those who favored widespread changes in government
10. French king who was executed during the Revolution
12. The French instrument for execution
15. The French national anthem
16. The period of the French Revolution from May, 1793, to August, 1794, during which thousands were executed
17. A member of the French political society that inaugurated the Reign of Terror during the French Revolution
18. Location of the French prison where the Revolution began in 1789
21. French legislators who sat in the center of the meeting hall, those who wanted some reforms but not extreme or excessive
22. French nobles who fled the country, living abroad and plotting against the Revolution

DOWN:

1. The five executives of the French government from October, 1795, to November, 1799
3. Site of the king's palace in France
4. The French middle class of society
6. French fortress that served as a jail for political prisoners, destroyed in 1789 to mark the beginning of the French Revolution
8. French queen who was executed during the Revolution
11. Aristocratic commander who was killed during the storming of the Bastille to begin the French Revolution
13. The red, white, and blue ribbon that the French revolutionaries adopted as their symbol
14. The capital of France
19. River in northeastern France, flowing 480 miles to the English Channel
20. Location of the execution of Louis XVI and Marie Antoinette

Name ______________________ Date ______________________

34. Revolution in France

35. NAPOLEON BONAPARTE

ACROSS:

1. Napoleon's economic policy that closed all ports on the European continent to British shipping
2. Scene of a naval battle off the southern coast of Spain in which the British defeated the French fleet in 1805
3. Napoleon's wife, whom he married in 1796 and divorced in 1809
4. Island in the Mediterranean Sea where Napoleon was born in 1769
5. British general who defeated Napoleon in 1815
6. Nickname given to Napoleon by his loyal troops
7. English admiral killed at the battle of Trafalgar in 1805
8. A feeling of pride in and devotion to one's country
9. Site of Napoleon's exile, 1814–1815, a tiny island off the Italian coast
10. Scene of Napoleon's final defeat, June 18, 1815
11. Russian czar who destroyed Moscow in 1812 rather than surrender it to the French
12. Cathedral where Napoleon crowned himself emperor on December 2, 1804
13. Napoleon's brother who was appointed king of Spain in 1808
14. Site of Napoleon's coronation
15. Spanish peasant fighters who ambushed French troops and then fled into hiding, a Spanish word meaning "little war"
16. Site of Napoleon's greatest victory, where French troops defeated the Austrian and Russian armies in December, 1805
17. Site of Napoleon's exile, 1815–1821, a remote island in the South Atlantic

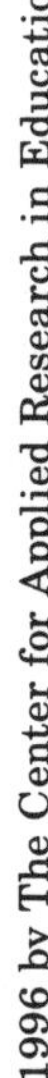

Name ______________________________ Date ____________________

35. Napoleon Bonaparte

Row	Letter
1	N
2	A
3	P
4	O
5	L
6	E
7	O
8	N
9	B
10	O
11	N
12	A
13	P
14	A
15	R
16	T
17	E

36. THE INDUSTRIAL REVOLUTION

ACROSS:

1. English cotton manufacturer, inventor of the water-powered spinning frame in 1769
5. Italian physicist who built one of the first electric batteries in 1800
10. U.S. scientist born in Scotland, inventor of the telephone in 1876
11. British mill worker who built the first spinning machines in the United States, called "the father of the American factory system"
15. U.S. inventor of the cotton gin in 1793
16. English inventor of the spinning mule in 1779
17. Italian inventor of a wireless telegraph system in 1895
18. English engineer who devised a process for eliminating impurities from pig iron in 1859
19. German inventor of an internal combustion engine that could power large vehicles such as trucks, ships, and locomotives
20. English physicist who discovered the properties of electromagnetism, which led to the construction of electric generators
23. A group of workers in a trade or industry who join together to bargain for better working conditions and higher wages
24. German scientist who devised an internal combustion engine that was fueled by gasoline in 1886
25. An organized work stoppage by employees, conducted for the purpose of improving wages and working conditions
27. English chemist who discovered a brilliant dye that could be made from coal, founder of the aniline dye industry
28. English weaver and inventor of the spinning jenny in 1764
29. U.S. inventor of interchangeable parts, identical components that can be used in place of one another in manufacturing
30. English novelist, author of *Hard Times,* in which he described life during the Industrial Revolution
31. French inventor of a power loom specially equipped for weaving figured textiles and controlled by a punched paper strip

DOWN:

2. English watchmaker who invented the flying shuttle in 1733
3. English scientific farmer who invented the seed drill in 1721
4. Scottish inventor and engineer who perfected the steam engine during the 1760's
6. English inventor who discovered a way to produce paper negatives in 1839, the basis of modern photography
7. English scientific farmer who devised the practice of crop rotation during the 1730's
8. French inventor of an early photographic process in 1839
9. U.S. inventor who developed a steamboat, the *Clermont,* in 1807
10. Rhode Island businessman who opened the first American factory in 1790 at Pawtucket
11. English engineer who perfected the locomotive, designer of the *Rocket* in 1829
12. English inventor of the power loom in 1785
13. English novelist, author of *Oliver Twist* and *David Copperfield,* in which he attacked the evils of child labor during the Industrial Revolution
14. U.S. inventor who constructed the first practical telegraph in 1837
17. Scottish engineer who devised a road surface made of crushed rock during the early 1800's
21. Country where the Industrial Revolution began during the 1700's
22. A demonstration by workers for the purpose of publicizing alleged grievances, persuading the public not to do business with the affected company
26. English physician who discovered vaccination in 1796

Name ______________________________ Date ______________________

36. The Industrial Revolution

37. REVOLUTIONS AND REACTIONS

The answers to the following clues are hidden in the puzzle. Circle the answer in the puzzle and then write the answer next to the correct number. Answers can be found horizontally, vertically, diagonally, and backward.

1. An international peace conference held in Austria in 1814
2. The French middle class that controlled the legislature and supported the king, the French word for townspeople
3. French delegate who attended the international peace conference in 1814
4. French laws passed in 1830 that dissolved the legislature, ended freedom of the press, and put new restrictions on the right to vote
5. Russian czar who attended the international peace conference in 1814
6. Austrian foreign minister who attended the international peace conference in 1814
7. During the 1800's, a philosophy that supported guarantees for individual freedom, political change, and social reform
8. European country that joined the Quadruple Alliance in 1815
9. The first European monarch to adopt middle class dress, called the "bourgeois monarch"
10. European country that established independence from the Ottoman Empire in 1829
11. English statesman who condemned the French Revolution because it brought about radical changes that destroyed traditional institutions, author of *Reflections on the Revolution in France*
12. German laws passed in 1819 that imposed press censorship and suppressed freedom of speech
13. European country that joined the Quadruple Alliance in 1815
14. Prussian king who attended the international peace conference in 1814
15. European country that established independence from the Netherlands in 1830
16. During the 1800's, a philosophy that supported the traditional order and resisted political and social change
17. European country that joined the Quadruple Alliance in 1815
18. British foreign minister who attended the international peace conference in 1814
19. French king who abdicated and fled to England during the July Revolution in 1830
20. During the 1800's, a feeling of pride for and devotion to a common cultural heritage regardless of political boundaries
21. European country that joined the Quadruple Alliance in 1815
22. French king who abdicated and fled to England during the revolution of 1848

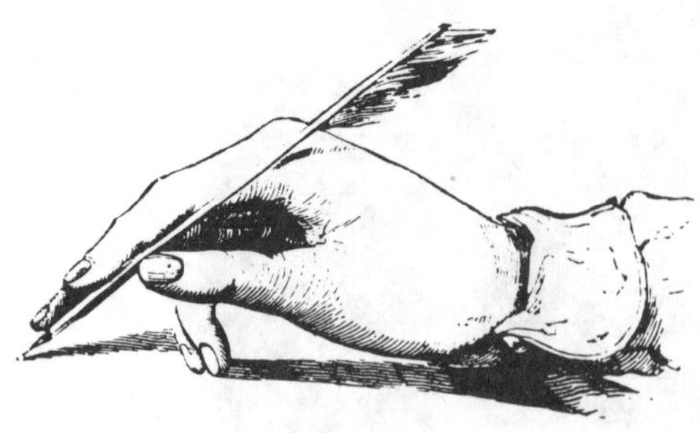

Name ______________________ Date ______________________

37. Revolutions and Reactions

H I L M O R I S T O W J C U R H I G E S A
S T M S I T A V R E S N O C T E N S T E A
A E U N I F M E T T E R N I C H V E R C S
I I T Y N R O R L L F O G L K S A E U N C
O N S F P E I S I O E G R U O B N H O A A
E X I S P D A B L U U D E C M A H P C N R
O M U A U E E N T I Y I S C T O G L E I L
G A U S T R I A E S N O S I R T A H E D S
R N R A A I P Z O P N A O P U N E I V R B
E R S L L C R I T H Y N F S H G R H A O A
N C I E L K E B N I A D V O R I E A H Y D
C S H X E W O L A L E B I E G E L S H L D
M C L A Y I A R I I K E E C R A T I D U E
O C K N R L N S S P O C N L R C S O P J C
M A N D A L M T S P E E N L G O A P J P R
O C H E N I E R U E C H A L A I C N D P E
R E N R D A T S R E D M U N D B U R K E E
I C H A L M A P A C T R I L S I H M F D S

1. ______________________
2. ______________________
3. ______________________
4. ______________________
5. ______________________
6. ______________________
7. ______________________
8. ______________________
9. ______________________
10. ______________________
11. ______________________
12. ______________________
13. ______________________
14. ______________________
15. ______________________
16. ______________________
17. ______________________
18. ______________________
19. ______________________
20. ______________________
21. ______________________
22. ______________________

38. LATIN AMERICAN INDEPENDENCE

ACROSS:

1. Ex-slave and revolutionary leader who drove the French forces from Hispaniola in 1801, later taken prisoner and died in France in 1803
2. The first Latin American country to free itself from European rule, the French colony on the island of Hispaniola in the Caribbean Sea
3. People of mixed European and African ancestry, part of the common class of Latin American society
4. Latin American country that declared its independence from Spain in 1818
5. Latin American revolutionary leader who helped win independence from Spain for Peru, Ecuador, Chile, and Argentina
6. The major religion in Latin America
7. U.S. president who promised to protect Latin American independence from European countries in 1823
8. People who were born in Latin America but whose ancestors came from Europe, wealthy landowners and lesser government officials
9. Latin American country that won its independence from Portugal peacefully in 1822
10. South American country that is named in honor of its revolutionary leader
11. Latin American revolutionary leader who helped free Venezuela from Spanish rule, often called "the Morning Star of Independence," later taken prisoner and died in Spain in 1816
12. One of the major languages spoken in Latin America
13. Latin American country that won its independence from Spain in 1816, homeland of a famous South American general and revolutionary leader
14. People of mixed European and Indian ancestry, part of the common class of Latin American society
15. A feeling of loyalty and devotion to one's own land and people
16. One of the first revolutionary leaders of Mexico, a priest who was captured by the Spanish and executed in 1811
17. Another of the major languages spoken in Latin America
18. Portuguese prince who became emperor of South America's largest country in 1822, South America's only monarch
19. Latin American country that won its independence from Spain in 1821, formerly called New Spain
20. Perhaps the best-known Latin American revolutionary leader, often called "the Liberator"
21. A dictator, usually an army officer, of a Latin American country
22. Another of the major languages spoken in Latin America
23. The privileged class of Latin American society, people who had been born in Spain or Portugal and held the most important positions in government and the Church
24. Site of the last major battle of the war for Latin American independence, December 9, 1824, in Peru
25. Latin American country that won its independence from Spain in 1821, homeland of "the George Washington of South America"

Name ______________________________ Date ______________________

38. Latin American Independence

39. THE TRIUMPH OF NATIONALISM

ACROSS:

3. Prussian prime minister appointed in 1862, known as "the Iron Chancellor," who created a united German empire
4. Italian nationalist who liberated Sicily and southern Italy from foreign control
6. Border province added to the German Confederation by the Franco-Prussian War
9. The German word for "emperor"
10. In 1871, the city that became the national capital of a united Italy
12. Site of the pope's palace in Italy
15. Italian nationalist and statesman, publisher of a newspaper called *Il Risorgimento (The Resurgence),* which eventually gave its name to the whole movement for Italian unity
16. Country that was forced to withdraw from the German Confederation during the Seven Weeks' War in 1866
18. The German term meaning "the politics of reality," used during the late 1800's to describe a tough, calculated brand of politics in which idealism played no part
20. Prussian king who was crowned the first emperor of the newly formed German empire in 1871
21. Border province added to the German Confederation during the war between Prussia and Denmark in 1864
22. Austrian territory lost to Italy during the Seven Weeks' War in 1866
23. Members of Prussia's wealthy landlord class, who held most government and military powers and dominated the Prussian parliament

DOWN:

1. The most industrial of the German states and whose army was by far the most powerful in central Europe
2. Another border province added to the German Confederation during the war between Prussia and Denmark in 1864
5. Italian patriot and general who worked to unite Italy, known as "The Red One"
7. The first king of a unified Italy, 1861–1878
8. Austria's capital, an important cultural center for German music, art, and literature during the early 1800's
11. French palace where King William I of Prussia was crowned emperor of the newly formed German empire on January 18, 1871
13. Another border province added to the German Confederation by the Franco-Prussian War
14. Italian nationalists led by Garibaldi, so named for the color of their uniforms
17. The German word for "empire"
19. Border province of France, containing rich coal and iron deposits, seized by Prussia in 1871

Name ______________________ Date ______________________

39. The Triumph of Nationalism

40. IMPERIALISM IN AFRICA

ACROSS:

3. Dutch colonists in South Africa, from the Dutch word for "farmer"
5. Scottish minister who went to Africa in 1814 to preach the Gospel and heal the sick
6. British colony in Africa on the north shore of Lake Victoria
8. European country that colonized Angola and Mozambique
10. Present-day name for the Belgian Congo
11. European country that colonized Rio de Oro and the Canary Islands
12. French explorer of Africa, the first European to cross the Sahara Desert (1827–1828)
15. British colonial statesman and financier who became rich in the diamond mines of South Africa, prime minister of the Cape Colony
16. One of only two African countries that remained free from European control, ruled by Menelik II from 1889 to 1913
18. European country that colonized Algeria and Tunisia
19. Site where diamonds were discovered in South Africa in 1867
21. The longest river in Africa
22. Scottish missionary who spent 30 years in central Africa
25. European country that colonized Libya and Eritrea
26. Disease that claimed many European lives in Africa before the discovery of quinine
27. The system in which an imperial power governs its colonies closely because it believes that the people are not able to govern themselves
30. Small Spanish colony in northwestern Africa
31. African country founded during the 1820's by former American slaves
34. British journalist and African explorer who found Dr. Livingstone in 1871
36. European country that colonized Rio Muni and northern Morocco
37. British general who conquered Sudan in 1898
38. British colony in west Africa
39. Sea located between Africa and Saudi Arabia

DOWN:

1. Italian colony in northern Africa
2. British colony in northern Africa
3. European country that colonized the Congo
4. Canal that was built to link the Mediterranean and Red Seas, providing a much shorter route from Europe to the Indian Ocean
7. Site where British and French forces in the Sudan almost went to war in 1898
9. Cattle disease that caused a disastrous famine in East Africa in the late 1880's, due to infected cattle imported from southern Europe
13. The domination by a country of the political, economic, or cultural life of another country or region
14. The policy whereby an imperial power tries to absorb colonies politically and culturally into the parent nation
17. A country whose foreign policy is controlled by an outside government
20. European country that colonized Sierra Leone and the Gold Coast
23. British explorer who trekked inland from the East African coast to discover the source of the Congo River, then traveled down the Congo to the Atlantic Ocean
24. European country that colonized Cameroons and Togo
28. French engineer who supervised the building of a canal to link the Mediterranean and Red Seas, completed in 1869
29. European country that had the most African colonies, one third of the continent and 64 million people to rule
32. Site of a European conference that drew boundary lines to divide up the continent of Africa (1884–1885)
33. European country that colonized Morocco and Equatorial Africa
35. The color usually used to represent the British empire on maps during the Age of Imperialism (the largest empire the world had ever known)

Name ______________________ Date ______________________

40. Imperialism in Africa

41. IMPERIALISM IN INDIA

ACROSS:

2. Port city on the southeastern coast of India
5. One of the major Indian exports during the Age of Imperialism
7. The first European to reach India by a sea route around Africa, 1498
8. One of the two dominant religions in India during the Age of Imperialism
11. Port city on the western coast of India
12. Another one of the two dominant religions in India during the Age of Imperialism
15. British general who ousted the French from India and founded British India
16. Britain's queen who took the title Empress of India in 1876
17. Portuguese port district on the western coast of India during the Age of Imperialism
18. The Indian custom of secluding women
20. The color of British combat uniforms adopted in India, from the Indian word for "dust"
21. A Hindu prince
22. Forbidden food of the Hindus
23. Indian soldiers who served in the British Indian Army, rebelling in 1857
24. Bay east of India

DOWN:

1. Forbidden food of the Muslims
3. British prime minister who called India "the brightest jewel in Her Majesty's Crown"
4. The chief of a tribal state in India
5. Port city on the northeastern coast of India
6. Another one of the major Indian exports during the Age of Imperialism
9. French settlement in southeastern India during the Age of Imperialism
10. Another one of the major Indian exports during the Age of Imperialism
13. Island south of India, acquired by the British in 1786 (now called Sri Lanka)
14. Indian nationalist who began the movement for independence from Britain in the early 1900's
17. River in northern India
19. Sea west of India

Name ______________________ Date ______________________

41. Imperialism in India

42. IMPERIALISM IN CHINA

ACROSS:

1. A rebellion of Chinese peasants in 1850, from the Chinese words for "great peace"
3. Country that controlled much of southwestern China and the port of Kwangchow
5. Chinese island taken over by Britain in 1842
7. Dynasty that ruled China from 1644 to 1911
8. Country that controlled much of central China and the port of Weihaiwei
11. Chinese river, called the "River of Sorrows" because its floods have caused much death and destruction, as in 1852
12. Leader of the Chinese nationalist movement, founder of the Kuomintang in 1912
14. Trade item that led to a war between China and Britain in 1839; a habit-forming narcotic made from the poppy plant
15. Country that controlled the Shantung Peninsula and the port of Kiaochow
16. Chinese island taken over by Japan in 1895, present-day Taiwan
19. The right of foreigners to be protected by the laws of their own nations
21. Port city in southern China controlled by Portugal
22. Chinese capital during the Age of Imperialism, present-day Beijing

DOWN:

2. One of the major Chinese exports during the Age of Imperialism
4. The first port where China granted Europeans trading rights
5. Chinese island controlled by France
6. Site where the British and Chinese signed a treaty in 1842, giving Britain the right to trade at Chinese ports
9. Country that controlled much of northern China and Port Arthur
10. American foreign policy proposed in 1899, protecting trading rights in China
13. Chinese secret group pledged to rid the country of "foreign devils," officially known as the Society of Righteous and Harmonious Fists
17. Continent where China is located
18. Another one of the major Chinese exports during the Age of Imperialism
20. Another one of the major Chinese exports during the Age of Imperialism

Name ______________________ Date ______________________

42. Imperialism in China

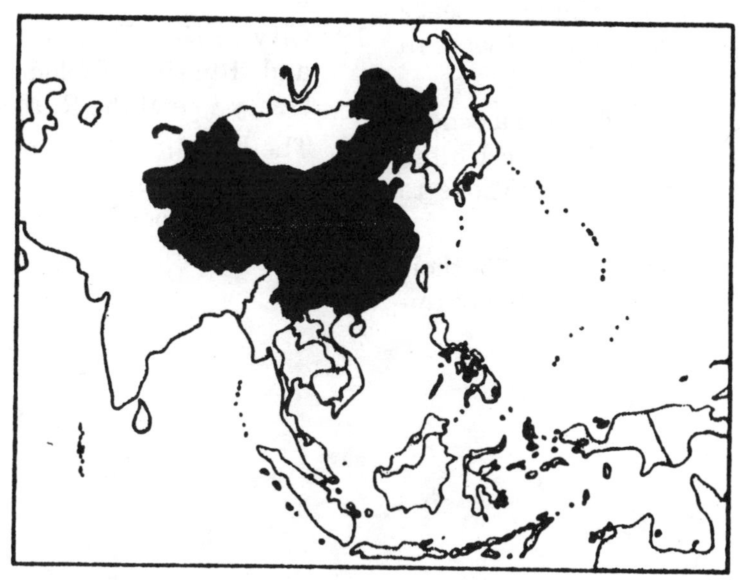

43. IMPERIALISM IN JAPAN

The answers to the following clues are hidden in the puzzle. Circle the answer in the puzzle and then write the answer next to the correct number. Answers can be found horizontally, vertically, diagonally, and backward.

1. The first Japanese port that was opened to European traders
2. U.S. naval commodore who opened Japan to American commerce in 1853
3. Country that went to war against Japan in 1904
4. The first European country that was allowed to trade in Japan
5. Treaty signed by Japan and the United States in 1854, opening Japanese ports to foreign trade
6. The major Japanese export during the Age of Imperialism
7. Site of the battle where the Japanese navy defeated the Russian Far Eastern Fleet in 1904
8. Emperor of Japan from 1867 to 1912
9. U.S. president who negotiated a peace agreement between Japan and Russia in 1905
10. Japanese statesman who drafted a constitution in 1889, after visiting the United States and several European nations to study their governments
11. Japanese warriors who lost much of their power and prestige during the Age of Imperialism
12. Port city on the eastern coast of Honshu island
13. Wealthy Japanese families who bought the chief industries and thereby came to dominate the Japanese economy during the Age of Imperialism
14. Japanese capital during the Age of Imperialism, present-day Tokyo
15. European country upon which the Japanese constitution was modeled
16. Name given to the reign of Emperor Mutsuhito, meaning "enlightened rule"
17. China's northeastern province that was rich in iron and coal, where rival claims led to the Russo-Japanese War in 1904
18. The capital of the Japanese Empire until 1868, a city on southwestern Honshu island
19. City in New Hampshire where Japanese and Russian diplomats worked out a treaty to end the Russo-Japanese War
20. The hereditary commanders of the Japanese army until 1868, known to foreigners as the "tycoon"

Name ______________________________ Date ____________________

43. Imperialism in Japan

```
C A R N A T D I O E C L K O A P
A E J O C H T U K A N A G A W A
A I R C W H H L O A E A S N O D
D Y N A M R E G D Y S D G C R O
M D T A U Y O M R A N A O C N K
M E R S C E D H L A E I G M R U
S R S R S Y O M L W A I C A G L
I I U R L A R R D I Y B S N N U
A M A T T H E W P E R R Y C T B
R U C C E H R H M L O L R H G P
R B A J T Y O N R I I A M U O Y
A O K E M D O O S N A D H R A A
E R N I L U S K E N R N T I M L
L I E A J P E V O M U S V A I J
D H L S C I V D S H M G E G H A
S O T O Y K E I E O A I O O S U
R T R X D A L M U G S M Y H U Z
R I S C F K T T Z A I B A T S U
A S B O T I H U S T U M H F T L
```


1. ______________________
2. ______________________
3. ______________________
4. ______________________
5. ______________________
6. ______________________
7. ______________________
8. ______________________
9. ______________________
10. ______________________
11. ______________________
12. ______________________
13. ______________________
14. ______________________
15. ______________________
16. ______________________
17. ______________________
18. ______________________
19. ______________________
20. ______________________

44. IMPERIALISM IN SOUTHEAST ASIA

ACROSS:

1. The world's second largest island, colonized by Britain, Germany, and the Netherlands during the Age of Imperialism
2. Southeast Asian country acquired by Britain piece by piece between 1820 and 1890 to protect the eastern frontier of India
3. An island south of the Malay Peninsula, colonized by Britain during the Age of Imperialism
4. An island of Indonesia, east of Borneo, colonized by the Netherlands during the Age of Imperialism
5. The third largest island in the world, colonized by Britain and the Netherlands during the Age of Imperialism
6. An island in the southeastern Malay Archipelago, colonized by Portugal and the Netherlands during the Age of Imperialism
7. An island in Indonesia, southeast of Sumatra, colonized by the Netherlands during the Age of Imperialism
8. Port city in the Philippine islands, site of the first major battle during the Spanish-American War
9. Natural resource exported from Southeast Asia during the Age of Imperialism
10. The only Southeast Asian country to escape European domination during the Age of Imperialism, present-day Thailand
11. A river in Southeast Asia, flowing 2,600 miles south to the China Sea
12. Cash crop exported from Southeast Asia during the Age of Imperialism
13. Port city in southern Burma, colonized by Britain during the Age of Imperialism
14. Sea between the Philippines and Borneo
15. Another cash crop exported from Southeast Asia during the Age of Imperialism
16. Another natural resource exported from Southeast Asia during the Age of Imperialism
17. An island in Indonesia, south of the Malay Peninsula, colonized by the Netherlands during the Age of Imperialism
18. French colony in Southeast Asia during the Age of Imperialism, present-day Vietnam, Laos, and Cambodia
19. U.S. commodore during the Spanish-American War who defeated the Spanish fleet in Manila Bay, the chief harbor in the Philippines
20. A part of Malaysia on northwestern Borneo, colonized by Britain during the Age of Imperialism
21. The capital of French Indochina during the Age of Imperialism, present-day Ho Chi Minh City
22. Another natural resource exported from Southeast Asia during the Age of Imperialism
23. Pacific island acquired by the United States as a result of the Spanish-American War
24. Another cash crop exported from Southeast Asia during the Age of Imperialism
25. Southeast Asian islands acquired by the United States as a result of the Spanish-American War
26. European country that colonized what is today called Laos, Cambodia, and Vietnam during the Age of Imperialism

Name ______________________________ Date ______________________

44. Imperialism in Southeast Asia

45. INVENTORS AND REFORMERS

The answers to the following clues are hidden in the puzzle. Circle the answer in the puzzle and then write the answer next to the correct number. Answers can be found horizontally, vertically, diagonally, and backward.

1. Scottish inventor who developed the first efficient steam engine in 1765
2. British nurse born in Italy who organized army hospitals during the Crimean War and founded the first school of professional nursing in the world
3. U.S. pioneers in aviation who launched the first powered airplane flight in 1903
4. U.S. scientist born in Scotland who invented the telephone in 1876
5. U.S. social reformer, preacher, and abolitionist
6. Belgian electrician who developed the first industrial dynamo in 1872
7. Italian inventor who developed a system of wireless telegraphy in 1895
8. U.S. inventor who developed the reaping machine in 1831
9. U.S. reformer who headed the North American Woman Suffrage Association
10. U.S. inventor who constructed the first practical telegraph in 1844
11. British suffragist who formed the Women's Social and Political Union in 1903
12. U.S. inventor who developed a steamboat, the *Clermont,* in 1807
13. U.S. inventor who originated a rubber vulcanization process in 1839
14. U.S. educator who founded the nation's first women's college, Mount Holyoke Female Seminary, in 1837
15. U.S. machinist who invented the sewing machine in 1846
16. American inventor who had more than 1,000 patents, including the phonograph and the first practical electric light bulb; called "the wizard of Menlo Park"
17. U.S. suffragist who led a group of reformers at the women's rights convention held in Seneca Falls, New York, in 1848
18. German inventor who produced the world's first motorcycle in 1885 and later manufactured cars that he named for a friend's daughter, Mercedes
19. U.S. inventor who developed a printing press in 1847 that could turn out 10,000 newspapers an hour
20. U.S. educator who established the first American college for training teachers in 1839
21. U.S. reformer who led a lifelong crusade to reform barbarous conditions in mental institutions
22. U.S. inventor who devised a sewing machine with a foot treadle
23. U.S. blacksmith who invented the steel plow in 1837
24. U.S. educator who opened the nation's first high school for girls in 1821
25. U.S. inventor who developed a repeating pistol
26. U.S. abolitionist who started a newspaper called *The North Star*
27. U.S. inventor who devised the cotton gin in 1793
28. U.S. suffragist who was arrested for trying to vote in the 1872 presidential election
29. U.S. automobile manufacturer who mass produced the Model T, reliable cars called "Tin Lizzies"
30. U.S. journalist, social reformer, and abolitionist; publisher and editor of his weekly newspaper, *The Liberator*

Name ______________________________ Date ____________________

45. Inventors and Reformers

```
R U E U E T C Y R U S M C C O R M I C K I A
O I L R T A H Y H I U H E R E E D N H O J A
P R I O T A E L I A S H O W E R E E I M A A
U S Z A A R O A A A A O R R H I A U A A A Y
I S A L C A E A E H N E N N A M E C A R O H
R A B I N A C A L S B E A A U C H L O Y E A
A L E X A N D E R G R A H A M B E L L L I N
N G T Z M S J A L O O O V E A R U M R Y N C
U U H E P U A I A R W U M M N C O A A O N C
I O C N A A M M U A N I J L R R O S S N H E
A D A O H A E I U T E A A E E W Y I U A N L
L K D B C U S A O E L U T E R U R F R O G A
A C Y E E I W U Y O L I A I O R M L O U A G
H I S G I A A I A E A C G A A D E A G R O N
O R T R R C T N W M N H O G C S M L S T D I
I E A A R D T R O T T T D L G O I S T R R T
D D N M A C O T W B H Y I O T E B L E O A H
G E T M C J T R R B O O O H L T I G M B L G
M R O E C L A O O L N D M M W E N R P E L I
V F N H A R T M L T Y B O A B I J D M R I N
C W A J D H M M E E H M M D S A L A J T W E
F E I O E R A U A S A E A C X E R E Y F A C
Z A T R B I A R U R W I A L E Y D V E U M N
D U S M L P V H C E M A T D L S E I V L M E
E N E L E V E O C L S N T Y I M A I S T E R
L B I O X S N A E I L R O T M X G K M O I O
F W Y C K I B R M N R N T R H A D N H N N L
S D E M M E L I N E P A N K H U R S T C M F
```

1. ____________________
2. ____________________
3. ____________________
4. ____________________
5. ____________________
6. ____________________
7. ____________________
8. ____________________
9. ____________________
10. ____________________
11. ____________________
12. ____________________
13. ____________________
14. ____________________
15. ____________________
16. ____________________
17. ____________________
18. ____________________
19. ____________________
20. ____________________
21. ____________________
22. ____________________
23. ____________________
24. ____________________
25. ____________________
26. ____________________
27. ____________________
28. ____________________
28. ____________________
30. ____________________

46. CURRENTS OF THOUGHT—I

ACROSS:

1. French postimpressionist artist (1839–1906) who tried to depict a mood or express an emotion in his paintings, such as *The Card Players*
2. English political economist (1806–1873) who supported reforms to correct the problems created by industrialization
3. English romantic poet (1788–1824) who died while fighting for the independence of Greece
4. English romantic poet (1770–1850) who glorified nature in his poem "The Tables Turned"
5. French romantic painter (1799–1863) who believed that the purpose of art was "not to imitate nature but to strike the imagination"
6. German physicist (1858–1947) who formulated the quantum theory
7. German biologist (1834–1914) who discovered that reproductive cells transmit biological characteristics to the next generation
8. Finnish composer (1865–1957) whose work gave people a heightened sense of nationalism
9. French realistic painter (1819–1877) who made no attempt to beautify life but instead reported it objectively
10. French artist (1814–1875) who painted the everyday lives of peasants and workers, such as *The Gleaners*
11. English romantic poet (1795–1821) who urged a return to a simple life, close to nature
12. French poet, novelist, and dramatist (1802–1885); author of *The Hunchback of Notre Dame*
13. French realistic painter and caricaturist (1808–1879) who attempted to show everyday life as it really was
14. French philosopher (1798–1857); founder of positivism and sociology
15. Austrian botanist (1822–1884) who formulated the laws of genetics
16. English novelist and poet (1840–1928) who portrayed nature as an impersonal force against which people had to struggle
17. English chemist and physicist (1766–1844) who theorized that all matter is made of tiny particles called atoms

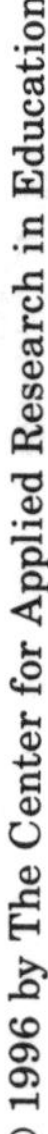

Name ______________________________ Date ____________________

46. Currents of Thought—I

1 C
2 U
3 R
4 R
5 E
6 N
7 T
8 S

9 O
10 F

11 T
12 H
13 O
14 U
15 G
16 H
17 T

47. CURRENTS OF THOUGHT—II

ACROSS:

1. English novelist (1812–1870) who was highly realistic in his portrayal of life in British cities, such as *Hard Times*
2. French physicist born in Poland (1867–1934); discoverer of radium and polonium, who won the Nobel Prize for Chemistry in 1911
3. Russian composer (1872–1915) who produced complex harmonies and rhythms
4. Scottish physicist (1831–1879) who discovered that electric and magnetic energy move in waves
5. French novelist (1799–1850) who realistically portrayed the aspects of life during the 1800's in a massive work called *The Human Comedy*
6. German composer (1770–1827) noted for such works as his Sixth Symphony, the *Pastoral*
7. Dutch postimpressionist painter (1853–1890) who used short, heavy brush strokes and bright colors to convey intense energy, such as *Starry Night*
8. French socialist (1811–1882) who proposed that workers set up cooperative workshops with financial support from the government, "from each according to ability, to each according to need"
9. French impressionist painter (1840–1926) who favored outdoor scenes for their natural light, such as *Gladioli*
10. British physicist born in New Zealand (1871–1937) who discovered that atoms were made up of smaller particles, a nucleus surrounded by one or more electrons
11. British manufacturer and utopian socialist (1771–1858) who established an industrial community in New Lanark, Scotland to test his ideas in 1800
12. German socialist leader and theoretician (1820–1895) who collaborated with Karl Marx to publish *The Communist Manifesto* in 1848
13. Italian operatic composer (1858–1924) who wedded his emotional music to melodramatic plots
14. French painter (1848–1903) whose colorful style was called postimpressionism
15. German physicist (1845–1923); discoverer of X-rays
16. English novelist (1797–1851); author of *Frankenstein*
17. U.S. composer born in Russia (1882–1971) whose ballet *The Rite of Spring* was first performed in Paris in 1913

Name ______________________ Date ______________________

47. Currents of Thought—II

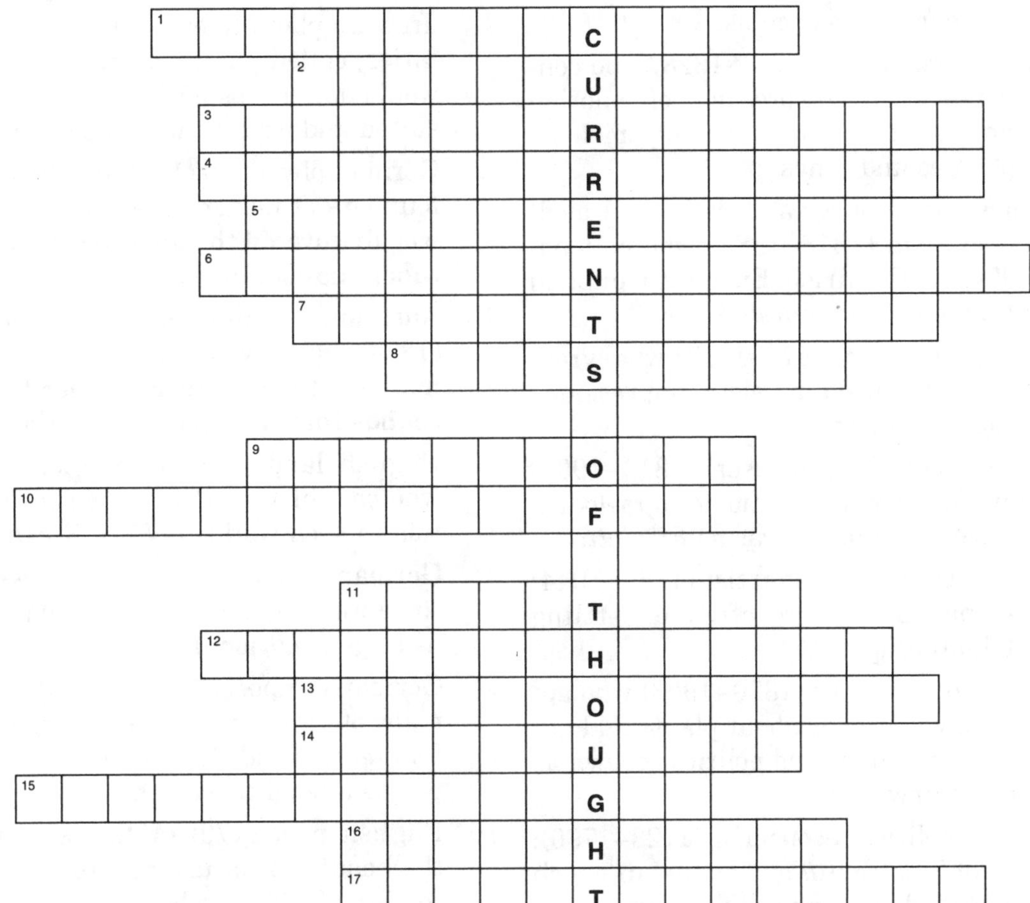

48. CURRENTS OF THOUGHT—III

ACROSS:

1. Spanish painter and sculptor (1881–1973); one of the founders of cubist art
2. Austrian composer (1797–1828) who concentrated on the expression of emotion rather than on form in warmly melodic symphonies and songs
3. German philosopher and theorist of modern socialism (1818–1883) who collaborated with Friedrich Engels to publish *The Communist Manifesto* in 1848
4. French composer (1875–1937) who wrote loosely structured musical impressions such as *The Waltz*
5. Italian operatic composer (1813–1901) who wedded emotional music to melodramatic plots in such operas as *Rigoletto*
6. Russian expressionist artist (1866–1944) whose paintings were often unsettling and frightening
7. English philosopher (1820–1903) who applied Darwin's ideas about plants and animals to economics and politics; known as a Social Darwinist
8. Scottish political economist (1723–1790); author of *The Wealth of Nations,* in which he supported laissez faire economics
9. Czech composer (1841–1904) whose work gave people a heightened sense of nationalism
10. French utopian socialist (1772–1837) who drew up plans to establish model communities, called phalansteries, where people would do the jobs for which they were best suited and would share the profits
11. German physician (1843–1910); one of the founders of modern medical bacteriology who discovered the organisms that caused tuberculosis and cholera
12. Austrian composer and conductor (1874–1951) who based his music on mathematical patterns rather than upon sounds that were pleasing to the ear
13. English landscape painter (1776–1837) who caught the romantic's sense of emotion in such works as *Hove Beach*
14. German composer (1810–1856) who wrote romantic melodies expressing emotion and feelings of nationalism
15. German composer (1813–1883) who based many of his operas, such as *Ring of the Nibelungen,* on old German legends that gave people a heightened sense of nationalism
16. English poet (1792–1822) who glorified the beauty of nature and urged a return to a simple life in rebellion against the ugliness of industrialization
17. U.S. physicist born in Germany (1879–1955); developed the theory of relativity

Name ______________________________ Date ____________________

48. Currents of Thought—III

1 C
2 U
3 R
4 R
5 E
6 N
7 T
8 S

9 O
10 F

11 T
12 H
13 O
14 U
15 G
16 H
17 T

49. CURRENTS OF THOUGHT—IV

ACROSS: ______________________________

1. Spanish composer and pianist (1860–1909) whose work gave people a heightened sense of nationalism
2. English romantic artist (1775–1851) who used the out-of-doors for the subjects of his paintings
3. Russian chemist (1834–1907) who organized a chart of all the known elements in 1869, called the Periodic Table
4. English political economist (1772–1823) whose ideas gave rise to what was called the Iron Law of Wages, inevitable cycles of population and wages
5. English surgeon (1827–1912); founder of antiseptic surgery
6. English philosopher (1748–1832) who argued that the government should intervene to improve living and working conditions
7. Russian novelist (1821–1881); author of *Crime and Punishment*
8. English naturalist (1809–1882) who presented a theory of evolution in his works *The Origin of Species* and *The Descent of Man*
9. English political economist (1766–1834) who supported laissez faire economics in his *Essay on Population*
10. Austrian neurologist (1856–1939) who founded the modern theory of psychoanalysis
11. Russian novelist and social reformer (1828–1910); author of *War and Peace*
12. German philosopher (1844–1900) who believed that some humans could and should evolve to a higher level called ubermenschen (supermen)
13. Russian physiologist (1849–1936) who began his work by studying the behavior of dogs
14. Russian poet (1799–1837) who based many works on traditional Russian folk tales, reflecting an upsurge of nationalism
15. French impressionist artist (1840–1919) who adopted a new technique of painting thousands of dabs of pure color onto the canvas
16. German painter (1867–1945) whose works depicted the bleak lives of workers and the miserable conditions of the early Industrial Revolution
17. French chemist (1822–1895); founder of modern bacteriology

Name ______________________ Date ______________________

49. Currents of Thought—IV

1 C
2 U
3 R
4 R
5 E
6 N
7 T
8 S

9 O
10 F

11 T
12 H
13 O
14 U
15 G
16 H
17 T

50. THE SPANISH-AMERICAN WAR

ACROSS:

2. Nickname of General John J. Pershing, which came from his years with the 10th Cavalry, an African-American regiment that fought in Cuba during the Spanish-American War
4. One of the last Spanish colonies in the Americas, located only 90 miles off the coast of Florida
5. Site where an American fleet sank a Spanish squadron on July 3, 1898, ending Spanish resistance in Cuba
7. U.S. army surgeon who proved the transmission of yellow fever by mosquitoes
10. Site of a U.S. naval station in Cuba
11. Site where the peace treaty was signed on December 10, 1898 to end the Spanish-American War
16. Spanish general who was sent to Cuba to put down the revolt for independence
17. Leader of the Filipino rebels fighting for independence from Spain
18. U.S. Speaker of the House who resigned his congressional seat in protest of colonial expansion
19. The most famous land battle in Cuba during the Spanish-American War
22. U.S. naval leader who sank the Spanish fleet stationed in Manila Bay; stating to an officer, "You may fire when ready, Gridley."
23. Capital of Spanish-owned Cuba
24. Caribbean island that became an independent nation as the result of the Spanish-American War
25. U.S. general who captured Puerto Rico during the Spanish-American War
27. Caribbean island that was acquired by the United States as a result of the Spanish-American War
29. Spanish diplomat who criticized the U.S. president in a private letter, stolen by a Cuban rebel and later published in the *New York Journal*
30. Publisher of the *New York World* whose sensational newspaper stories called for a war to liberate Cuba from Spanish rule
32. A volunteer unit in the Spanish-American War, a mixed crew of cowboys, college students, and adventurers

DOWN:

1. Port on the southeastern coast of Cuba, site of a major naval battle during the Spanish-American War
3. Pacific islands that were acquired by the United States as a result of the Spanish-American War
4. Spanish naval leader in the Caribbean during the Spanish-American War
6. Pacific island that was acquired by the United States as a result of the Spanish-American War
8. U.S. Secretary of State who called the fighting with Spain a "splendid little war"
9. Leader of the First Volunteer Cavalry Regiment during the Spanish-American War, who had resigned as assistant secretary of the navy in order to fight
12. Cash crop of Cuba, in which American industrialists had invested millions of dollars
13. U.S. military leader in Cuba during the Spanish-American War, officer of the 10th Cavalry
14. Captain of the U.S. battleship that exploded in Havana's harbor on February 15, 1898
15. U.S. battleship that mysteriously exploded on February 15, 1898, killing 260 American sailors
20. Nickname that the American press dubbed the Spanish general in Cuba because of his brutal treatment of prisoners and his cruel policies
21. U.S. naval leader in the Caribbean during the Spanish-American War
22. Spanish minister to the United States who resigned just prior to the Spanish-American War
23. Publisher of the *New York Journal* whose sensational newspaper stories called for a war to liberate Cuba from Spanish rule
26. U.S. president during the Spanish-American War
28. U.S. military officer in Puerto Rico during the Spanish-American War
31. U.S. artist who illustrated reporters' dispatches during the Spanish-American War

Name ______________________________ Date ______________________

50. The Spanish-American War

51. THE PANAMA CANAL

ACROSS:

2. A section of a canal enclosed by gates at either end, within which the water depth may be varied to raise or lower boats from level to level
3. A narrow piece of land extending into a body of water and connecting two larger land masses
5. European country that unsuccessfully attempted to dig a canal across Panama in 1882
7. Author of *The Path Between the Seas,* an exciting account of the building of the Panama Canal
10. U.S. president when the construction of the Panama Canal began
12. Port near the Pacific end of the Panama Canal, capital of Panama
14. U.S. Army medical officer who led a program that eliminated yellow fever in Panama
15. An eight-mile cut of the Panama Canal through Culebra Mountain in the southeastern canal zone, named after an American army engineer
19. U.S. Army engineer who supervised the construction of the Panama Canal
21. U.S. warship that was sent to support Panama in its revolution for independence
22. Port town at the Pacific end of the Panama Canal

DOWN:

1. Passenger-cargo steamship that completed the first trip through the Panama Canal on August 15, 1914
2. European engineer who attempted to dig a canal across Panama but failed due to a lack of money, inadequate tools, and disease
4. Disease that threatened workers digging the Panama Canal
6. Country from which Panama declared its independence on November 3, 1903
8. U.S. president who agreed to a series of treaties granting Panama control over the canal zone by the year 2000
9. Lake that makes up part of the Panama Canal route
11. British author who called the building of the Panama Canal "the greatest liberty Man has ever taken with Nature"
13. Port town at the Caribbean end of the Panama Canal
14. U.S. physician who mounted a campaign to eliminate malaria and bubonic plague in Panama
16. U.S. president when the construction of the Panama Canal was completed
17. U.S. Secretary of State who negotiated the treaty that gave the United States the canal zone
18. The width (in miles) of the U.S. canal zone that stretches across Panama
20. The number of years that it took to construct the Panama Canal, at a cost of $400 million and thousands of lives

Name ______________________ Date ______________

51. The Panama Canal

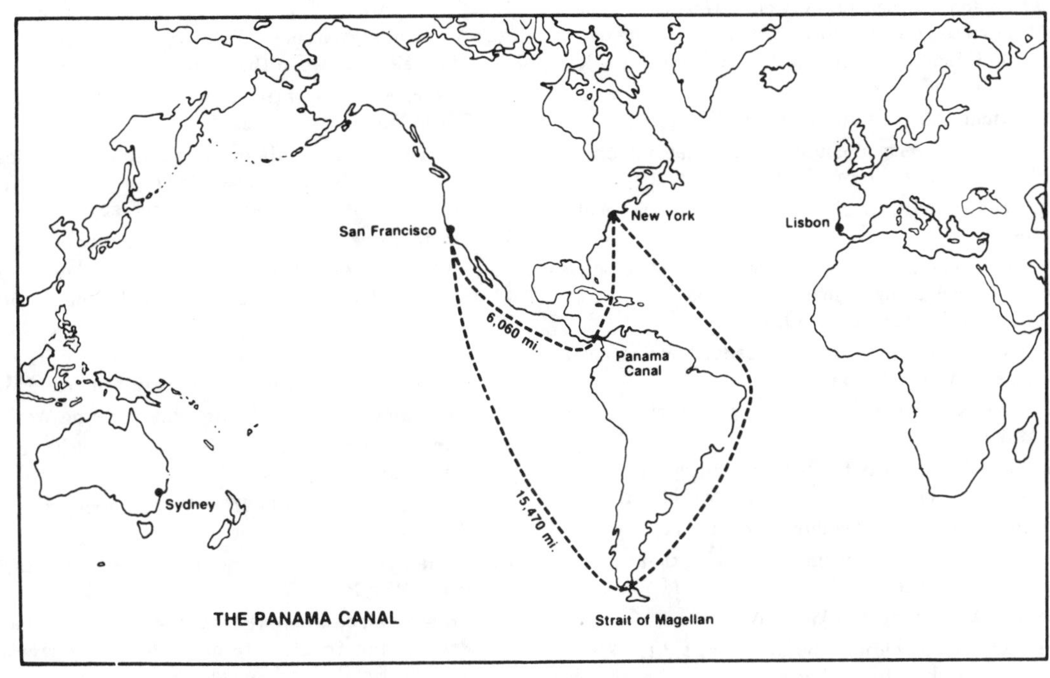

52. WORLD WAR I

The answers to the following clues are hidden in the puzzle. Circle the answer in the puzzle and then write the answer next to the correct number. Answers can be found horizontally, vertically, diagonally, and backward.

1. British passenger ship that was torpedoed by a German submarine on May 7, 1915, killing 1,200 passengers, including 139 Americans
2. Village in northeastern Poland, scene of a major Russian defeat by German forces in August 1914
3. Serbian nationalist who assassinated the archduke and archduchess of Austria on June 28, 1914
4. Grim nickname given to the area between the trenches that were dug during World War I
5. French general, commander in chief of the Allied armies during World War I
6. Location of the assassination of the archduke of Austria on June 28, 1914
7. Town in northeastern France on the Meuse River, scene of several battles during World War I
8. Name given to Germany and Austria-Hungary during World War I because of their geographic location in the heart of Europe
9. British king during World War I
10. Name given to the battle lines between France and Germany during World War I
11. Germany's foreign secretary who attempted to persuade Mexico to join the war on the German side in exchange for Germany's help to get back Mexico's lost land in Texas and Arizona
12. Popular American song during World War I
13. One of the newly formed countries that became an independent nation as the result of World War I
14. Russian ruler during World War I, executed by revolutionaries in 1917
15. River in northeastern France, scene of a decisive battle where the French army stopped the German advance toward Paris on September 12, 1914
16. French passenger ship that was torpedoed by a German submarine in March 1916
17. British representative at the peace treaty that ended World War I
18. Another one of the newly formed countries that became an independent nation as the result of World War I
19. Nickname of aerial battles during World War I
20. Another one of the newly formed countries that became an independent nation as the result of World War I
21. Emperor of Austria during World War I
22. African-American soldier who was awarded the Croix de Guerre, a high military honor from the French government
23. Nickname of a German cannon that hurled an 1800-pound shell a distance of nine miles, named after the wife of Gustav Krupp, the German munitions manufacturer
24. Another one of the newly formed countries that became an independent nation as the result of World War I
25. U.S. naval leader during World War I who devised the convoy system to protect merchant ships crossing the Atlantic
26. Archduke of Austria whose assassination on June 28, 1914, led to the outbreak of World War I
27. Nickname of a U.S. infantryman during World War I
28. Emperor of Germany during World War I who, after his nation's defeat, abdicated and fled to exile in the Netherlands
29. River in northern France, scene of several battles during World War I
30. The name given to Great Britain, France, and Russia during World War I
31. Site where a treaty was signed between Germany and Russia in March 1918, which ended the war between the two countries
32. An international organization established after World War I for the preservation of world peace
33. Gas-filled airships developed by Germany to drop bombs behind the enemy line, named after the designer
34. Russian revolutionaries who took control of the government in November 1917 and pledged to make peace with Germany
35. Commander of the U.S. army during World War I, called Black Jack
36. A town in northern France, site of the signing of armistices between the Allies and Germany in 1918
37. French representative at the peace treaty that ended World War I
38. A series of proposals drawn up by U.S. President Wilson that outlined his goals for a just and lasting peace "to make the world safe for democracy"
39. Another one of the newly formed countries that became an independent nation as the result of World War I
40. Commander of the French army during World War I, called Papa
41. Another one of the newly formed countries that became an independent nation as the result of World War I
42. Nickname of German submarines during World War I
43. Name given to the battle lines between Russia and Germany during World War I
44. Commander in chief of the German army during World War I
45. Italian representative at the peace treaty that ended World War I
46. French palace where the leaders of the victorious Allied Powers met in 1919 to sign the peace treaties that would officially end World War I
47. British passenger ship that was torpedoed by a German submarine on March 28, 1915
48. Russian revolutionary leader who took control of the government in November 1917
49. Another one of the newly formed countries that became an independent nation as the result of World War I
50. U.S. president during World War I

Name ______________________________ Date ____________________

52. World War I

```
N E E D H A M R O B E R T S G N I H S R E P J N H O J
A I K A V O L S O H C E Z C A L L I E D P O W E R S B
Y L F I N L A N D E G R O E G D Y O L L D I V A D T I
L U L A C E N T R A L P O W E R S S N S P S P W O M G
E S G A L M P T L E K L D C O A I U N M O O V E U S B
A I N O T A F E S O J Z N A R F D C J E L M E S G B E
G T O A S V B C N R F C A J G R A J R A A J M T H B R
U A S E L L I A S R E V L D E R P S N C N W K E B C T
E N L A F D A A S H A G R V S I E D T D D N G R O Z H
O I I D R A I V T A L M O B C J M B B A L R A N Y A A
F A W S A A E R I C H V O N L U D E N D O R F F T R K
N S W K N I J G E A I O I U E M E M Y E Z B E R N N S
A M O I Z A N E R U S R R E M A A M G A N S U O O I V
T I R V F S B O V O P R O S E R C E M C T N B N R C O
I S D E E B U A T O E A T I N N S T A O B U A T F H T
O M O H R R U S L S E G T E C E O Y N B S C X T N O I
N A O S D Y T I S A E N I N E L R I M I D A L V R L L
S I W L I E R H F E F R V U A S A I J G A B T G E A T
W L G O N V C W E O X J F O U R T E E N P O I N T S S
P L L B A R T H U R Z I M M E R M A N N T M L C S J E
E I S G N D R G E D E K S M L E H L I W R E S I A K R
B W J M D O G F I G H T S C N O M A N S L A N D E J B
S N I L E P P E Z L I T H U A N I A E N G E I P M O C
F E R D I N A N D F O C H G E R F F O J S E U Q C A J
```


1. ____________
2. ____________
3. ____________
4. ____________
5. ____________
6. ____________
7. ____________
8. ____________
9. ____________
10. ____________
11. ____________
12. ____________
13. ____________
14. ____________
15. ____________
16. ____________
17. ____________
18. ____________
19. ____________
20. ____________
21. ____________
22. ____________
23. ____________
24. ____________
25. ____________
26. ____________
27. ____________
28. ____________
29. ____________
30. ____________
31. ____________
32. ____________
33. ____________
34. ____________
35. ____________
36. ____________
37. ____________
38. ____________
39. ____________
40. ____________
41. ____________
42. ____________
43. ____________
44. ____________
45. ____________
46. ____________
47. ____________
48. ____________
49. ____________
50. ____________

53. RUSSIA IN REVOLUTION

ACROSS: ______________________________

2. In 1922, the new capital of the U.S.S.R., an inland city that was safer from foreign invasion
6. The mountainous region on the southern border of the Russian empire, birthplace of Joseph Stalin
8. Name used by Russian socialist revolutionaries until March 1918
11. Nickname of the Russian Communists, which stood for the bloodshed of violent revolution
12. A major naval base in northwestern Russia where sailors staged a revolt in March 1921
15. The urban working class of Russia, the Latin word used by Karl Marx to describe the "have nots"
18. The youngest daughter of Nicholas II, presumedly executed by revolutionaries in July 1918, but a legend persists that she escaped to the West
19. A Soviet commission that worked as secret police against counterrevolution
20. A workers' council that has political powers and organizes political activities
21. The official newspaper of the Communist party
23. The last czar of Russia, who gave up the throne in March 1917 and was executed by revolutionaries in July 1918
26. Chief leader of the Russian socialist revolutionaries, head of the U.S.S.R. from 1917 to 1924
27. The new name taken by Russian socialist revolutionaries in 1918, from the writings of Karl Marx that described workers who had seized power of the economy
28. The name used by Iosif Vissarionovich Dzhugashvili, which means "man of steel" in Russian; successor of Lenin

DOWN: ______________________________

1. A council of workers, soldiers, and intellectuals formed by Russian revolutionaries in 1917
3. The bleak region of northeastern Russia that lies in Asia, where many opponents of the Communist party were exiled to forced-labor camps
4. The name used by Lev Davidovich Bronstein, an important figure during the Russian revolutionary movement and organizer of the 1917 takeover
5. An international organization formed in Russia in 1919 for extending the scope of socialism
7. Site in Moscow where Lenin's body, now embalmed, lies in a mausoleum, where thousands of people visit it every year
9. Russian monk who advised Nicholas II and his wife, assassinated in December 1916
10. The former name of what was Leningrad and is now known as St. Petersburg
12. A prosperous Russian peasant who employed labor and opposed the Soviet collectivization of farms
13. Russian revolutionist who organized and led the Red Army, second only to Lenin in popularity with the revolutionaries
14. Czarina of Russia, executed by revolutionaries in July 1918
16. The new name given to Russia by socialist revolutionaries in 1922
17. Communist newspaper
18. The youngest child of Czar Nicholas, executed by revolutionaries in July 1918
22. The only son of Nicholas II, who suffered from hemophilia, a blood disorder called "the royal disease"
24. The name used by Vladimir Ilyich Ulyanof, socialist revolutionary who returned to Russia in April 1917 after seventeen years in exile
25. The former Russian national assembly elected indirectly by the people, dissolved during the revolution of 1917

Name ______________________ Date ______________

53. Russia in Revolution

54. SHIFTS IN WORLD POWER

ACROSS:

1. Hindu political and spiritual leader in the Indian movement for independence
2. Persian army officer who seized control of the government in 1921, took the title of shah for himself in 1925, and changed the name of his country from Persia to Iran in 1935
3. Chinese general who became president of the Nationalist Republic of China in 1928
4. Turkish nationalist and founder of modern Turkey who overthrew the last Ottoman emperor and became president in 1923
5. Indian word meaning "Great Soul," the title of respect given to Gandhi during the Indian movement for independence
6. Self-proclaimed king of Saudi Arabia who named the Arab nation after his family in 1932
7. Revolutionary leader who took control of Mexico in 1917; assassinated in 1920
8. Nationalist leader who overthrew the last emperor of China and became president of the new Republic of China
9. Indian word meaning "home rule," the watchword of the Indian nationalists
10. Mexican president who was assassinated in 1928
11. Indian word meaning "hold fast to the truth," a movement characterized by nonviolent resistance and noncooperation
12. U.S. president who promised to respect the rights of Latin American countries under his "Good Neighbor Policy"
13. Austrian journalist who founded an organization to work for the establishment of a homeland for Jews in Palestine
14. One of the most famous Mexican revolutionists, an agrarian leader who stated, "It is better to die on your feet than to live on your knees."
15. Jewish nationalists who wanted a homeland in Palestine
16. Indian nationalist leader and later the first prime minister
17. Ruthless general who ruled Venezuela for nearly thirty years after seizing power in 1908, boasting "All Venezuela is my cattle ranch."
18. Name given to the founder of modern Turkey, meaning "father of the Turks"

Name ______________________ Date ______________________

54. Shifts in World Power

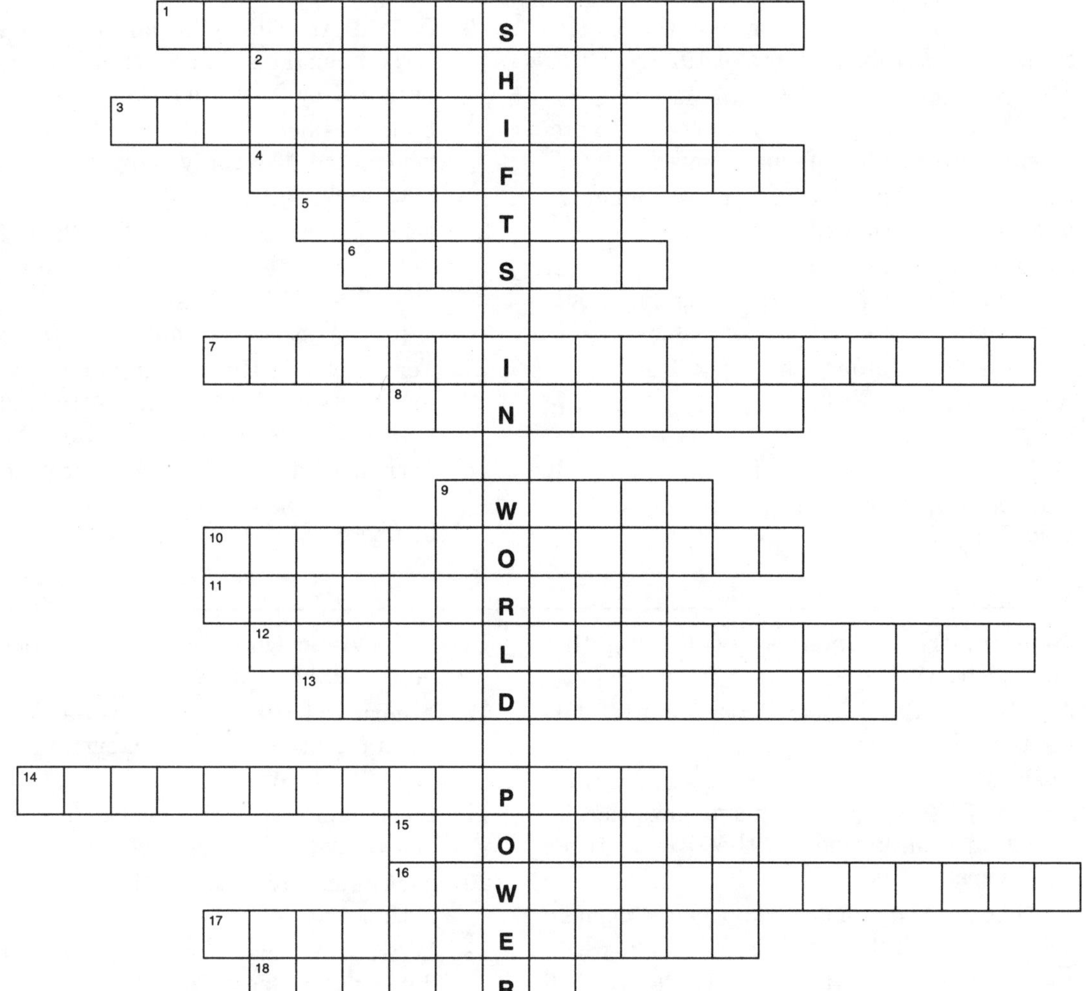

55. THE YEARS BETWEEN THE WARS

ACROSS:

1. U.S. president when the Great Depression began
3. The popular music that swept the United States and Europe during the 1920's
4. The government relief program used in Great Britain during the Great Depression to provide sustenance for the unemployed
9. U.S. president after World War I who promised a "return to normalcy"
10. Swiss town where France and Germany signed a treaty in 1925 promising they would never again make war against each other
11. A fast dance popular during the 1920's
13. Austrian premier who was assassinated in 1934
16. Location of the world's first commercial radio station, KDKA, which began broadcasting in 1920
18. English motion picture actor who was popular in the United States during the 1920's
19. In 1929, the financial capital of the world, located near the southern tip of Manhattan Island in New York City
21. U.S. president during the Great Depression who stated, "The only thing we have to fear is fear itself."
24. English novelist, author of *To the Lighthouse*, in which characters come to life through complex internal monologues
26. Popular U.S. jazz trumpeter during the 1920's
27. Term given to the growing fear that communist uprisings were being plotted against the United States and western Europe
28. Term used during the 1920's for young women trying to appear sophisticated in dress and behavior

DOWN:

1. Popular African-American poet and author during the 1920's
2. Another popular African-American poet during the 1920's
3. Irish novelist, poet, and short story writer, author of *Ulysses,* a 1,500 page novel that focused on a single day in the lives of three Dubliners
5. British poet, dramatist, and critic born in the United States, author of "The Waste Land," a long poem that pictured a world drained of hope and faith
6. Polish general who led a revolt in 1926 and set himself up as dictator
7. German playwright and poet, author of *The Three Penny Opera,* which criticized capitalism and middle class ideas
8. Spanish painter and sculptor active in France, the founder of cubism
12. Aviation pioneer, the first woman to fly across the Atlantic
14. U.S. aviator who made the first solo transatlantic flight in 1927
15. American banker and statesman who worked out a plan to strengthen Germany's economy after World War I
17. Los Angeles suburb that became the motion picture capital of the world during the 1920's
20. Nickname given to the first motion pictures with sound
22. Migrant farmworkers who left the Dust Bowl during the Great Depression to seek work elsewhere
23. U.S. attorney general who launched a series of raids to round up suspected radicals and communists after World War I
25. An unusual artistic movement in the 1920's that scorned traditional artistic forms as meaningless in a world turned upside down by the senseless slaughter of war, from the French word meaning "hobby horse"

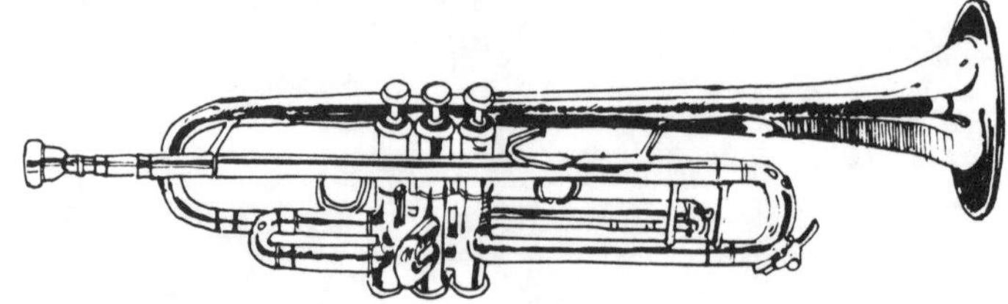

Name ______________________ Date ______________

55. The Years between the Wars

1 2 3 4 5 6 7 8 9 10 11 12 13 14 15 16 17 18 19 20 21 22 23 24 25 26 27 28

56. THE RISE OF TOTALITARIAN STATES

ACROSS:

1. The first of Europe's totalitarian dictators
4. The first European country to have a fascist government
5. The German "master race" that Hitler insisted was destined to rule inferior peoples
7. Name given to November 9, 1939, when Nazi mobs looted Jewish shops, burned synagogues, and beat Jews on the streets and in their homes, the German word meaning "the night of broken glass"
9. The German state secret police under Hitler's regime, noted for the brutality of its methods
11. The title applied to Adolf Hitler by his adherents, the German word for "leader"
13. Totalitarian nation that invaded Manchuria in 1931 and withdrew from the League of Nations in March 1933
14. The title applied to Benito Mussolini by his adherents, the Italian word for "leader"
15. The bent cross adopted as the symbol of the National Socialist German Workers' Party
16. A political movement that believes in an extreme form of nationalism, denying individual rights, insisting upon the supremacy of the state, and advocating dictatorial one-party rule
17. Name given to the supporters of Benito Mussolini who roamed the streets of Italy beating up Communists and Socialists, from the color that was part of their uniforms

DOWN:

1. A book written by Adolf Hitler in 1924, setting forth his views on the superiority of the Germans and the decadence of democracy, German words meaning "My Struggle"
2. Russian ruler who organized a totalitarian state during the 1930's
3. Spanish general who seized power in 1939 and ruled as a totalitarian dictator for more than thirty years
6. Hitler's minister of propaganda who made radio stations play military music and speeches glorifying the German state
8. Country where Hitler was born in 1889
10. Name given to the members of the National Socialist German Workers' Party
12. German word meaning "empire"
13. Religious group labeled by Hitler as inferior, unfit to be part of the great German empire

Name ____________________ Date ____________________

56. The Rise of Totalitarian States

57. WORLD WAR II

The answers to the following clues are hidden in the puzzle. Circle the answer in the puzzle and then write the answer next to the correct number. Answers can be found horizontally, vertically, diagonally, and backward.

1. U.S. naval base in Hawaii that was attacked by the Japanese on December 7, 1941, "a date which will live in infamy"
2. German dictator and leader of the Nazi Party, called "der Fuhrer"
3. The sudden, massive attacks of tanks and airplanes used by Germany during World War II, the German word meaning "lightning war"
4. Italian dictator and leader of the Fascist Party, called "Il Duce"
5. Soviet dictator during World War II, called "Uncle Joe"
6. The name given to Great Britain, France, the Soviet Union, and the United States during World War II
7. U.S. president when World War II ended
8. Island in the North Pacific, scene of an American victory over the Japanese in April 1945
9. American commander in Asia who promised "I shall return" as he evacuated U.S. troops from the Philippines in 1941
10. City in southwestern Poland, site of the largest Nazi death camp during World War II
11. U.S. admiral in the Pacific during World War II
12. Japanese emperor during World War II
13. Town in northern France where the French leaders surrendered to Germany on June 22, 1940; the same site where Germans had been forced to sign the armistice ending World War I
14. The genocidal destruction of Jews by Nazi Germany during World War II
15. The name given to Germany, Italy, and Japan during World War II
16. Japanese city devastated by the first atomic bomb used in warfare; August 6, 1945
17. U.S. general during World War II
18. Scene of one of the decisive battles of World War II, June 3, 1942, a turning point in the Pacific war
19. The first European capital to be freed from Nazi control; June 4, 1944
20. U.S. battleship upon which the Japanese formally surrendered on September 2, 1945
21. Site where German troops surrendered to the Soviets on January 31, 1943
22. German general during World War II, called "the Desert Fox"
23. Japanese suicide missions in which a pilot crashed his plane loaded with explosives into an American ship, the Japanese word meaning "divine wind"
24. U.S. president when World War II began
25. Japanese admiral who led the attack on Hawaii on December 7, 1941
26. Scene of the evacuation of British forces from France during World War II; May 26–June 4, 1940
27. British general during World War II, called "Monty"
28. Site of the first Allied offensive in the Pacific, a savage struggle in the Solomon Islands that lasted from July 1942 to February 1943
29. French leader of the Vichy Regime, convicted of treason in 1945
30. U.S. admiral in the Atlantic during World War II
31. A village in northern Egypt, site of a decisive British victory during World War II
32. British prime minister during World War II who stated, "I have nothing to offer but blood, toil, tears, and sweat."
33. Provisional capital of France during the German occupation in World War II
34. Site of the Allied beachhead in the invasion of Italy during World War II
35. Japanese general during World War II
36. Soviet commander during World War II
37. U.S. general during World War II, called "Old Blood and Guts"
38. Code name for June 6, 1944, the Allied invasion of Normandy, France
39. French general who formed an underground movement known as the Free French, whose resistance fighters made heroic efforts to sabotage the Nazis
40. Scene of a conference of Roosevelt, Churchill, and Stalin in February 1945; a port city on the Black Sea
41. Island in the North Pacific, scene of an American victory over the Japanese in February 1945
42. Allied commander in chief in Europe during World War II, called "Ike"
43. Site where a second atomic bomb was dropped on Japan on August 9, 1945
44. The German air force during World War II

Name ______________________________ Date ____________________

57. World War II

```
A U S C H W I T Z L L I H C R U H C I T S
I R U O S S I M S M N E I S E N H O W E R
R G P Y Z H U K O V L I C A S H M M O L U
O I Z N A P I Y A L T A L I D I O P J A H
M J N M A L L I E S S I X A D R N I I L T
E P O T U A T L P R A A R W T O T E M A R
J M T T X S F A E P B G A H V S G G A M A
T O L I Y E S L A H N Y A D D H O N T E C
N L S O T I H O R I H E U N A I M E S I A
E U E G U A D A L C A N A L Z M E L U N M
Z F C V F E K A H I K G S N R A R L A M R
A T P F E R T Y A I N E A E T C Y U C J E
K W I E O S H J R E Y I L B U A W A O C R
I A L M T C O K B L I T Z K R I E G L K A
M F E T I A S O O M I L E M M O R E O J A
A F D V O N I L R H O K I N A W A D H F H
K E A B M J G N T H G I R W N I A W L B P
D Y A M A M O T O M W C J S N A M U R T S
```

1. ________	16. ________	31. ________
2. ________	17. ________	32. ________
3. ________	18. ________	33. ________
4. ________	19. ________	34. ________
5. ________	20. ________	35. ________
6. ________	21. ________	36. ________
7. ________	22. ________	37. ________
8. ________	23. ________	38. ________
9. ________	24. ________	39. ________
10. ________	25. ________	40. ________
11. ________	26. ________	41. ________
12. ________	27. ________	42. ________
13. ________	28. ________	43. ________
14. ________	29. ________	44. ________
15. ________	30. ________	

58. POST-WORLD WAR II

The answers to the following clues are hidden in the puzzle. Circle the answer in the puzzle and then write the answer next to the correct number. Answers can be found horizontally, vertically, diagonally, and backward.

1. The worldwide peacekeeping organization created after World War II
2. European nation that was divided into four occupation zones after World War II
3. The alliance formed in 1949 between the United States and Western European countries that pledged military support to one another in case any member was attacked
4. The name given to the unfriendly rivalry between the United States and the Soviet Union, which was neither true peace nor outright war
5. U.S. diplomat who urged a policy of containment in response to Soviet expansion, applying political, economic, and military pressure to hold the Soviets within their current boundaries
6. The alliance system formed in 1955 that linked the Soviet Union and Eastern European countries
7. U.S. president who ordered tons of supplies to be airlifted into West Berlin to prevent their submission to the Soviet Union
8. Part of Palestine that was proclaimed as a Jewish national state in 1948
9. Chinese Communist leader who became the chairman of the People's Republic of China in 1949
10. U.S. Secretary of State who devised a plan to offer massive economic aid to European countries and stop the spread of communism
11. Capital of the Federal Republic of Germany, known as West Germany
12. Eastern European countries whose policies were dictated or heavily influenced by the Soviet Union
13. Soviet leader who died in 1953
14. Eastern European country that unsuccessfully attempted to oust its Soviet-controlled government in 1956
15. The southern German town where the Allies put the surviving Nazi leaders on trial for "crimes against humanity"
16. The term coined to describe the barrier of censorship and secrecy imposed by the Soviet Union between its sphere of influence and the rest of the world
17. Capital of the German Democratic Republic, known as East Germany
18. Pacific islands that were granted full independence from the United States in 1946
19. Chancellor of the German Federal Republic after World War II
20. British statesman who first used the phrase "iron curtain" to stand for the division of Europe after World War II
21. British prime minister after World War II
22. An island off the coast of southeastern China, where Chiang Kai-shek and other Nationalist leaders fled from the Communists in 1949
23. Asian nation that received its independence from Great Britain in 1947
24. World War II general who was elected president of the United States in 1952
25. Site of the permanent headquarters of the new international peacekeeping organization formed after World War II
26. Asian peninsula that was divided after World War II, with a Soviet puppet government in the north and an American-supported government in the South
27. Yugoslavia's Communist leader who kept his country independent of the Soviet Union after World War II
28. U.S. Senator who charged thousands of Americans of being Communist supporters during the 1950's

Name ______________________________ Date ____________________

58. Post-World War II

```
B A V N N M P L S M A O T S E T U N G L
F S J T A T D A C M R A W D L O C I P B
N E A E W E R C N C E R N N Y R M A Y N
I N T N I V A A L L I H C R U H C T A A
Z I O N A R T S D C S M A X V O N R I G
M P S B T O S E C E E G R E T N L U S E
J P P H U N I T E D N A T I O N S C B R
L I Y A L N E I O U H A T B I U B N Y M
C L M L E B I L H S O T U E W F M O M A
J I A C A E S L N B W G R E B M E R U N
F H B H R V L E A N E W Y O R K C I T Y
C P C A S E O T I T R R I K E O N U R Z
M O N T I R U A T E S W L N O D E D U T
H T C A P W A S R A W U N I I R R S M F
R I S A T T S M U N J A N A N F E M A A
M J A S O O D F S E N L E R K S C A N M
```

1. ______________________ 15. ______________________
2. ______________________ 16. ______________________
3. ______________________ 17. ______________________
4. ______________________ 18. ______________________
5. ______________________ 19. ______________________
6. ______________________ 20. ______________________
7. ______________________ 21. ______________________
8. ______________________ 22. ______________________
9. ______________________ 23. ______________________
10. ______________________ 24. ______________________
11. ______________________ 25. ______________________
12. ______________________ 26. ______________________
13. ______________________ 27. ______________________
14. ______________________ 28. ______________________

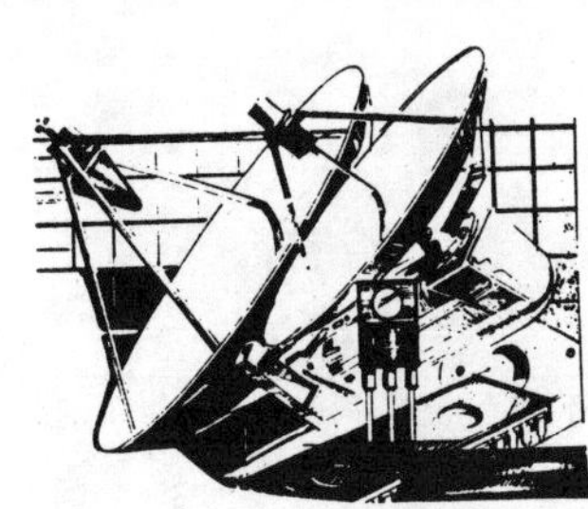

59. THE COLD WAR TURNS HOT

ACROSS:

1. U.S. president when the Korean War began
2. U.S. Secretary of State during the Korean War
3. Communist China's foreign minister during the Korean War
4. American general who commanded the United Nations forces during the Korean War
5. English translation of the word "Korea"
6. River that separates Korea from China
7. Commander of the U.S. Eighth Army during the Korean War
8. Body of water west of Korea
9. Pacific island where President Truman and General MacArthur met in October 1950
10. Leader of the Republic of Korea, known as South Korea
11. Parallel of latitude where Korea was divided after World War II, with a communist government supported by the Soviets in the north and an American-supported government in the south
12. Capital of the Republic of Korea
13. An agreement to stop fighting; ending the hostilities in Korea on July 27, 1953
14. Capital of the Democratic People's Republic of Korea
15. Leader of the Democratic People's Republic of Korea, known as North Korea
16. Site of a surprise amphibious invasion by U.S. marines in Korea during September 1950
17. Body of water east of Korea
18. U.S. president when the Korean War ended

Name ______________________________ Date ____________________

59. The Cold War Turns Hot

1 T
2 H
3 E
4 C
5 O
6 L
7 D
8 W
9 A
10 R
11 T
12 U
13 R
14 N
15 S
16 H
17 O
18 T

60. NATIONALISM IN AFRICA

ACROSS:

4. Republic in western Africa, formerly French Sudan
5. Republic in central Africa, formerly the southern part of the UN Trust Territory of Ruanda-Urundi
8. Republic in central Africa, formerly the Belgian Congo, that received its independence in 1960
9. Republic in northeastern Africa that received its independence in 1956
11. Republic in north central Africa, formerly part of French Equatorial Africa, that received its independence in 1960
12. West African nation that received its independence from Great Britain in 1965
14. Site of a huge dam constructed on the Nile River in Egypt, completed in 1970 with aid from the Soviet Union
16. Republic in northwestern Africa, a former French colony that established independence in 1962
19. A language spoken by many East Africans, basically Bantu with a mixture of Arabic elements
20. The policy of racial segregation and discrimination against nonwhites in the Republic of South Africa
23. Republic in northern Africa that became independent from Italy in 1951
24. East African nation that achieved independence from Great Britain in 1962
27. The motto of Kenya, a Swahili expression meaning "a pulling together of all races"
29. Republic in western Africa, formerly Portuguese West Africa, recognized as an independent nation in 1975
30. African nation that achieved independence in 1963, formerly British East Africa
31. Libyan leader who overthrew the established monarchy in 1969, strongly supporting the Arab nations in the Middle East that opposed Israel
32. African republic formed when Tanganyika was united with Zanzibar in 1964, formerly German East Africa

DOWN:

1. The last country of Africa to gain its independence, formerly German Southwest Africa
2. Republic in west central Africa that received its independence from France in 1960
3. Anglican Archbishop who received the Nobel Peace Prize as recognition for his courageous fight against segregation in South Africa
6. Republic in northern Africa that received its independence from France in 1956
7. An enclave, administratively part of Angola, on the west coast of Africa between the Republic of Congo and the Republic of Zaire
8. Republic in south central Africa, formerly Northern Rhodesia
9. Emperor who was returned to the Ethiopian throne when the Italians were defeated during World War II
10. West African nation that celebrated its independence from Great Britain in 1960; the most populous nation in Africa
13. West African country that received its independence from France in 1960
15. Leader of the African National Council, the major black political party in South Africa, who was imprisoned in 1964
17. Republic in western Africa, the first black African nation to win its independence, formerly the British colony known as the Gold Coast
18. Republic in central Africa, formerly the northern part of the UN Trust Territory of Ruanda-Urundi
21. The longest river in Africa, rising in Lake Victoria and flowing 3,500 miles north to the Mediterranean Sea
22. Republic on the west coast of central Africa, formerly part of French Equatorial Africa
25. Republic in western Africa that established independence from France in 1958
26. President of the United Arab Republic, 1958–1970, who brought the Suez Canal under Egyptian control
28. Republic in west central Africa, independent from France since 1960

Name ______________________ Date ______________________

60. Nationalism in Africa

61. DEVELOPMENTS IN THE MIDDLE EAST

The answers to the following clues are hidden in the puzzle. Circle the answer in the puzzle and then write the answer next to the correct number. Answers can be found horizontally, vertically, diagonally, and backward.

1. One of the three major religions practiced in the Middle East
2. Site of the U.S. embassy in Iran where militants seized 52 Americans on November 4, 1979, and held the hostages for 444 days before releasing them
3. Egyptian president who seized control of the Suez Canal in 1956
4. Mideast nation where civil war broke out between Christians and Muslims in 1975
5. Brief fighting in 1967 when the Israelis defeated the armies of Egypt, Syria, and Jordan and occupied much new territory
6. U.S. president who helped negotiate a peace agreement between Egypt and Israel in 1979
7. City in Israel that is sacred to all three of the major religions in the Middle East
8. Egyptian president who recognized Israel's right to exist in 1979, assassinated in 1981
9. Organization formed by Mideast nations in 1960 to set levels for oil production and a common pricing policy on oil (abbr.)
10. Mideast nation whose population is over eighty percent Jewish
11. Muslim religious leader who established a new regime in Iran in 1979
12. Site of a huge dam on the Nile River in Egypt, completed in 1970 with Soviet aid
13. Israeli prime minister who signed a peace settlement with Egypt in 1979
14. A radical Arab group that conducted a terrorist campaign against Israel during the 1970's (abbr.)
15. Another one of the three major religions worshiped in the Middle East
16. Israeli prime minister from 1969 to 1974
17. Mideast peninsula occupied by Israel after the 1967 war and returned to Egypt as part of the Camp David agreement in 1979
18. Site of the U.S. embassy in Lebanon that was bombed by terrorists in April 1983
19. Arab leader who proclaimed the West Bank an independent Palestinian state in November 1988
20. Another one of the three major religions worshiped in the Middle East

Name ______________________________ Date ____________________

61. Developments in the Middle East

T O B R I E M A D L O G E O R

A N E L I Z A Y E A B L A R O

D J I M M Y C A R T E R P H A

A N R U T O L T N A U Y O S N

S T U A C E P O V S T R W I O

R H T R A L N L P I R A I M N

A M A R S A X L N X N S H E A

W S S U B A O A Y D L I Z L B

N I G E B M I H C A N E M A E

A A L I M T D K M Y O M A S L

J D S U S T G H I W M A L U A

S U F I E R N O W A J L O R C

D J R H N A A M P R N S R E F

R H R M W A M E L E I I P J W

C A Q S B K I I L N C O S C H

N S A B D E L N A S S E R L O

T A F A R A R I S A Y A G M B

1. ______________________________ 11. ______________________________

2. ______________________________ 12. ______________________________

3. ______________________________ 13. ______________________________

4. ______________________________ 14. ______________________________

5. ______________________________ 15. ______________________________

6. ______________________________ 16. ______________________________

7. ______________________________ 17. ______________________________

8. ______________________________ 18. ______________________________

9. ______________________________ 19. ______________________________

10. ______________________________ 20. ______________________________

62. CHANGE AND CONFLICT IN ASIA

ACROSS: ______________________________

1. Communist guerrilla forces supported by North Vietnam
2. Japanese emperor who died on January 7, 1989; succeeded by his son Akihito
3. Indian prime minister elected in 1966 and assassinated in 1984
4. U.S. president who visited China in 1972, establishing normal diplomatic relations after more than twenty years of hostility
5. Asian nation that became independent in December 1971, formerly East Pakistan
6. Chinese Communist leader who died in 1976; succeeded by Deng Xiaoping
7. Port city on southern Honshu island, Japan; site of the first World's Fair ever held in Asia, Expo 70
8. Asian nation that became independent in August 1950, formerly the Dutch East Indies
9. Asian nation that exploded its first nuclear device in 1974
10. American general who commanded the occupation forces in Japan from 1945 to 1952
11. Former capital of South Vietnam, captured by Communist troops in 1975 and renamed Ho Chi Minh City
12. Asian nation that exploded its first atom bomb in 1964
13. South Asian nation that was invaded by Soviet troops in 1979
14. The first prime minister of India, 1947–1964
15. Chinese capital where thousands of students demonstrated against Communist rule in 1989
16. Asian nation that fell to Communist forces in April 1975, formerly known as Cambodia
17. Asian nation that became independent on August 15, 1947, formerly part of the British colony of India
18. Communist leader and president of North Vietnam from 1945 to 1969
19. Filipino president who fled the country in 1986, charged with fraud and corruption
20. Indian political and spiritual leader who was killed in January 1948 by a Hindu fanatic who opposed efforts to establish peace between Hindus and Muslims
21. Independent Asian nation created by the union of former British colonies in 1963
22. Asian nation that received its independence from the United States on July 4, 1946
23. Island south of the Malay Peninsula that became an independent nation in 1965

Name ______________________________ Date ____________________

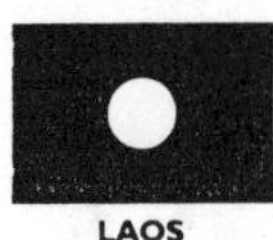
LAOS

62. Change and Conflict in Asia

MALAYSIA

INDONESIA

KOREA, SOUTH

1	C
2	H
3	A
4	N
5	G
6	E
7	A
8	N
9	D
10	C
11	O
12	N
13	F
14	L
15	I
16	C
17	T
18	I
19	N
20	A
21	S
22	I
23	A

NEPAL

PHILIPPINES

SINGAPORE

63. THE WORLD IN CHANGE

The answers to the following clues are hidden in the puzzle. Circle the answer in the puzzle and then write the answer next to the correct number. Answers can be found horizontally, vertically, diagonally, and backward.

1. Britain's first woman prime minister, known as "The Iron Lady"
2. Ohio university where four students were killed by National Guardsmen in May 1970 during a demonstration against the Vietnam War
3. Soviet dissident who published *The Gulag Archipelago* in 1973, an account of life in prison camps
4. Cuban leader during the Cuban Missile Crisis
5. The leader of Solidarity, an independent Polish labor union
6. Agreement signed by the United States and the Soviet Union in 1972, limiting the number of nuclear warheads and missiles that each country would keep (abbr.)
7. French socialist who won the presidency in 1981, the first leftist government in France since the 1930's
8. Heir to the British throne who married Lady Diana Spencer on July 29, 1981
9. Site of an unsuccessful invasion of Cuba in April 1961, launched by Cuban exiles trained and armed by the United States
10. French president who retired in 1969 and died the following year
11. The world's fastest-growing city and site of the world's worst air pollution
12. The first American president to visit the Soviet Union since World War II
13. Eastern European nation that was invaded by the Soviet Union on August 20, 1968
14. The first woman to be appointed to the United States Supreme Court
15. Soviet leader during the Cuban Missile Crisis
16. Pope who was wounded in an assassination attempt in 1981
17. The easing of international tension, especially between the Soviet Union and the United States, from the French word meaning "relaxation"
18. Soviet leader who signed the Intermediate Nuclear Forces Treaty with the United States on December 8, 1987, which called for the destruction of 1,752 Soviet missiles
19. Spanish dictator who died in 1975; succeeded by Juan Carlos
20. The name given to the series of events that led to the resignation of U.S. President Richard Nixon
21. Chilean poet, the first Latin American writer to win the Nobel Prize for Literature
22. Site of the 1980 Olympics, boycotted by the United States after the Soviet invasion of Afghanistan
23. Portuguese leader who died in 1970, after ruling as dictator since the 1930's
24. Soviet leader who signed the Strategic Arms Limitation Treaty with the United States in 1972, which froze for five years the number of offensive missiles held by the two countries
25. Site of a brief war between Argentina and Great Britain in 1982
26. U.S. president during the Cuban Missile Crisis
27. Soviet dissident who won the Nobel Prize for Peace in 1975 for his efforts in support of human rights
28. European nation that withdrew from NATO in 1966
29. West German prime minister who won the Nobel Prize for Peace for his role in normalizing East-West relations with his policy called "Ostopolitik"
30. U.S. president who signed the Intermediate Nuclear Forces Treaty with the Soviet Union on December 8, 1987, which called for the destruction of 859 American missiles

Name ______________________ Date ______________

63. The World in Change

T R A B A Y O F P I G S J W U O B S
S T E R D E T E N T E O O M R A D A
S M I A V N M I A R H C L T Y N C I
E A N N E I J L C N S E S O A R O V
L T L D H X A G P O C A F L R E A O
R O L T C O I A M N C P S O V A E R
A L M A H N U B A R I I N A O G E A
H B I A S L U R I G D N X I N A C H
C R T I U S F I S N O Y D E N N E K
E E T A R U A E A C I N A U M A B A
C Z E C H O S L O V A K I A J N G S
N H R T K E K A A B M U L X A D O B
I N R C A L H M O Z W O C S O M R A
R E A H A T E I A W A L E S A N B C
P V N F J M S S U S F R A N C O A O
C R D A N Y S T I N E H Z L O S C A
T H A T C H E R N A D L R A T R H E
E T A G R E T A W E C N A R F D E R
A I D E G A U L L E K D O W E R V S

1. ______________
2. ______________
3. ______________
4. ______________
5. ______________
6. ______________
7. ______________
8. ______________
9. ______________
10. ______________
11. ______________
12. ______________
13. ______________
14. ______________
15. ______________
16. ______________
17. ______________
18. ______________
19. ______________
20. ______________
21. ______________
22. ______________
23. ______________
24. ______________
25. ______________
26. ______________
27. ______________
28. ______________
29. ______________
30. ______________

64. A NEW AGE OF EXPLORATION

ACROSS:

1. American space shuttle launched successfully in 1988, giving new impetus to the U.S. space program
3. The first U.S. civilian to fly on a space shuttle mission
4. New Hampshire school teacher who was killed in the explosion of a U.S. space shuttle on January 28, 1986
7. Site of the U.S. control center for spacecraft missions
9. One of the test pilots who set a new aviation record by flying nonstop around the world in December 1986
10. The first person sent into orbit, a Soviet cosmonaut in 1961
13. One of the pilots of America's first space shuttle
16. Site of the U.S. launching center for spacecraft
19. American unmanned spacecraft that landed on the planet Mars in 1976
21. U.S. agency that regulates the American space program (abbr.)
22. America's three-man spacecraft
23. America's one-man spacecraft
25. The second American astronaut to step on the surface of the moon, July 20, 1969
26. Another one of the pilots of America's first space shuttle
27. The first African-American astronaut in space
28. The first American astronaut sent into space
29. Another one of the U.S. test pilots who set a new aviation record by flying nonstop around the world in December 1986
30. Utah senator who flew on a U.S. space shuttle mission in 1985

DOWN:

2. A scientific research station launched by the United States in 1973 that remained aloft until 1979
3. America's two-man spacecraft
5. California desert where the first American space shuttle landed on April 15, 1981
6. Soviet spacecraft that docked with an American spacecraft in orbit around the earth in 1975
8. The first space satellite to orbit the earth, launched by the Soviet Union in October 1957
11. The first American to orbit the earth
12. The first American female astronaut in space
13. U.S. space shuttle that exploded after takeoff on January 28, 1986, killing all seven crew members
14. The first American astronaut to step on the surface of the moon, July 20, 1969
15. The Lunar Expedition Module that landed on the surface of the moon on July 20, 1969
17. The first U.S. space shuttle, launched on April 12, 1981
18. The first American spacecraft that was sent into orbit in 1958
19. American unmanned spacecraft that photographed the planet Saturn in August 1981
20. The second American astronaut sent into space
24. U.S. Air Force base in California where the space shuttles land

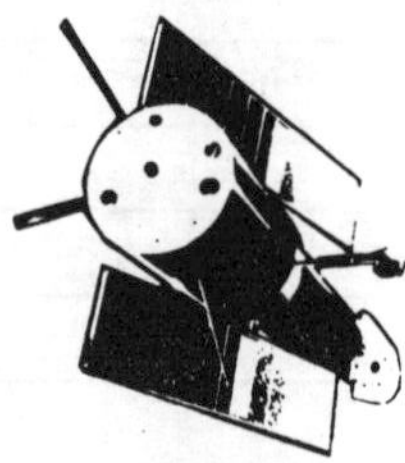

Name ____________________ Date ____________________

64. A New Age of Exploration

65. FAMOUS QUOTATIONS IN WORLD HISTORY

The answers to the following clues are hidden in the puzzle. Circle the answer in the puzzle and then write the answer next to the correct number. Answers can be found horizontally, vertically, diagonally, and backward.

1. Austrian foreign minister who remarked, "When France sneezes, all Europe catches cold."
2. U.S. president during World War I who stated, "We must make the world safe for democracy."
3. Roman emperor who boasted, "I found Rome built of sundried brick; I leave her clothed in marble."
4. Chairman of the Second Continental Congress who stated, "I shall sign so boldly the king shall read it without his glasses," upon the adoption of the American Declaration of Independence
5. Union general during the Civil War who stated, "War is hell," describing his destruction in the South
6. U.S. astronaut who remarked, "That's one small step for a man, one giant leap for mankind," after setting foot on the surface of the moon on July 20, 1969
7. Popular U.S. president whose slogan was "The buck stops here."
8. British prime minister during World War II who said, "Never was so much owed by so many to so few," expressing the gratitude of the British people to the Royal Air Force
9. American patriot who stated, "Give me liberty or give me death," prior to the Revolutionary War against Great Britain
10. British biologist who suggested the theory of "survival of the fittest"
11. U.S. president who described his foreign policy in Latin America with the phrase, "Speak softly and carry a big stick."
12. Ancient Greek philosopher whose motto was "Know thyself."
13. U.S. president during the Civil War who began his most famous speech with the words, "Four score and seven years ago"
14. U.S. general who promised, "I shall return," upon evacuating American troops from the Philippines during World War II
15. British king who remarked, "I sent a boy to do a man's job," after the American victory in the Revolutionary War
16. U.S. president who declared, "Millions for defense but not one cent for tribute," after a French attempt to bribe American diplomats during the XYZ Affair
17. American patriot who warned colonists, "The British are coming," during the Revolutionary War
18. U.S. president during the Great Depression who stated, "All we have to fear is fear itself."
19. British prime minister who remarked, "Oh God! It is all over," after the American victory in the Revolutionary War; then he resigned
20. U.S. president who stated, "Ask not what your country can do for you, ask what you can do for your country," during his inauguration in 1961
21. U.S. president who called December 7, 1941 "a date which will live in infamy," following the Japanese attack on Pearl Harbor
22. American leader during the Revolutionary War who stated, "One could trail my army by the blood of their ragged feet."

Name ______________________________ Date ____________________

65. Famous Quotations in World History

```
T E N A R M S T R O N G G R O E G
I R A H A H A N C O W R E V E R E
N O M A C A R H I B A I C O F H O
U O U A U G U S T U S X L H R A R
W S R J D R S L N L H I C S V G G
K E T T C A E A P O I I S E O M E
G V A H H V M Y D E N N E K C N H
D E I C E R D S R R G A C A S E J
N L B S E E C E E N T M W O N H G
L T O H N N V T M C O U C R L A S
G O S N I E T A H E N R Y M O N E
R H E W R E R D B L A T T A C C H
D K R J M A C A R T H U R H N O J
S A C P O K I M E L E W A N I C L
D R Z B R O O S E V E L T R L K G
```

1. ______________________
2. ______________________
3. ______________________
4. ______________________
5. ______________________
6. ______________________
7. ______________________
8. ______________________
9. ______________________
10. ______________________
11. ______________________
12. ______________________
13. ______________________
14. ______________________
15. ______________________
16. ______________________
17. ______________________
18. ______________________
19. ______________________
20. ______________________
21. ______________________
22. ______________________

66. WORLD HISTORY NICKNAMES

ACROSS:

1. Duke of Normandy who defeated England in 1066, known as "the Conqueror"
2. Italian Fascist dictator during World War II, called "Il Duce"
3. Scandinavian adventurer who colonized Greenland, called "the Red"
4. Latin American revolutionary leader often called "the Liberator"
5. Florentine banker and patron of the arts, known as "the Magnificent"
6. English king, 1509–1547, who asserted royal supremacy over the Catholic Church in England, known as "Defender of the Faith"
7. Leader of a fierce nomadic people from Central Asia who attacked Europe during the fifth century, called "the Hun"
8. French king, 1643–1715, who built the spectacular palace at Versailles, called "the Sun King"
9. Leader of thousands of poor, unarmed peasants on the first Crusade to the Holy Land, called "the Hermit"
10. Ancient country of Asia comprising the region between the Tigris and Euphrates rivers, called "the Fertile Crescent"
11. European nation called "the Third Reich" during World War II
12. Portuguese prince and patron of explorers and sea expeditions, known as "the Navigator"
13. City on the Bosporus, called "the second Rome"
14. German Nazi dictator during World War II, called "der Fuhrer"
15. Founder of the German Empire, called "the Iron Chancellor"
16. Countries on the large peninsula of southeastern Europe, called "the powder keg of Europe" prior to World War I
17. Greek conqueror of the Persian Empire, known as "the Great"
18. Czar of Russia, 1547–1584, called "the Terrible"
19. German general during World War II, called "the Desert Fox"
20. The founder of modern Turkey, called Ataturk, or "father of the Turks"
21. English king who supervised a new translation of the Bible, sometimes described as "the most learned fool in Christendom"

Name ______________________ Date ______________________

66. World History Nicknames

1 W
2 O
3 R
4 L
5 D

6 H
7 I
8 S
9 T
10 O
11 R
12 Y

13 N
14 I
15 C
16 K
17 N
18 A
19 M
20 E
21 S

67. WORLD HISTORY POTPOURRI—I

ACROSS:

2. Scottish inventor who patented the first efficient steam engine
6. Pope who crowned Charlemagne the first Holy Roman Emperor
8. Inventor of the flashlight
10. First element in the periodic table
11. The holy city of Islam that contains the Black Stone
13. Country where the Grimm brothers collected fairy tales
16. In the Bible, the first man
18. Southeast Asian country between Bangladesh and Thailand
19. In Greek mythology, the fellow travelers of Jason
20. Robinson Crusoe's trusted servant
22. English physician who discovered the vaccination for smallpox
24. Bacteriologist who developed the first effective vaccine in preventing polio
25. Mythological giant with 100 eyes
26. The first man to successfully predict the return of a comet
28. South African physician who performed history's first heart transplant
29. Roman poet who wrote the "Aeneid"

DOWN:

1. The sacred book of the Muslims
3. The major artery in the human body
4. Planet that is closest to the earth
5. Name of the ancient Cretan civilization
7. The world's fastest four-legged animal
9. Planet whose orbit is closest to the sun
12. Angel who announced the birth of Christ
14. Explorer who named the Pacific Ocean
15. Pilot of the first airplane to exceed the speed of sound
17. Norwegian explorer who discovered the South Pole
20. Austrian physician who developed psychoanalysis
21. Location of the Taj Mahal
23. Roman emperor who committed suicide
24. The former name of Thailand
27. A festival garland of flower blossoms worn in Hawaii

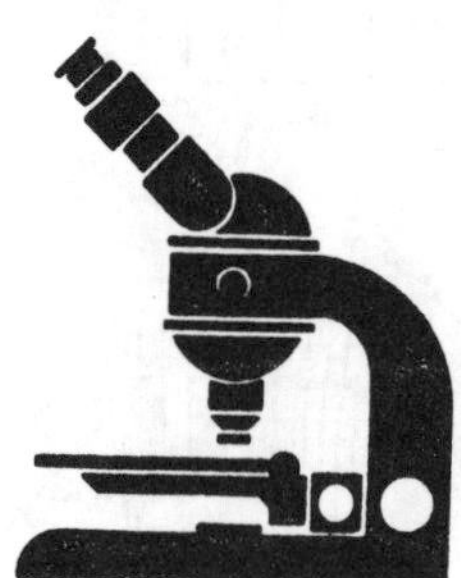

Name ______________________ Date ______________

67. World History Potpourri—I

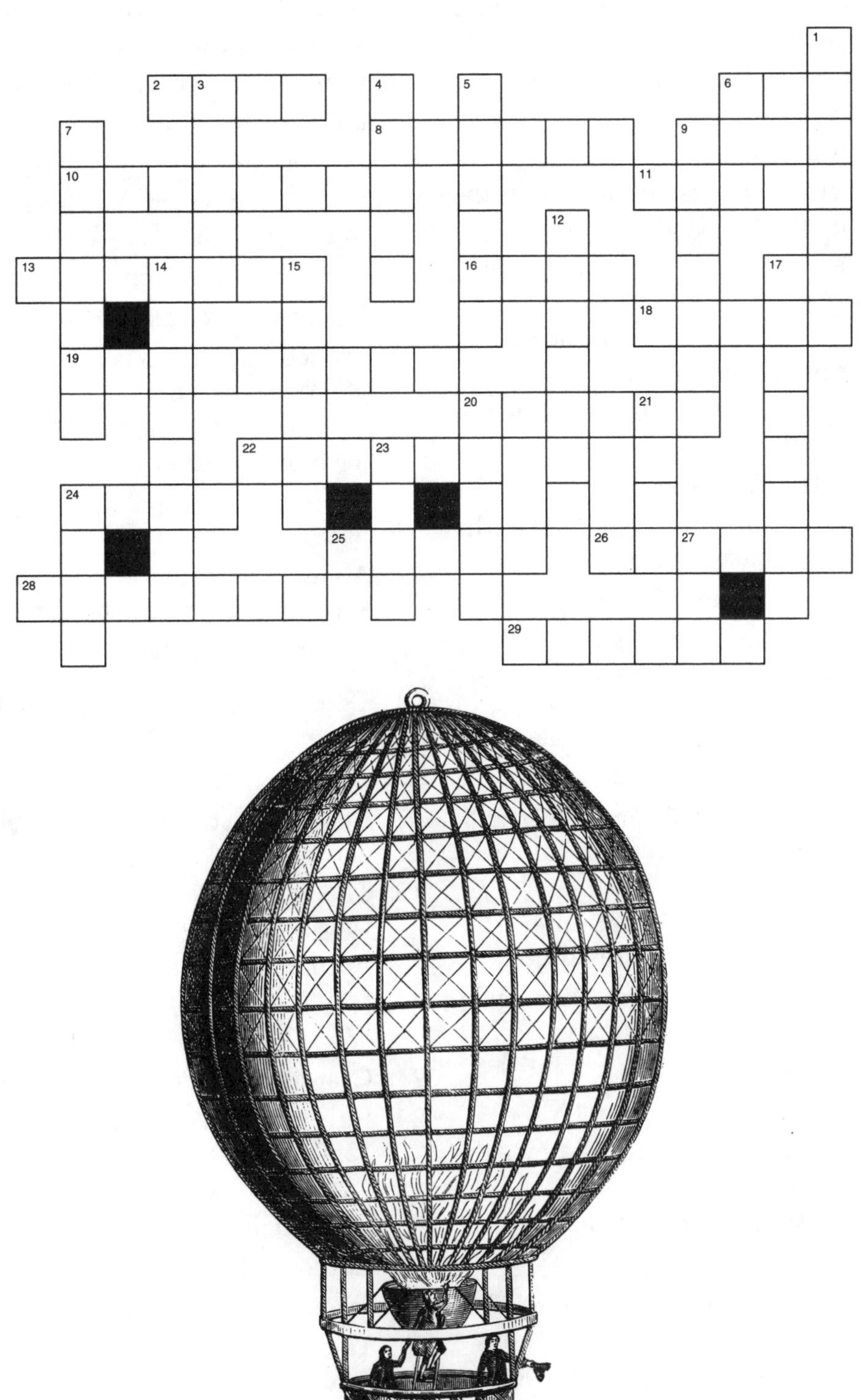

68. WORLD HISTORY POTPOURRI—II

ACROSS:

4. King of Babylonia who conquered Judea and destroyed Jerusalem
8. The fourth Muslim caliph and adopted son of Muhammad
9. The first American in space
10. German printer who is credited with the invention of movable type
12. Germany's most powerful battleship during World War II
14. Greek philosopher who was condemned to death for heretical teaching
17. Country that developed silk production in about 1500 B.C.
18. Native country of Copernicus
20. The ruling Chinese dynasty when the Great Wall was completed
21. Native country of Marie Curie
22. Author of *A Midsummer Night's Dream*
24. New York island that served as the chief U.S. immigration station from 1892 to 1943
25. Scottish scientist who discovered penicillin
26. Shakespearean play that contains the words "To be or not to be"
30. Explorer for which America was named
31. Author of *Gulliver's Travels*
32. Country in which the Renaissance began in about 1300
35. Ancient Chinese philosopher and teacher
37. Hindu word meaning "works" or "deeds"
38. French explorer who discovered the St. Lawrence River
40. The number of times a Muslim reserves for prayer each day
41. The remaining portion of a meteor that has fallen to earth
42. Abbey where the coronations of English kings and queens take place
43. The founder of Buddhism

DOWN:

1. American patriot and diplomat who said, "In this world nothing is certain but death and taxes."
2. A piece of metal or rock that enters the earth's atmosphere from outer space
3. First person to make a solo nonstop flight from New York to Paris
5. A wild dog of Australia
6. Site of the palace built by Louis XIV
7. The first explorer to reach India by sailing around Africa
10. The former Portuguese port on the west coast of India
11. The mythological creature who turned people to stone
13. Name for a Japanese pilot who made a suicidal crash attack during World War II
15. The high citadel of Athens, Greece
16. The remains of a plant or animal formed in rock, coal, or other natural material
17. European astronomer who first thought the sun to be the center of the solar system
19. The legislative assembly of certain countries, such as Japan
23. Author of the theory of evolution
27. Name of the German air force during World War II
28. Czar of Russia called "the Terrible"
29. European artistic style of painting from 1550 to 1750
33. Family of bankers who ruled Florence, Italy during the 1400's and 1500's
34. Author of the *Iliad* and the *Odyssey*
36. Inventor of the modern-day assembly line
38. The first king to jointly rule England and Scotland
39. Author of *The Wealth of Nations*

Name ______________________ Date ______________

68. World History Potpourri—II

69. WORLD HISTORY POTPOURRI—III

ACROSS: ____________________

1. Ancient city in Italy that disappeared after the eruption of Mt. Vesuvius in 79 A.D.
4. Country that boasts the world's oldest national flag
7. Native country of the painter known as "El Greco"
9. Author of *Alice in Wonderland*
13. The center of the theater district in London
15. The father of modern medicine
17. The second largest planet
19. The number of continents on earth
20. Seventeenth-century Italian astronomer, mathematician, and physicist
23. Author of *Das Kapital*
25. The hardest naturally occurring substance known to mankind
26. Author of *A Christmas Carol*
28. Name of the spaceship that made the first manned flight around the moon
32. The tutor of Alexander the Great
34. In the Bible, the man who lived to be 969 years old
36. Christopher Columbus's flagship on his first voyage to the New World
37. The one food item that pandas need daily to survive
38. Author of *Moby Dick*
39. Name for the Hindu "heaven"

DOWN: ____________________

1. Native country of Marie Curie
2. City where Pablo Picasso did most of his work
3. The first country that used Arabic numerals
4. French philosopher who said, "I think, therefore I am"
5. The name given to Great Britain, France, the Soviet Union, and the United States during World War II
6. In the Bible, the mountain where Noah's ark finally came to rest
8. Name of the first U.S. satellite launched in 1958
10. Paris museum that holds the portrait of Mona Lisa
11. Russian composer who was the guest conductor when Carnegie Hall opened on May 5, 1891
12. Name the ancient Romans gave to the common people
14. The name of Magellan's ship
16. Country that defeated the Spanish Armada in 1588
17. Canal that links the Red Sea to the Mediterranean
18. The most abundant metal in the earth's crust
21. U.S. army surgeon who proved the transmission of yellow fever by mosquitoes
22. The scale used to measure earthquakes
24. The tree on which silkworms feed
27. An underground chamber in Rome where early Christians were buried
29. The highest ranking group in the traditional Indian caste system
30. The first book of the Bible
31. U.S. state that was first named the Sandwich Islands by Captain Cook
33. In Greek mythology, the god of light
35. Yugoslav Communist leader who died in 1980

Name ______________________ Date ______________________

69. World History Potpourri—III

70. WORLD HISTORY POTPOURRI—IV

ACROSS:

2. In the Bible, the first woman
5. The monster that is still being reported in a lake in Scotland
6. A lightweight wood produced by a South American tree
8. Country where the Aswan Dam is located
9. Author of *The Scarlet Letter*
13. Mathematician who formulated the law of gravitation
14. Author of *Les Miserables*
16. The messenger god of Zeus
18. The smallest planet
19. The name of Henry Hudson's ship
20. The sea between Egypt and Arabia
21. The study of the original development of humankind
24. A sleeveless garment of camel's or goat's hair cloth worn in Arabia
27. Founder of the Mormon church in 1830
28. Name of the Jewish feast of lights
30. Heir to the Hapsburg empire who was assassinated on June 28, 1914
31. The ancient religion of Japan meaning "The Way of the Gods"
32. One of the competing branches that developed within Islam

DOWN:

1. Inventor of the electric battery
3. The greatest oil-producing country of South America
4. Planet that takes 248 years to go around the sun
7. Author of "The Pit and the Pendulum"
10. Site of the battle where Napoleon was defeated in 1815
11. Attila the _____
12. Country that is the origin of the Doberman Pinscher
15. The name of Sir Francis Drake's ship
17. The father of Pocahontas
22. Nineteenth-century Frenchman who proved that airborne germs caused infections
23. The largest living bird
25. Alloy produced from a combination of copper and zinc
26. Nationality of Rembrandt
29. Spanish artist who painted the picture *Persistence of Memory* that included limp watches

Name ______________________ Date ______________________

70. World History Potpourri—IV

71. WORLD HISTORY POTPOURRI—V

The answers to the following clues are hidden in the puzzle. Circle the answer in the puzzle and then write the answer next to the correct number. Answers can be found horizontally, vertically, diagonally, and backward.

1. The first man in space
2. French heroine in the Battle of Orleans in 1429
3. National origin of Copernicus and Marie Curie
4. Legendary outlaw of medieval England who robbed from the rich and gave to the poor
5. Author of *Journey to the Center of the Earth*
6. Art museum in Paris that contains the portrait of Mona Lisa
7. The first woman to cross the Atlantic by airplane, in 1928
8. A lightweight wood produced by a South American tree
9. U.S. inventor who developed the reaping machine in 1834
10. Ship canal opened in 1869 to link the Red Sea and the Mediterranean
11. French sculptor of *The Thinker*
12. Religious sect known as the Society of Friends
13. Author of "The Battle Hymn of the Republic"
14. Alloy made from a combination of copper and zinc
15. One of the Native American leaders in the Battle of the Little Big Horn
16. In Greek mythology, the kidnapper of Helen, thus causing the Trojan War
17. The most widely practiced religion in India
18. Author of *Pilgrim's Progress*
19. Alloy made from a combination of copper and tin
20. Founder of the American Red Cross
21. Frenchman who won the 1952 Nobel Peace Prize for his work in Africa
22. The ninth planet in the order from the sun
23. American explorer who flew over the South Pole in 1926
24. The first Englishman to sail around the world
25. The second most abundant element in the earth's atmosphere
26. Prime Minister who stated this was "their finest hour" to inspire the British people during World War II
27. The youngest person to ever serve as president of the United States
28. Country where the Acropolis and Mount Olympus are located
29. German astronomer who discovered that the orbits of the planets were ellipses
30. The number of colors in a rainbow
31. Country where the Aswan Dam is located
32. U.S. inventor of the frozen food process in 1925
33. One of the Native American leaders in the Battle of the Little Big Horn
34. The longest bone in the human body
35. Country where the Taj Mahal is located
36. Head of the Secret Service of the Third Reich during World War II
37. Egyptian monument having a human head and a lion's body
38. Roman general who led the invasion of Britain
39. The first U.S. woman to travel in space
40. Mexican general who led the siege against the Alamo in 1836

Name ______________________________ Date ____________________

71. World History Potpourri—V

T R A H R A E A I L E M A J L F A E S I L M
E O B P T H E O D O R E R O O S E V E L T S
K U C L E E C E E R G E C A U A D M I E X I
A F I U W G O L H U Z I Y A V J N H U N E U
R N J T O D Y S A N H Q R C R F C O I R A D
D D O O H N I B O R W K U B E R J H F P N N
S N H T D L S R D A E C S A U R P D A A O I
I A A C R K B U A N E N M H K S L R O P R H
C Y N E A A L B E R T S C H W E I T Z E R C
N N N T W A B J O Z C N C E H S R U R E C D
A U E J A I H A L A O B O N B D A S D D R J
R B S U I A N M R T I R R A L I S I R Y U A
F N K L L S N D S A M S M A R E R D B L M R
T H E I U A E N I I L D I D S Y E D E R E O
R O P U J S I V A A N C C U L S R S S A F X
C J L S K W E R E A S I K L R A V S S E O Y
S W E C B D C G L N B N A C H E M L E W Y G
C C R A Z Y H O R S E S L C R T A F K V M E
N P A E G Y P T S I T T I N G B U L L F E N
C T A S E B F N I D O R E T S U G U A C O N
N I R A G A G I R U Y S H O A H S P C L B K
S J W R M G N R E L M M I H H C I R N I E H

1. ____________________
2. ____________________
3. ____________________
4. ____________________
5. ____________________
6. ____________________
7. ____________________
8. ____________________
9. ____________________
10. ____________________
11. ____________________
12. ____________________
13. ____________________
14. ____________________
15. ____________________
16. ____________________
17. ____________________
18. ____________________
19. ____________________
20. ____________________
21. ____________________
22. ____________________
23. ____________________
24. ____________________
25. ____________________
26. ____________________
27. ____________________
28. ____________________
29. ____________________
30. ____________________
31. ____________________
32. ____________________
33. ____________________
34. ____________________
35. ____________________
36. ____________________
37. ____________________
38. ____________________
39. ____________________
40. ____________________

72. WORLD HISTORY POTPOURRI—VI

ACROSS:

1. The galaxy in which the earth is located
2. English author who created Sherlock Holmes
3. U.S. president who was blind in his left eye
4. The first country to be profoundly affected by the Industrial Revolution
5. Author of "The Rime of the Ancient Mariner"
6. *Time* magazine's "Man of the Year" for 1938
7. A moving river of ice
8. The legislative body of Israel
9. Village in western Portugal where the Virgin Mary was reportedly seen on six occasions
10. The study of organisms and their environment
11. English colonist who married Pocahontas in 1614
12. Country where Hammurabi lived
13. Italian artist who painted the *Madonna del Granduca* in 1505
14. The form of mathematics that uses the tangent, cotangent, secant, and cosecant functions
15. Author of *The Spirit of Laws*
16. German family famed for steel and armaments manufacturing during World Wars I and II
17. One of the major British universities established in the 1300's
18. Body of water off of New Brunswick that is known for its high tides
19. Body gland that produces insulin
20. City where the world's oldest sundried mud bricks can be found
21. German physicist who developed an instrument for detecting radioactivity

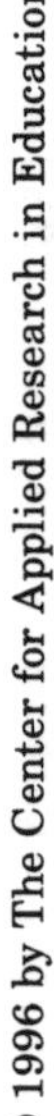

Name ______________________ Date ______________

72. World History Potpourri—VI

Clue	Letter
1	W
2	O
3	R
4	L
5	D
6	H
7	I
8	S
9	T
10	O
11	R
12	Y
13	P
14	O
15	T
16	P
17	O
18	U
19	R
20	R
21	I

73. WORLD HISTORY POTPOURRI—VII

ACROSS:

1. The first American writer to win a Nobel Prize in 1930
2. Author of *The Social Contract*
3. King of Judea who had all the infants under the age of two killed in Bethlehem at the time of Christ
4. The chief deity of the Aztecs
5. One of the major British universities established in the 1300's
6. The number of sides in an octagon
7. The first dog to orbit the earth
8. The Jewish New Year, celebrated in September or early October
9. The form of mathematics that uses rhombus, hypotenuse, and parallelogram
10. In Norse mythology, the god of war, thunder, and strength
11. In Roman mythology, the goddess of grain
12. Author of the poem "Rubaiyat"
13. Country that was once called Abyssinia
14. Founder of the Salvation Army
15. Dutch artist who painted a self-portrait showing his bandaged ear
16. *Time* magazine's "Man of the Year" in 1939 and 1942
17. In Greek mythology, the god of love
18. The only child born on the *Mayflower*
19. In Greek mythology, the messenger of the gods
20. Famous battle where Napoleon was defeated in 1815
21. The unit of measurement that was used for Noah's ark

Name ______________________________ Date ____________________

73. World History Potpourri—VII

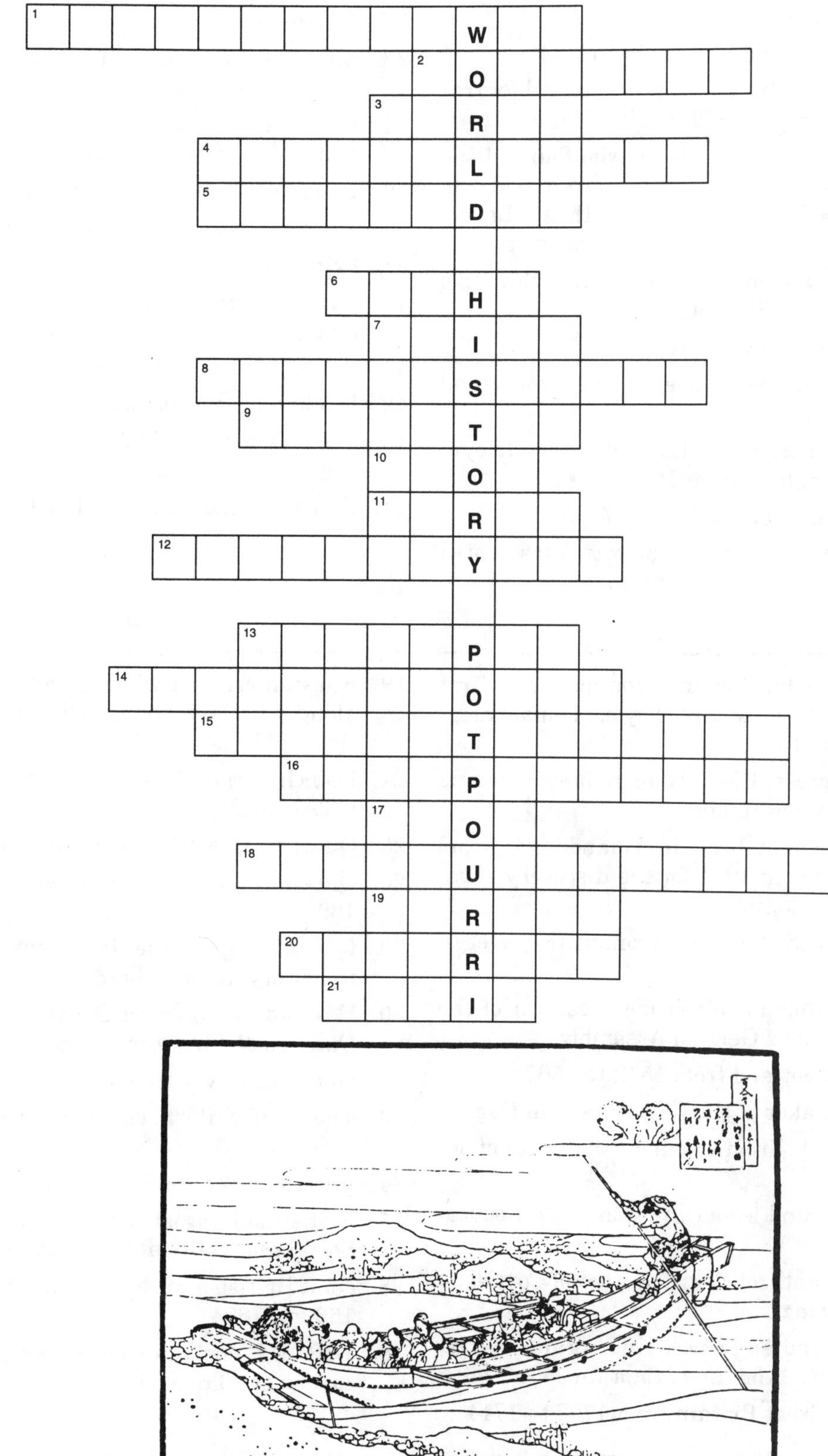

74. WOMEN IN WORLD HISTORY

ACROSS:

3. Name of the first, fifth, and sixth wives of Henry VIII of England
6. Queen of England from 1553 to 1558
8. American suffragist who was arrested for trying to vote in the 1872 presidential election
9. British nurse born in Italy who founded the first school of professional nursing in the world; known as "The Lady with the Lamp" during her service in the Crimean War
11. The first woman justice on the Supreme Court of the United States
12. Wife of Ivan the Terrible
17. American Indian guide to the Lewis and Clark expedition
20. Daughter of Henry VIII and Anne Boleyn, queen of England from 1558 to 1603
21. British author of *Wuthering Heights*
22. Prime minister of India who was assassinated in 1984
23. Famous Russian ballerina who died in 1931
27. American author of *Uncle Tom's Cabin*
28. Empress of Russia from 1762 to 1796; known as "the Great"
31. American author of *The Good Earth* and Nobel Prize winner in 1938
36. Queen of France who was guillotined in 1793
37. The first woman to fly across the Atlantic
38. Prime minister of Israel from 1969 to 1974
40. Spanish queen who supported the first Atlantic crossing of Christopher Columbus
41. British author of *Frankenstein*
42. Filipino president inaugurated in 1986
43. The only wife of a U.S. president to also be the mother of a U.S. president
44. Founder of the American Red Cross Society

DOWN:

1. American educator who founded the first women's college, Mount Holyoke Female Seminary, in 1837
2. T'ang empress, the only woman ever to rule China in her own name
3. French chemist born in Poland and Nobel Prize winner in 1911 for the discovery of radium and polonium
4. The first U.S. female astronaut to travel in space
5. The first woman to become president of the United Nations General Assembly
7. Queen of Scotland from 1542 to 1567
10. Reputed maker of the first American flag
13. American abolitionist called "the Moses of her people"
14. U.S. nurse and leader in birth control education
15. American anthropologist, author of *Coming of Age in Samoa*
16. American Indian princess in Virginia who reputedly saved the life of Captain John Smith
18. Queen of Great Britain from 1702 to 1714
19. Russian czarina who was executed in 1918, along with her husband Nicholas and their five children
24. French national heroine known as "the Maid of Orleans"
25. Queen of Great Britain from 1837 to 1901
26. Queen of the Hawaiian Islands from 1891 to 1893
29. Queen of Egypt, the first woman ruler known to history, around 1478 B.C.
30. U.S. novelist born in Germany, author of *All Quiet on the Western Front*
32. Queen of Egypt from 51 to 30 B.C.
33. The first child born in America of English parents
34. American deaf and blind lecturer
35. British suffragist who founded the Women's Social and Political Union in 1903
38. Joint British sovereign with William III from 1689 to 1694
39. Wife of Menelaus whose abduction by Paris caused the Trojan War

Name ______________________ Date ______________

74. Women in World History

75. BIBLICAL NAMES IN WORLD HISTORY

ACROSS:

3. Woman who was one of the ancestors of King David
4. The apostle believed to be the author of the first Gospel
8. The niece of Herod who was given the head of John the Baptist as a reward for her dancing
9. Hebrew woman who, as the queen of Persia, delivered her people from destruction
15. One of the four archangels named in Hebrew tradition
17. Son of David and the tenth century B.C. king of Israel, noted for his wisdom
19. Man in the Bible who had many sufferings but kept his faith in God
20. Philistine giant who was killed by David
21. The outcast son of Abraham and Hagar
22. One of the twelve apostles
23. Hebrew prophet and lawgiver who freed the Israelites from slavery in Egypt
26. The first man in the Bible
27. The youngest son of Jacob and ancestor of one of the twelve tribes of Israel
30. Brother of Moses and first high priest of the Hebrews
31. The first king of Israel
34. Hebrew prophet of the sixth century B.C.
37. One of the twelve apostles and the betrayer of Jesus
38. Son of Adam and Eve and brother of Cain
39. Patriarch and founder of the Hebrew people
41. Son of Isaac and Rebekah and the elder twin brother of Jacob
42. A prophet who was held captive in Babylon and delivered by God from a den of lions
43. One of the four archangels named in Hebrew tradition
44. One of the apostles, the chief early Christian missionary to the Gentiles
46. Hebrew prophet who spent three days in the belly of a great fish
47. Hebrew prophet of the eighth century B.C.
51. Son of Jacob who rose to high office in Egypt after being sold into slavery by his brothers
52. Mistress and betrayer of Samson
54. Evangelist believed to be the author of the second Gospel
56. The son of Isaac and Rebekah and younger twin brother of Esau
57. The wife of Isaac and mother of Esau and Jacob
58. The sister of Lazarus and Martha, mother of Jesus

DOWN:

1. Physician and companion of the apostle Paul, believed to be the author of the third Gospel
2. King of Israel in the ninth century B.C.
5. The first woman in the Bible
6. The author of several New Testament epistles
7. Builder of the ark in which he, his family, and living creatures of every kind survived the Flood
10. Apostle who demanded proof of Christ's resurrection
11. Hebrew judge who appointed Saul and then David king
12. One of the twelve apostles
13. One of the archangels named in Hebrew tradition
14. In the Old Testament, a patriarch commanded by God to build an ark that saved every kind of animal from the Flood
16. Hebrew leader who succeeded Moses during the settlement of the Israelites in Canaan
18. Hebrew hero who fought against the Philistines
23. The sister of Lazarus and Mary and friend of Jesus
24. The wife of Abraham and mother of Isaac
25. A youth who slew Goliath and succeeded Saul as the king of Israel
28. Queen of Israel and wife of Ahab who was noted for her wickedness
29. One of the four archangels named in Hebrew tradition
32. The brother of Mary and Martha who was raised by Jesus from the dead
33. The mistress of Abraham
35. King of Israel and husband of Jezebel
36. One of the twelve apostles
37. Hebrew prophet of the sixth and seventh centuries B.C.
40. The elder son of Adam and Eve who killed his brother Abel
44. One of the twelve apostles
45. Hebrew prophet of the sixth century B.C.
46. The Baptist prophet and baptizer of Jesus
48. The son of Abraham and father of Jacob
49. One of the twelve apostles, believed to be the author of the fourth Gospel
50. Hebrew prophet of the ninth century B.C.
53. The mother of Ishmael
55. Progenitor of the human race

Name ______________________ Date ______________

75. Biblical Names in World History

76. MYTHOLOGICAL NAMES IN WORLD HISTORY—I

ACROSS:

1. In Greek and Roman mythology, the god of sunlight, music, prophecy, and poetry
3. The goddess of flowers in Roman mythology
8. Poet and musician in Greek mythology who tried to rescue his wife Eurydice from Hades by charming Pluto and Persephone with his lyre
9. The Muse of heroic poetry in Greek mythology
11. Son of Laius and Jocasta who in Greek mythology killed his father and married his mother not knowing their identities
13. The god of forests, pastures, flocks, and shepherds in Greek mythology who was represented as having the legs, ears, and horns of a goat
14. The goddess of agriculture in Greek mythology
15. A whirlpool off the coast of Sicily personified in Greek mythology as a female monster
18. Chief of the Greek army during the Trojan War
21. In Greek mythology, a beautiful youth loved by the goddess of the moon and granted eternal youth through eternal sleep
23. In classical legend, the Trojan hero of the *Aeneid*
24. The god of thunder, weather, and crops in Norse mythology
26. Hero in Greek mythology, second in bravery only to Achilles during the Trojan War
28. Hero in Greek mythology noted for his strength and for performing twelve gigantic labors imposed on him by Hera
29. The goddess of victory in Greek mythology
32. The god of medicine in Greek mythology
33. Son of Priam and Hecuba, a Trojan hero killed by Achilles in Greek mythology
34. The god of war in Roman mythology
35. A legendary Dutch mariner condemned to sail the seas until Judgment Day
38. In Greek mythology, a Phoenician princess who was carried off by Zeus disguised as a white bull
41. God of the north wind in Greek mythology
43. In Greek mythology, an ivory statue of a maiden brought to life by Aphrodite after its sculptor, Pygmalion, had fallen in love with it
45. Hero in Greek mythology who killed the Minotaur and conquered the Amazons
46. The queen of heaven in Roman mythology, wife of Jupiter and goddess of light, birth, women, and marriage
48. Son of Mars in Roman mythology who was the twin brother of Remus and the founder of Rome
51. In Greek mythology, the wife of Orpheus, whom he attempted to bring back from Hades but failed because he looked back at her
52. The son of Hermes and Aphrodite who in Greek mythology became united with the nymph Salmacis into a single body
54. A daughter of Tantalus in Greek mythology who while weeping for her slain children was turned by Zeus into a stone from which her tears continued to flow
55. Titan in Greek mythology forced to bear the heavens on his shoulders
56. The god of the sea in Roman mythology
60. King of Sparta, brother of Agamemnon, and husband of Helen of Troy in Greek mythology
61. The goddess of love and beauty in Roman mythology
62. A Cyclops in Greek mythology who was blinded by Odysseus
63. Woman with magic powers in Greek mythology who helped Jason obtain the Golden Fleece

DOWN:

2. The god of the dead and the underworld in Greek mythology
4. King of Thebes who in Greek mythology was killed by his son Oedipus
5. A sculptor in Greek mythology who fell in love with a statue that was then brought to life by Aphrodite
6. In Greek mythology, the chief god and ruler of the sky and weather
7. The wife of Agamemnon in Greek mythology
9. The goddess of agriculture in Roman mythology
10. In Greek mythology, the son of Priam and Hecuba who carried off Helen of Troy, wife of Menelaus, thus causing the Trojan War
12. In Greek mythology, the king of Troy during the Trojan War
14. In Roman mythology, goddess of the forest, childbirth, and the moon
16. Legendary queen of Carthage who fell in love with Aeneas and killed herself when he left her
17. In Greek legend, a king who had the power of turning whatever he touched into gold
19. The goddess of wisdom in Greek mythology
20. The god of fire and metalworking in Greek mythology
22. Legendary Swiss patriot commanded to shoot an apple from his son's head with bow and arrow
25. In Greek legend, a daughter of Agamemnon and Clytemnestra who persuaded her brother Orestes to kill their mother to avenge their father's murder
26. The god of medicine in Roman mythology
27. Goddess of the moon, wild animals, and hunting in Greek mythology
30. In Norse mythology, the wife of Odin and the goddess of marriage and the hearth
31. A Titan in Greek mythology who was punished by Zeus for stealing fire from heaven and giving it to human beings
33. The wife of Priam and mother of Paris in Greek mythology
36. God of commerce, eloquence, travel, and theft who served as the messenger of the other gods in Roman mythology
37. The god of war in Greek mythology
39. A legendary German magician who sold his soul to the devil
40. The god of gates and doors and of beginnings and endings in Roman mythology who is usually pictured as having two opposite faces
42. In Greek mythology, a youth beloved by Aphrodite for his beauty and killed by a wild boar
44. The goddess of wisdom in Roman mythology
47. The god of love in Roman mythology
49. In Norse mythology, the god of war, art, culture, and the dead
50. The god of marriage in Greek mythology
52. In Greek mythology, the wife of Zeus and goddess of women and marriage
53. A god of agriculture in Roman mythology
57. The god of love in Greek mythology
58. In Greek mythology, the winged goddess of victory
59. A queen of Sparta in Greek mythology who was courted by Zeus in the form of a swan

Name ______________________________ Date ______________________

76. Mythological Names in World History—I

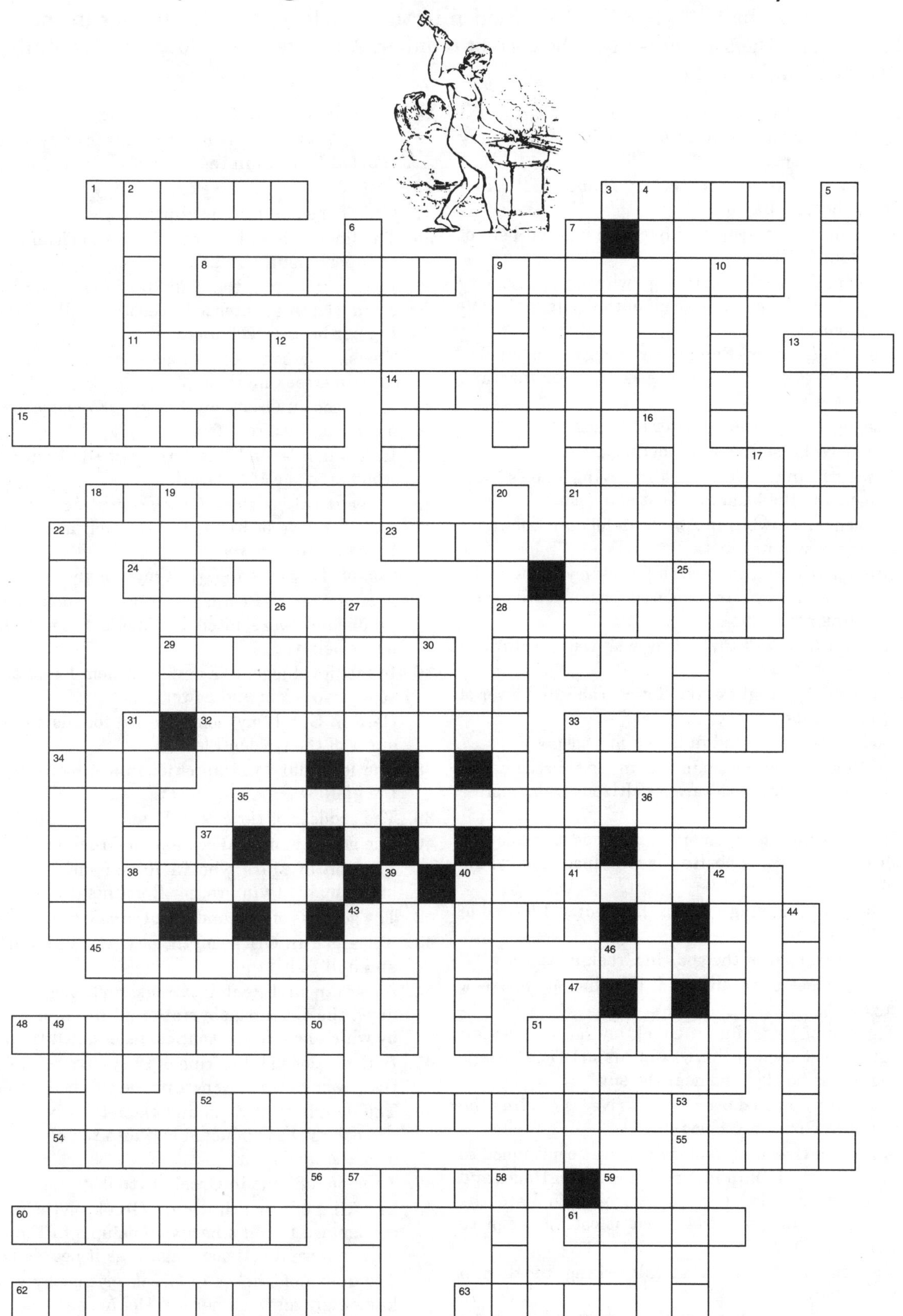

77. MYTHOLOGICAL NAMES IN WORLD HISTORY—II

The answers to the following clues are hidden in the puzzle. Circle the answer in the puzzle and then write the answer next to the correct number. Answers can be found horizontally, vertically, diagonally, and backward.

1. The foremost Greek hero of the Trojan War, killed by an arrow Paris shot into his right heel, his only vulnerable spot
2. A monster in Greek mythology shaped half like a man and half like a bull
3. Legendary sixth-century British king and hero of the Round Table
4. A woman in Greek mythology who out of curiosity opened a box and let loose all of the evils that trouble humans
5. The chief god in Roman mythology, husband of Juno and the god of light, the sky and weather, and of the state
6. The legendary Greek writer of fables
7. A winged horse in Greek mythology
8. A monster in Greek mythology having a lion's body, wings, and the head and bust of a woman
9. A legendary cowboy in American folklore known for his extraordinary feats
10. King of Ithaca and hero in Greek mythology who after the Trojan War wandered for ten years before reaching home
11. A Titan in Greek mythology who was overthrown by his son Zeus
12. A legendary knight of the Round Table and lover of Queen Guinevere
13. God of the west wind in Greek mythology
14. An English gentlewoman who in legend rode naked through Coventry to save its citizens from oppressive taxes
15. In Greek mythology, a six-headed sea monster who dwelt in a cave opposite the whirlpool Charybdis off the coast of Sicily
16. A prophet and magician in the medieval legend of King Arthur
17. The messenger of the gods in Greek mythology
18. The goddess of reward and punishment in Greek mythology
19. The son of Daedalus in Greek mythology who fell into the sea when the wax of his artificial wings melted as he flew too near the sun
20. A Titan who ruled over a great river encircling the earth in Greek mythology
21. A king in Greek mythology who was condemned to stand up to his chin in a pool of water in Hades and beneath fruit-laden branches, only to have the water or fruit go out of reach at each attempt to drink or eat
22. The god of fire and metalworking in Roman mythology
23. A Titan in Greek mythology who supported the heavens on his shoulders
24. The god of love in Greek mythology
25. A queen of Sparta in Greek mythology who was courted by Zeus in the form of a swan
26. God of the sea in Greek mythology
27. God of the sun in Greek mythology
28. The famous hero lumberjack in American folklore, of superhuman size and strength
29. In Greek legend, the daughter of Oedipus and Jocasta who was sentenced to death for illegally burying her brother Polynices
30. The sky personified as a god and father of the Titans in Greek mythology
31. A sea god in Greek mythology who was capable of assuming different forms
32. In English legend, the knight of the Round Table who found the Holy Grail
33. A beautiful youth in Greek mythology who pined away for love of his own reflection and was then turned into a flower
34. God of the winds in Greek mythology
35. A daughter of Priam in Greek mythology whose prophecies were fated by Apollo to be true but never believed
36. In medieval legend, a devil to whom Faust sold his soul for wisdom and power
37. Hero in Greek mythology noted for his successful quest of the Golden Fleece
38. The legendary Indian chief in a famous poem by Longfellow
39. The goddess of flowers in Roman mythology
40. The god of wine and ecstasy in Greek mythology
41. The son of Mars who in Roman mythology was killed by his twin brother Romulus
42. The goddess of love and beauty in Greek mythology
43. A sea god in Greek mythology who was half man and half fish
44. Athenian architect in Greek mythology who devised the Cretan Labyrinth and inventor of wings by which he and his son Icarus escaped from it
45. In Greek legend, the king of Phrygia who was given the power to turn everything he touched into gold
46. The daughter of Zeus and Demeter who in Greek mythology was abducted by Pluto to rule with him over the underworld
47. The wife of Zeus in Greek mythology
48. The king of Corinth who in Greek mythology was condemned to roll a heavy stone up a hill in Hades only to have it roll down again as it neared the top
49. The queen of Thebes in Greek mythology who unknowingly married her son Oedipus
50. The god of war in Greek mythology

Name ______________________________ Date ______________________

77. Mythological Names in World History—II

```
J E F E R J U P I T E R N S O L C I N
Z D A H A L A G M O R O I T E W J O A
E H N O S C O C A S S A N D R A S A R
P O S E I D O N P A U M A H R I E T C
H T R Y I D O O J D N E I E E L L S I
Y A S V P T S O R I O P S C Y L L A S
R N A P I E T I D O R H P A T I I C S
U T U R A N U S S N C i V I S B H O U
S I T R G N U A I Y I S S U N S C J S
I G A D B N D L C S E T L O L O A C R
N O F L A I R O A U Y O K C R C R L U
H N S E M E P E R S E P H O N E A A A
I E C P M P D H U A S H H E M P N N T
A O R U H T R A S A S E A U P O E C O
W F A M K I T O L E P L S I S E M E N
A S L H E L N T T U P E G A S U S L I
T O E O A S A X O E S S J R T M U O M
H R T S R P A U L B U N Y A N H A T J
A E S U L A T N A T O S E S S Y L U F
```

1. ______________
2. ______________
3. ______________
4. ______________
5. ______________
6. ______________
7. ______________
8. ______________
9. ______________
10. ______________
11. ______________
12. ______________
13. ______________
14. ______________
15. ______________
16. ______________
17. ______________
18. ______________
19. ______________
20. ______________
21. ______________
22. ______________
23. ______________
24. ______________
25. ______________
26. ______________
27. ______________
28. ______________
29. ______________
30. ______________
31. ______________
32. ______________
33. ______________
34. ______________
35. ______________
36. ______________
37. ______________
38. ______________
39. ______________
40. ______________
41. ______________
42. ______________
43. ______________
44. ______________
45. ______________
46. ______________
47. ______________
48. ______________
49. ______________
50. ______________

78. POPULAR NAMES IN WORLD HISTORY

ACROSS:

2. The name of six kings of Great Britain and two kings of Greece
3. The name of twelve popes
8. The name of five popes, two czars of Russia, and a fourth-century Christian bishop
10. The name of eight popes, a czar of Russia, and the king of Macedon who conquered the Persian Empire
11. The name of six kings of France and the father of Alexander the Great
13. The name of three Holy Roman emperors and the first king of Prussia
17. The name of eight kings of England, including "Beauclerc," "Bolingbroke," and "the Huckster"
19. The name of eighteen kings of France and a Holy Roman emperor
20. The name of the first, fifth, and sixth wives of Henry VIII of England, the wife of Peter the Great, and an empress of Russia
22. The name of two kings of Great Britain, one who was the first Stuart king and one who was deposed
24. The name of nine kings of England, including "the Confessor," "the Peacemaker," and "Longshanks"
25. The name of two queens of England and a queen of Scotland

DOWN:

1. The name of twenty-one popes, a king of England, a king of Portugal, and a king of Poland
3. The name of five kings of Spain and the Duke of Edinburgh, husband of Queen Elizabeth II of England
4. The name of eight popes
5. The name of six popes, a czar of Russia, and a king of Greece
6. The name of sixteen popes and a Frankish bishop and historian
7. The name of nine popes and an English monk called "the Apostle of Germany"
9. The name of fifteen popes and an Italian monk who founded a religious order
12. The name of thirteen popes
14. The name of three kings of England, including "Crouchback" and "the Lion-Hearted"
15. The name of ten kings of France, two kings of Great Britain, a king of Sweden, and a Holy Roman emperor
16. The name of four kings of England, including "the Conqueror," "Rufus," and "the Sailor King"
18. The name of two English kings, one who was murdered in the Tower of London and one who abdicated and became the Duke of Windsor
21. The name of four kings of France, a Holy Roman emperor, and a Portuguese prince who was a patron of explorers and sea expeditions
23. The name of thirteen popes and a Byzantine emperor called "the Isaurian"

Name ______________________ Date ______________________

78. Popular Names in World History

79. FOREIGN WORDS AND PHRASES—I

ACROSS:

1. Latin phrase meaning "always faithful"—motto of the U.S. Marine Corps
2. Hawaiian word meaning "love," "greetings," or "farewell"
3. Latin phrase meaning "second self"
4. Latin phrase meaning "always prepared"—motto of the U.S. Coast Guard
5. Latin phrase meaning "one out of many"—used on the Great Seal of the United States and on several U.S. coins
6. French word meaning "townspeople" or "the middle class"
7. French phrase meaning "on the contrary"
8. German word meaning "life world" or "world of lived experience"
9. Japanese word meaning "good-bye"
10. Italian phrase meaning "what will be, will be"
11. Italian word meaning "till we meet again" or "farewell"
12. Latin word meaning "still higher"—motto of New York
13. Latin phrase meaning "God enriches"—motto of Arizona
14. German word meaning "wonderful"
15. German word meaning "your health"—used as a toast or an expression of good will to someone who has just sneezed
16. French phrase meaning "enjoy your meal" or "good appetite"
17. Hawaiian word meaning "thank you"
18. Greek word meaning "I have found it"—motto of California
19. French phrase meaning "a false step," "mistake," or "error"
20. Latin phrase meaning "have the body"—a writ issued to bring a detained person before a court
21. Spanish phrase meaning "Spanish spoken"
22. Latin phrase meaning "the existing state of affairs"

Name ______________________________ Date ____________________

79. Foreign Words and Phrases—I

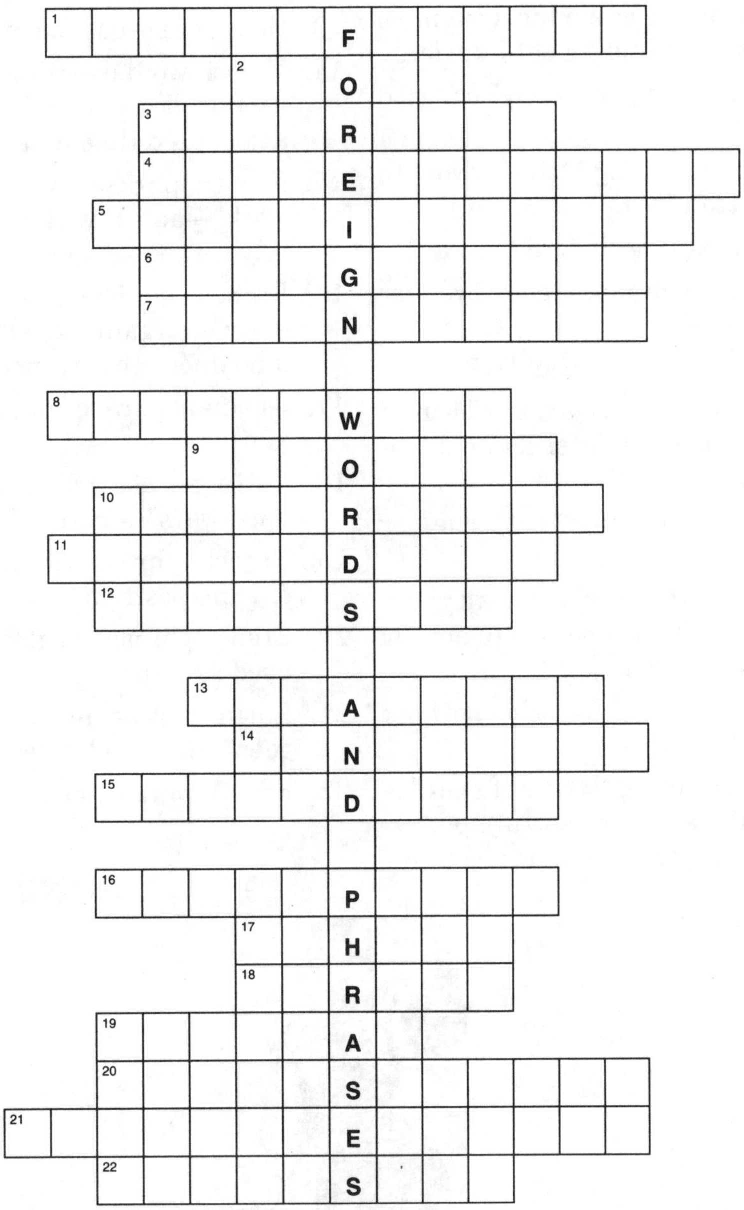

80. FOREIGN WORDS AND PHRASES—II

ACROSS:

1. French phrase meaning "to let to do"—used to describe an economic system in which the government does not interfere
2. French word meaning "good day" or "good morning"
3. Latin phrase meaning "thus ever to tyrants"—motto of Virginia
4. Latin phrase meaning "before the war"
5. Spanish word meaning "good-bye" or "farewell"
6. Italian phrase meaning "good day"
7. French word meaning "relaxation"—used to describe the easing of international tensions
8. German phrase meaning "not true" or "isn't it so"
9. Latin word meaning "under penalty"—a judicial writ requiring a person to appear in court to give testimony
10. Latin word meaning "I direct"—motto of Maine
11. French phrase meaning "stroke of state"—used to describe a sudden seizure of government, often accompanied by violence
12. French word meaning "good evening"
13. Spanish phrase meaning "good-bye"
14. French word meaning "betake yourself"—used to describe an appointed meeting at a specified time and place
15. French phrase meaning "outside of the work"—any of various savory foods generally served as appetizers before a meal
16. French word meaning "to undertake"—one who organizes and assumes the risk of a business or enterprise
17. German phrase meaning "German spoken"
18. Latin phrase meaning "to the stars by hard ways"—motto of Kansas
19. French phrase meaning "on guard"—a fencing position
20. French phrase meaning "to your health"—used as a toast
21. Latin phrase meaning "it grows as it goes"—motto of New Mexico
22. French phrase meaning "if you please"

Name ______________________ Date ______________________

80. Foreign Words and Phrases—II

FOREIGN WORDS AND PHRASES

1, 2, 3, 4, 5, 6, 7, 8, 9, 10, 11, 12, 13, 14, 15, 16, 17, 18, 19, 20, 21, 22

81. VOCABULARY WORDS IN WORLD HISTORY

The answers to the following clues are hidden in the puzzle. Circle the answer in the puzzle and then write the answer next to the correct number. Answers can be found horizontally, vertically, diagonally, and backward.

1. A soldier who fights in any country's army for pay
2. The situation in which a single company controls an entire industry
3. A person who is learning a trade or craft from a master and who works without pay except for room and board
4. A series of rulers from a single family
5. To resign as ruler
6. A government under which citizens with the right to vote choose their leaders
7. A tax on goods imported from another country
8. A temporary alliance between groups who are usually on different sides
9. The belief that the wealth of a country should be shared equally among all its citizens
10. An overall rise in the prices of goods and services
11. South Africa's legal system of rigid separation between blacks and whites
12. A territory that was administered on behalf of the League of Nations until it was judged ready for independence
13. An agreement to stop fighting
14. The practice of lending money for interest
15. A person whose ideas are incorrect in the opinion of the Church
16. A skilled worker who makes goods by hand
17. Compensation paid after a war by a defeated nation for the damages it caused other nations
18. A person who dies or suffers for his or her beliefs
19. A ship developed in the 1400's with triangular sails for tacking into the wind and square sails for running before the wind
20. The intentional killing of an entire people
21. One-sided information designed to convince people of a certain point of view
22. A political and military system based on the holding of land, with an emphasis on local protection, local government, and local self-sufficiency
23. A final demand that, if not met, will end negotiations and lead to war
24. The leader of a family or tribe who rules by paternal right
25. A public announcement of a policy
26. A government controlled by church leaders
27. A person who believes that all governments are evil and should be overthrown
28. The period of time before the beginning of written records
29. A ruler with unlimited power
30. An economic system characterized by the investment of money in business ventures with the goal of making a profit
31. The policy of making concessions in the hope of avoiding war
32. A ruler who governs oppressively or brutally
33. The ability to read and write
34. Payment to a church of ten percent of a person's income
35. The right to vote
36. The way of life that a group of people develops and passes on to its children, including language, tools, skills, and traditions
37. The temporary banishment from society or from a particular group
38. The relationship between living things and their environment
39. The policy whereby an imperial power tries to absorb colonies politically and culturally
40. A person who speaks out against a government or expresses an opinion that differs from that held by the general society

Name ______________________________ Date ____________________

81. Vocabulary Words in World History

N O I T A L F N I C A P I T A L I S M
A R T I S A N C I L B U P E R I T I S
P A T R I A R C H C E L A T E T H E I
P Y A A W G H Y A M Y T R N A E E D L
R Y R A N E C R E M T I M E C R O I A
E H C U R B A O C M S M I D U A C E D
N E O E S V M T R H A A S I S C R H U
T W T R E U A S A B N T T S U Y A T E
I I U L E R M I A B Y U I S R S C R F
C J A D I P E H P B D M C I Y T Y A S
E A C F O R A E P M I I E D C T R P S
T Y F E U P B R E L R A C I R O Y A O
E A G T P R O P A G A N D A E B T U C
S T L O T M A T S T R E M Y T H R A I
C U A D L Y I A E L I T I T H E A I A
C I F D T O R T M Y L O P O N O M L L
E E T F N L C A E A G E N O C I D E I
M D B E R A I E N T S F L S E E C E S
W A I S R A M W T T S I H C R A N A M
H I T C E E G O S T R A C I S M A S O
E H T I T N H E O N O I T I L A O C W

1. ______________
2. ______________
3. ______________
4. ______________
5. ______________
6. ______________
7. ______________
8. ______________
9. ______________
10. ______________
11. ______________
12. ______________
13. ______________
14. ______________
15. ______________
16. ______________
17. ______________
18. ______________
19. ______________
20. ______________
21. ______________
22. ______________
23. ______________
24. ______________
25. ______________
26. ______________
27. ______________
28. ______________
29. ______________
30. ______________
31. ______________
32. ______________
33. ______________
34. ______________
35. ______________
36. ______________
37. ______________
38. ______________
39. ______________
40. ______________

82. IMPORTANT YEARS IN WORLD HISTORY—B.C.

ACROSS: ________________

2. Augustus became emperor of Rome
4. Hatshepsut declared herself pharaoh of Egypt
6. Shang dynasty began in China
9. Cleopatra committed suicide
10. Kingdom of Israel was divided
12. Rome defeated Carthage in the First Punic War
14. City-states appeared in Sumer
15. Confucius was born in China
18. Siddhartha Gautama (Buddha) was born in India
20. First Olympic games were held in Greece
21. Israel became a kingdom
22. Phoenicians developed a writing system
23. Bronze Age began

DOWN: ________________

1. Nebuchadnezzar of Babylon captured Jerusalem
2. Great Wall of China was completed
3. The Great Silk Road opened from China to the West
5. Sparta defeated Athens in the Peloponnesian War
7. Persian Empire began
8. Egypt was absorbed into the Roman Empire
11. Virgil wrote *Aeneid*
12. Ashoka inherited the throne of India
13. Hittites learned to use iron
14. Upper and Lower Egypt joined
16. Hammurabi established a code of laws
17. Great Pyramid completed in Egypt
18. Rome established a republic
19. Hannibal invaded Italy during the Second Punic War

Name ______________________________ Date ____________________

82. Important Years in World History—B.C.

83. IMPORTANT YEARS IN WORLD HISTORY—0–1500

ACROSS: ____________________

3. Jesus of Nazareth was executed
4. Vasco da Gama reached India by sailing around Africa
6. Ming dynasty moved the capital of China to Peking
8. Muhammad was born in Arabia
11. Ferdinand and Isabella united Spain
12. Columbus discovered the West Indies
14. Pope Urban II initiated the Crusades
16. Dante wrote *The Divine Comedy*
19. Roman Empire in the west ended and the Dark Ages began
20. Treaty of Verdun divided Charlemagne's empire into three kingdoms
21. King John of England signed the Magna Carta
23. The Hundred Years' War began between France and England
25. Charlemagne was crowned King of the Franks
27. Golden Age of Japan began
28. Amerigo Vespucci explored the east coast of South America

DOWN: ____________________

1. Johann Gutenberg printed the Bible with movable type
2. St. Augustine became the first Archbishop Canterbury
3. Roman Emperor Constantine converted to Christianity
5. Charlemagne was crowned Holy Roman Emperor
7. Marco Polo returned from China
9. Charles Martel defeated the Muslims at the Battle of Tours
10. Ottoman Turks captured Constantinople
13. Normans invaded and conquered England
15. Byzantine Emperor Justinian codified Roman laws
17. The War of the Roses began in England
18. The Black Death broke out in Europe
21. John Cabot explored the east coast of North America
22. Golden Age of China began
24. Constantine reunited the eastern and western Roman Empires
26. Italian city of Pompeii was destroyed by the eruption of Mt. Vesuvius

Name ______________________ Date ______________

83. Important Years in World History—0–1500

84. IMPORTANT YEARS IN WORLD HISTORY—1500–1800

ACROSS:

1. Louis XIV, "the Sun King," died in France
3. The Thirty Years' War began in Europe
5. The capital of Russia was transferred to St. Petersburg
8. Holland proclaimed independence from Spain
9. England defeated the Spanish Armada
10. Montezuma became ruler of the Aztec Empire
11. England founded the Virginia colony at Jamestown
12. Thomas Jefferson drafted the Declaration of Independence
13. The first Dutch settlers reached the Cape of Good Hope
14. Cortes began his conquest of Mexico
17. The Pilgrims reached New England
18. Sir Isaac Newton discovered the law of gravity
20. Peter the Great began to westernize Russia
21. The first British convicts arrived at the penal colony in Australia
22. Copernicus suggested that the earth was not the center of the universe
23. Pizarro conquered the Incas of Peru
24. Treaty of Paris ended the American Revolutionary War

DOWN:

2. The first permanent theater was built in London
4. Parliament drafted a Bill of Rights for England
6. Galileo made the first thermometer
7. Cervantes wrote *Don Quixote*
8. George Washington became the first president of the United States
9. Sir Francis Drake began his voyage around the world
10. The French and Indian War began
12. One of Magellan's Portuguese ships completed its sail around the world
13. England seized New Netherlands from the Dutch
14. Spanish colonists founded St. Augustine, Florida
15. Martin Luther began a religious revolt in Germany
16. The French Revolution began with the storming of the Bastille
17. King Charles I of England was beheaded
18. Henry VIII established the Church of England
19. King Louis XVI of France was beheaded

Name ______________________ Date ______________

84. Important Years in World History—1500–1800

85. IMPORTANT YEARS IN WORLD HISTORY—1800–1900

ACROSS: ______________________________

2. Texas declared independence from Mexico
5. Karl Marx published *The Communist Manifesto*
6. Gold was discovered in California
7. Serfdom was abolished in Russia
10. The United States declared war against Great Britain
11. Irish potato famine began
12. The Mexican War began
13. The United States purchased the Louisiana Territory from France
14. Napoleon was defeated at the Battle of Waterloo
16. Marie Curie discovered radioactivity
19. Slavery ended in the United States
20. The first transatlantic telegraph cable was laid
24. Gold was discovered in Victoria, Australia
25. Sepoy Rebellion against British rule began in India
26. Treaty of Guadalupe Hidalgo ended the Mexican War
27. The Crimean War began
28. Bismarck of Prussia united Germany as a nation

DOWN: ______________________________

1. Britain suppressed native troops in the Indian Mutiny
2. Napoleon's invasion of Russia was repulsed
3. The American Civil War began
4. Americans began trade with the Japanese
8. Samuel Morse invented the telegraph
9. British captured Capetown from the Dutch
10. Napoleon became emperor of France
12. The Spanish-American War began
14. Alexander Graham Bell invented the telephone
15. Mexico won independence from Spain
16. The Suez Canal opened in Egypt
17. The United States purchased Alaska from Russia
18. British settlers reached New Zealand
19. Charles Darwin published *On the Origin of Species*
21. Treaty of Ghent ended the War of 1812
22. The Franco-Prussian War ended
23. Greece won independence from Turkey

Name ______________________ Date ______________________

85. Important Years in World History—1800–1900

86. IMPORTANT YEARS IN WORLD HISTORY—1900–1990

ACROSS: ______

1. Sun Yat-sen became the first president of the Republic of China
3. Armistice ended World War I
5. Finland declared independence from Russia
7. AIDS epidemic began
8. Berlin Wall was erected
10. Panama Canal opened
11. United States proclaimed the Open Door Policy for China
13. World War II ended
14. Soviet Union invaded Afghanistan
16. Treaty of Portsmouth ended the Russo-Japanese War
17. Organization of Petroleum Exporting Countries (OPEC) was founded
18. Hungary declared itself an independent republic
19. Warsaw Pact formed in eastern Europe
20. Ireland gained independence from Great Britain
21. Estonia declared independence from Russia
22. World War I began in Europe
23. India received independence from Great Britain
26. Soviets launched the first spacecraft, *Sputnik*
27. Korean War began
29. The first American rocketed into space
31. Mussolini came to power in Italy
32. American astronauts landed on the moon
34. United States proclaimed the Good Neighbor Policy for Latin America
35. World War II began in Europe
36. Bolshevik Revolution in Russia
37. Spanish Civil War began
38. Communists led by Mao Tse-tung overthrew the Chinese government

DOWN: ______

1. Berlin Wall was opened
2. U.S. forces invaded Panama
4. Lithuania declared independence from Russia
6. Boxer Rebellion in China
8. United States entered World War II
9. Treaty of Versailles officially ended World War I
10. United Nations was founded
11. East Pakistan seceded from Pakistan as Bangladesh
12. Bay of Pigs invasion in Cuba
13. Cuban Missile Crisis
14. Japanese Emperor Hirohito died
15. Suez Canal Crisis
16. Women received the right to vote in the United States
18. United States entered World War I
19. *Lusitania* sunk by German submarine
20. Israel was proclaimed a Jewish state
21. Alaska and Hawaii became states of the Union
22. European Common Market was organized
24. U.S. stock market crash set off a worldwide economic depression
25. Iran freed American hostages held in the U.S. Embassy
26. Japanese attacked Pearl Harbor, Hawaii
27. Martin Luther King, Jr. and Robert Kennedy were assassinated
28. Persian Gulf Crisis
30. Hitler came to power in Germany
32. Philippines were granted independence by the United States
33. North Atlantic Treaty Organization (NATO) was founded

Name ______________________ Date ______________

86. Important Years in World History—1900–1990

87. COUNTRIES OF THE WORLD—LATIN AMERICA

ACROSS: ______

7. Latin American country where the Andes Mountains reach their greatest average heights
9. Central American country that has the largest population
10. The second largest country in Latin America
12. Latin American country whose shape is one of the most unusual in the world (2,650 miles long and 225 miles wide)
13. Latin American country that is a self-governing commonwealth of the United States
17. The only South American country that has borders on both the Caribbean Sea and the Pacific Ocean
19. The isthmus connecting North and South America
22. The most densely settled country in Central America
23. Latin American country that has the highest capital in the world (11,910 feet)
25. The largest island in the Caribbean Sea
26. A former Dutch colony that gained its independence in 1975
28. The smallest republic in South America
29. Central American country that does not border the Caribbean Sea
30. Central American country that has the highest standard of living

DOWN: ______

1. South American country that was formerly named British Guiana
2. Latin American country that has the highest per capita income
3. Central American country that has the highest literacy rate
4. Country that has the largest city of the West Indies
5. The third largest country in Latin America
6. The poorest country in Latin America
8. Latin American country that has the most rapid rate of population increase
11. The farthest east of all of the islands of the West Indies
14. The largest country in Latin America
15. The third largest island in the Caribbean Sea
16. Caribbean islands where Columbus landed in 1492
18. Central American country that does not border the Pacific Ocean
20. Central American country that has the least industry
21. Central American country that was formerly named British Honduras
24. South American country that leads in the production of coffee
27. Country that has the largest city in the Andes Mountains

Name ______________________ Date ______________________

87. Countries of the World—Latin America

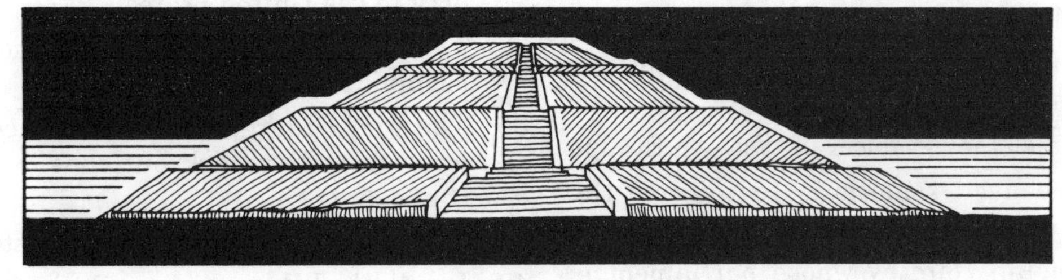

88. COUNTRIES OF THE WORLD—EUROPE

The answers to the following clues are hidden in the puzzle. Circle the answer in the puzzle and then write the answer next to the correct number. Answers can be found horizontally, vertically, diagonally, and backward.

1. Scandinavian country that has the largest glacier in Europe and the world's most northern capital
2. Central European country where people speak German and are over eighty-five percent Roman Catholic
3. European country where the roots of the democratic system of government developed
4. A tiny European country located on the Rhine River between Switzerland and Austria
5. The largest nation in Western Europe
6. European country that gained independence from the United Kingdom in 1949, the "Emerald Isle"
7. The largest country in Eastern Europe
8. The largest Scandinavian country
9. Western European country where almost fifty percent of the land lies below sea level
10. The world's smallest micro-state, home of the Pope and the center of the Roman Catholic religion
11. One of the four political divisions of the United Kingdom
12. European country that ranks number one in the world in olive production
13. The major food exporter of Eastern Europe
14. The smallest Scandinavian country
15. A small country in the Pyrenees Mountains between Spain and France
16. The leading steel producer in Western Europe
17. The name used sometimes to refer to the Netherlands
18. Scandinavian country whose parliament is over 1,000 years old, the oldest in the world
19. European country that is the world's leading producer of cork
20. European country that was the center of the Renaissance
21. Western Europe's leading fishing nation
22. Western European country where some of the most important battles of World War I and World War II were fought, even though it declared neutrality
23. Eastern European country between Poland and Hungary
24. Western Europe's number one citrus-fruit producer
25. Central European country called the "savings bank of the world"
26. One of the four political divisions of the United Kingdom
27. A small island nation located in the middle of the Mediterranean Sea
28. Western Europe's leading agricultural nation
29. The most densely populated Scandinavian country
30. European country whose art, philosophy, and science formed the basis of Western civilization
31. Country that has the lowest per capita income in Western Europe
32. One of the four political divisions of the United Kingdom
33. The least developed and poorest country of Eastern Europe
34. European country where the first Olympic Games were held in 776 B.C.
35. Western Europe's largest oil exporter
36. European country that gave the Statue of Liberty to the United States
37. The oldest country in Europe and the oldest republic in the world
38. The world's largest island, located quite far away from Denmark but considered part of that country
39. The most populous country in Eastern Europe
40. Landlocked European country surrounded by France, Germany, and Belgium
41. Scandinavian country whose paper mills produce over one million tons of Western Europe's newsprint each year
42. The most densely populated independent nation in the world
43. One of the four political divisions of the United Kingdom
44. The largest Scandinavian country in population

Name ____________________ Date ____________________

88. Countries of the World—Europe

L O N R O M D V A T I C A N C I T Y R

U D E N M A R K O N I R A M N A S G A

B D N A L L O H N E R E D O S D S E F

S N O R W A Y D E O N T B C N O P R H

E A R R O D N A D A E G E A A M A M P

A S T Y O A B N E G C A L B A N I A E

V I H Z L A A U W E E R G A C M N N A

L I E E W A I A S C E T I E N S W Y A

P R R I T A T R S H R S U S P D M D L

T I N C P J L I T A G E M A P E N X O

A L I E C H T E N S T E I N E A G I M

R Y R L D G N A S L U N F K L F I D E

L A E A N E I Y D O P A T R M R N N D

A W L N A M W N L V A N E A A A L I N

G R A D L D A S H A R Z L M L N A N A

U O N L N L E L U K T T E N I C C G L

T N D A E S C L T I A I I E W E R E T

R A L C E S E S W A O F L D O E R T O

O O I B R W E S G R U O B M E X U L C

P H U N G A R Y G T J I O C A N O M S

F U S L L A G U T R O P E P O L A N D

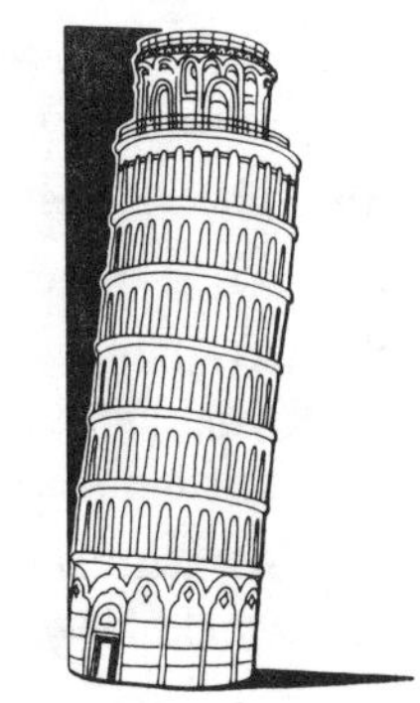

1. ____________________
2. ____________________
3. ____________________
4. ____________________
5. ____________________
6. ____________________
7. ____________________
8. ____________________
9. ____________________
10. ____________________
11. ____________________
12. ____________________
13. ____________________
14. ____________________
15. ____________________
16. ____________________
17. ____________________
18. ____________________
19. ____________________
20. ____________________
21. ____________________
22. ____________________
23. ____________________
24. ____________________
25. ____________________
26. ____________________
27. ____________________
28. ____________________
29. ____________________
30. ____________________
31. ____________________
32. ____________________
33. ____________________
34. ____________________
35. ____________________
36. ____________________
37. ____________________
38. ____________________
39. ____________________
40. ____________________
41. ____________________
42. ____________________
43. ____________________
44. ____________________

89. COUNTRIES OF THE WORLD—AFRICA

ACROSS:

2. North African country that became independent from France in 1962
9. African country that began in 1822 as a settlement for freed American slaves
10. Africa's most populous country
12. African country that is the world's largest exporter of phosphates, fertilizers valued for their phosphoric acid
13. African country formerly named Southern Rhodesia
18. African country that has the largest petroleum reserves
19. The richest country in equatorial Africa
21. African country formerly named Nyasaland
22. African country that holds about half of the world's supply of coumbite, a metal used to harden stainless steel
28. African country where the longest river in the world flows into the Mediterranean Sea
29. African country that is one of the world's largest copper producers
30. Location of Mt. Kilimanjaro and Lake Tanganyika
33. African country formerly named German East Africa
34. The largest country in Africa
36. African country formerly named the Gold Coast
38. The last country of Africa to gain its independence
40. African country that was once part of French Equatorial Africa
41. The third largest country in Africa
42. African country that faces both the Gulf of Aden and the Indian Ocean

DOWN:

1. African country formerly named French Sudan
3. African country that was never colonized by a European power
4. African country that faces both the Mediterranean Sea and the Atlantic Ocean
5. African country that is ninety-three percent desert
6. African country formerly named the Belgian Congo
7. West African republic that became independent from France in 1960
8. A landlocked country completely surrounded by the Republic of South Africa
11. North African country that has adopted an aggressive variety of Islam, supporting radical causes all around the world
14. African country formerly named Dahomey
15. The first black African nation to win its independence
16. African country that faces both the Mediterranean Sea and the Red Sea
17. African country where the ancient city of Timbuktu flourished as a center of Muslim learning and culture
20. African country formerly named German Southwest Africa
23. Home of the Organization of African Unity
24. African country formerly named Bechuanaland
25. Country that is Africa's favorite tourist attraction
26. Location of the Serengeti plains and the archaeological site of Olduvai, where evidence of some of the earliest human settlements has been discovered
27. African country formerly named Northern Rhodesia
29. African country that was ruled by Belgium for fifty-two years
30. African country where the ancient city of Carthage controlled trade throughout the Mediterranean
31. African country formerly named Basutoland
32. African country that was once governed jointly by Britain and Egypt
35. African country where Dr. Albert Schweitzer founded the famous missionary hospital at Lambarene
37. African country that was granted independence from France in 1960
39. North-central African country that gained complete independence from France in 1960

Name ______________________ Date ______________________

89. Countries of the World—Africa

90. COUNTRIES OF THE WORLD—THE ORIENT

The answers to the following clues are hidden in the puzzle. Circle the answer in the puzzle and then write the answer next to the correct number. Answers can be found horizontally, vertically, diagonally, and backward.

1. Asian country where more students graduate from high school than in any other country in the world
2. Asian country formerly named Siam
3. Asian country that was granted independence from Britain and separated from India in 1947
4. Asian country that is the world's leading rice producer
5. Southeast Asian country where the United States fought its longest war in history
6. Asian country that includes more than 7,000 islands
7. Asian peninsula divided into two countries at roughly the 38th parallel
8. Asian country formerly named Ceylon
9. The former name of Cambodia
10. Asian country that occupies the largest total land area of any archipelago in the world
11. Asian country that is the world's second leading producer of tea
12. The only landlocked country in Southeast Asia
13. Asian country that has the second largest population in the world
14. Asian country that is the world's chief exporter of rice
15. Southeast Asian country whose population is more than seventy-five percent Chinese
16. Asian country that has the largest fishing industry in the world
17. Asian country whose extreme isolation led to the idea of Shangri La, an imaginary hidden utopia or paradise
18. Asian country that is one of the world's poorest and most crowded nations
19. Asian country that gained its independence from China in 1946
20. Country that has the largest city in Southeast Asia
21. Asian country that is the world's third largest wheat producer
22. Asian country whose population is more than eighty percent Roman Catholic
23. Asian country whose population is about ninety percent Muslim
24. Country that is the center of trade and banking for Southeast Asia
25. Asian country that is the world's third largest producer of tin
26. Asian country that was granted independence from Britain in 1947
27. Asian country whose population is more than ninety-five percent Buddhist
28. Asian country that became independent from the Dutch in 1950
29. Asian country that produces the world's largest supply of rubber
30. Southeast Asian country that was granted independence from France in 1954
31. Asian country that leads the world in the production of tungsten, a metal used in hardening steel
32. A rich but tiny independent nation on the north side of the island of Borneo
33. Asian country formerly named East Pakistan
34. The oldest democracy in Asia
35. Asian country that ranks number one in the world in the production of automobiles, televisions, cameras, and motorcycles
36. Asian country formerly named the Netherlands East Indies
37. Location of Mount Everest, the world's highest mountain
38. Asian country that has the longest continuous history of any people on earth
39. Asian country that was invaded by the Soviet Union in 1979
40. The only country in Southeast Asia that has not been ruled by a European colonial power
41. A cluster of coral islands southwest of Sri Lanka that gained independence from Britain in 1965
42. Asian country that leads the world in the production of burlap, a material made from the fiber of the jute plant
43. Southeast Asian country that gained its independence from France in 1953, now known as Cambodia
44. Asian country that left the Federation of Malaysia in 1965 and became an independent country
45. Asian nation that became independent from the United States in 1946
46. The most populated nation in the world
47. Asian country that is the world's leading tin-mining nation
48. Asian nation that was granted its independence from the British in 1948, now known as Myanmar
49. Asian country where more than 250 different languages are spoken on the various islands
50. Asian country formerly named Formosa

Name ______________________ Date ______________

90. Countries of the World—The Orient

A B I L A I S E N O D N I L S E
I K A N S C A M A N T E I V H R
L A N I S I S O F N N A T U H B
O M A N D Y N I G B K I P F X M
G P W N W O E G H N O D Y A K A
N U I B A N G L A D E S H O N L
O C A N U I A L N P C K R S D D
M H T R T R I T I E O E V E N I
E E B A R R M L S N A R R A A V
C A Y N S M O A T I A N E S L E
D H D A E V I D A C K P O A I S
P H I L I P P I N E S A A R A L
G E O N R G A E M I L J P J H O
E B I L A M A L A Y S I A E T S

1. ______________
2. ______________
3. ______________
4. ______________
5. ______________
6. ______________
7. ______________
8. ______________
9. ______________
10. ______________
11. ______________
12. ______________
13. ______________
14. ______________
15. ______________
16. ______________
17. ______________
18. ______________
19. ______________
20. ______________
21. ______________
22. ______________
23. ______________
24. ______________
25. ______________
26. ______________
27. ______________
28. ______________
29. ______________
30. ______________
31. ______________
32. ______________
33. ______________
34. ______________
35. ______________
36. ______________
37. ______________
38. ______________
39. ______________
40. ______________
41. ______________
42. ______________
43. ______________
44. ______________
45. ______________
46. ______________
47. ______________
48. ______________
49. ______________
50. ______________

Name ______________________________ Date ____________________

91. CAPITAL CITIES OF THE WORLD—LATIN AMERICA

Circle the names of the capital cities in the puzzle and then write the name of each capital next to the correct country. Answers can be found horizontally, vertically, diagonally, and backward.

```
T A S K O E D I V E T N O M E S L I M B
O B E I S M Y A P A R A M A R I B O L C
A U N N S A N J O S E A Z I M L N E J E
L E N G M I N R R O P O G A I T N A S J
T N E S U P V S T L B E L M P B N O P M
E O Y T I C A L A M E T A U G A J K O S
Y S A O A B E G U L R C H J S N L A R N
T A C N E U I E P B V A A S A C T I T W
I I N Q A C G E R X V A A S R O F L O O
C R K A U J Y A I A H U D Z G E L I F T
O E C G V I O G N I M O D O T N A S S E
C S E A J A T A C A F S B S R J B A P G
I T M E R I H O E N M A A P O V N R A D
X Y T I C A M A N A P N L T W J E B I I
E C A S U N C I O N J J I A U A D Y N R
M B A P M E D A W O E U N A P O M L E B
S E G R O E G T S C Q A N N I A T I F A
M T G E O R G E T O W N C A K I Z O L S
```

1. ________________ Guatemala
2. ________________ Uruguay
3. ________________ Belize
4. ________________ Bolivia
5. ________________ Mexico
6. ________________ Guyana
7. ________________ Chile
8. ________________ Panama
9. ________________ Peru
10. ________________ Haiti
11. ________________ Brazil
12. ________________ Cuba
13. ________________ Ecuador
14. ________________ Jamaica
15. ________________ Grenada
16. ________________ Trinidad and Tobago
17. ________________ French Guiana
18. ________________ Dominican Republic
19. ________________ Nicaragua
20. ________________ Puerto Rico
21. ________________ Argentina
22. ________________ El Salvador
23. ________________ Costa Rica
24. ________________ Venezuela
25. ________________ Honduras
26. ________________ Paraguay
27. ________________ Bahamas
28. ________________ Colombia
29. ________________ Suriname
30. ________________ Barbados

Name ______________________________ Date ____________________

92. CAPITAL CITIES OF THE WORLD—EUROPE

ACROSS:

1. Capital of Sweden
5. Capital of the Netherlands
6. Capital of Northern Ireland
7. Capital of Iceland
10. Capital of Ireland
13. Capital of Finland
15. Capital of Romania
16. Capital of Luxembourg
19. Capital of Switzerland
21. Capital of Holland
25. Capital of Bulgaria
27. Capital of Bulgaria
31. Capital of Ireland
32. Capital of Poland
33. Capital of Greece
34. Capital of Germany
37. Capital of Belgium
38. Capital of Denmark
39. Capital of Austria

DOWN:

2. Capital of Norway
3. Capital of Spain
4. Capital of France
8. Capital of Malta
9. Capital of Portugal
11. Capital of Romania
12. Capital of Austria
14. Capital of Switzerland
17. Capital of Italy
18. Capital of Russia
20. Capital of Scotland
22. Capital of Albania
23. Capital of the Netherlands
24. Capital of Great Britain
26. Capital of Hungary
28. Capital of Portugal
29. Capital of the Czech Republic
30. Capital of France
35. Capital of Italy
36. Capital of Switzerland

Name ______________________________ Date ____________________

93. CAPITAL CITIES OF THE WORLD—AFRICA

Circle the names of the capital cities in the puzzle and then write the name of each capital next to the correct country. Answers can be found horizontally, vertically, diagonally, and backward.

S N A I R O B I A T Y R K A N O C E S

M A H M A L A B O N D J A M E N A B I

O J A R A L A P M A K E M O L U D A G

Y D R A E L N G O I L A G I K P D N A

D I A N O S T Z O L T G S M R B I J B

E B R M O G A D I S H U I E Y E S U O

B A E J S U N V R A B A T E W B A L R

M L O U A G A D O U G O U G R E B U O

B A I C E Z N K M O R O N I L S A R N

A C C B Z I A O C I U O I U Y O B E E

B R A A R E R C A H L P S G L T A S T

A K R I X E I I A I O A D N A U L A N

N B H I R A V S L R K T H A G P U M W

E L D A U O O I T A U I T B O A W K O

D N E O R G K O L R A B N A S M E D T

F I M N D T N A A L I R M S A O I A E

C A O A I O O A M R E P I U H C I K E

S M T F V U M U B A C B O D J A C A R

L E O O B A L A M B B C N L R U S R F

L Y A O U N D E O A F I A P I N B A A

I G S E R L A N E T W D J I B O U T I

1. ____________ Liberia
2. ____________ Mali
3. ____________ Gabon
4. ____________ Algeria
5. ____________ Ghana
6. ____________ Zaire
7. ____________ Gambia
8. ____________ Nigeria
9. ____________ Congo
10. ____________ Egypt
11. ____________ Niger
12. ____________ Benin
13. ____________ Uganda
14. ____________ Morocco
15. ____________ Kenya
16. ____________ Chad
17. ____________ Guinea
18. ____________ Malawi
19. ____________ Libya
20. ____________ Zambia
21. ____________ Togo
22. ____________ Sudan
23. ____________ Rwanda
24. ____________ Senegal
25. ____________ Tunisia
26. ____________ Sierra Leone
27. ____________ Mozambique
28. ____________ Burundi
29. ____________ Botswana
30. ____________ Mauritania
31. ____________ Burkina Faso
32. ____________ Zimbabwe
33. ____________ Tanzania
34. ____________ Equatorial Guinea
35. ____________ Somalia
36. ____________ Cote D'Ivoire
37. ____________ Namibia
38. ____________ Cape Verde Islands
39. ____________ Guinea-Bissau
40. ____________ Ethiopia
41. ____________ Swaziland
42. ____________ Lesotho
43. ____________ Comoro Islands
44. ____________ Cameroon
45. ____________ Angola
46. ____________ Djibouti
47. ____________ Madagascar
48. ____________ South Africa
49. ____________ Sao Tome and Principe
50. ____________ Central African Republic

Name ______________________________ Date ______________________

94. CAPITAL CITIES OF THE WORLD—THE ORIENT

ACROSS: ____

1. Capital of Bangladesh
2. Capital of Afghanistan
3. Capital of Singapore
4. Capital of Vietnam
5. Capital of Nepal
6. Capital of Myanmar
7. Capital of Malaysia
8. Capital of Sri Lanka
9. Capital of Taiwan
10. Capital of Laos
11. Capital of Bhutan
12. Capital of China
13. Capital of Pakistan
14. Capital of Mongolia
15. Capital of Cambodia
16. Capital of India
17. Capital of North Korea
18. Capital of Indonesia
19. Capital of Philippines
20. Capital of South Korea
21. Capital of Thailand
22. Capital of Japan

95. MOUNTAINS OF THE WORLD—I

ACROSS:

5. Volcano in western Italy
6. The highest peak in Turkey
9. The highest peak in New Zealand
10. The highest peak in the Philippines
12. The highest peak in the Appalachian Mountains
13. Volcano in eastern Sicily
14. The highest peak in Australia
16. The highest peak in the Pyrenees Mountains
17. The highest peak in Canada
18. The highest peak in Sicily
21. The highest peak in Greece
23. Volcano in the Philippines
25. According to the Bible, the traditional resting place of Noah's ark
26. According to the Bible, the mountain where the Law was given to Moses
27. The highest mountain on the south island of New Zealand
29. The highest peak in Japan
30. The second highest peak in North America
32. The highest peak in the Rocky Mountains of the conterminous United States
34. The highest peak in Spain
35. The highest peak in the Philippines
36. The highest peak in the Canadian Rockies
37. Volcano in the northwestern United States

DOWN:

1. An extinct volcano on Honshu island, Japan
2. Mountain in the United States on which are carved gigantic faces of four American presidents
3. Mountain in the Alps on the Swiss-Italian border
4. Mountain in Hawaii that is considered the wettest place in the world, receiving more than 460 inches of rain per year
7. The highest peak in the Alps
8. Volcano in the Philippines
11. The highest peak in Africa
15. The highest peak in Wales
18. The highest peak in the world
19. The highest peak in Japan
20. The highest mountain in New South Wales, Australia
22. The highest peak in France
24. The highest peak in North America
28. An active volcano in Hawaii
31. An active volcano in southeastern Alaska
33. An active volcano in southeastern Luzon, Philippines

Name ______________________________ Date ____________________

95. Mountains of the World—I

96. MOUNTAINS OF THE WORLD—II

The answers to the following clues are hidden in the puzzle. Circle the answer in the puzzle and then write the answer next to the correct number. Answers can be found horizontally, vertically, diagonally, and backward.

1. Mountain chain extending the length of the Italian peninsula
2. Mountain system in southeastern Europe between the Black Sea and the Caspian Sea
3. Mountain system in western South America extending from Panama to Tierra del Fuego
4. Mountain range on the border of Norway and Sweden
5. Mountains in Russia, usually thought of as the dividing line between Europe and Asia
6. Mountain range in central Asia on the northern border of Afghanistan and Pakistan
7. Mountain range in southeastern Siberia
8. Mountain system in Mexico
9. Mountains in northwestern Spain
10. Mountains in southern Iran
11. Mountains in northwestern Africa extending from southwestern Morocco to northern Tunisia
12. Mountains in northern England
13. Mountains in eastern Europe along the boundary between Poland and the eastern Czech Republic
14. Mountains in northern Iran
15. Mountains in northern Scotland
16. Mountain system in southern Europe
17. Mountains in southwestern Alaska
18. Mountains in southwestern Spain
19. Mountains in northwestern Canada
20. Mountains in western North America extending from Alaska to New Mexico
21. Mountains in central Spain
22. Mountains in northeastern France
23. Mountain system in southern Asia on the borders of India, Tibet, Nepal, and Bhutan
24. Mountains on the French-Spanish border extending from the Bay of Biscay to the Mediterranean Sea
25. Mountain system in eastern North America extending from southern Quebec to central Alabama
26. Mountain system in western China
27. Mountain range in southeastern Spain
28. Mountains in western Wales
29. Mountain range on the eastern coast of North and South Korea
30. Mountain system along the border of the Czech Republic and Poland
31. Two mountain chains in southern India
32. Mountain range in northeastern Siberia
33. Mountain range along the border of the Czech Republic and Germany
34. Mountain range in southern Siberia
35. Mountains in western Greece
36. Mountain chain in the Balkan Peninsula dividing Bulgaria from Macedonia
37. Mountains in central China
38. Mountain system in Asia along the border between Mongolia and western China
39. Mountains in northern Turkey
40. Mountain range in southeastern Russia
41. Mountain range in northern India and Pakistan
42. Mountain range along the border of India and Myanmar
43. Mountain range extending along the boundary between France and Switzerland
44. Mountain range in southern Turkey

Name ______________________________ Date ____________________

96. Mountains of the World—II

Z A G R O S A M Y L O K J O L E N E
N P O N T I C A V A K S A L P S I K
A E S U I S U D N I P U E L E A S U
I N A I R B M A C L O R N G T P Y S
R N H S E A D V A A D U S L L A N K
B I I O L R L E I A U O A A U S I O
A N M R B S R N M T V C Y T E N R K
T E A G U A D A R R A M A E H E A W
N S L A R O R R M N H U N S S R P I
A G A Z Z R R R D O R E D E U O E N
C R Y L E T E E J U R A E J K S N K
R A A I T R S I S Y A E S U U T N E
H M S K O A O S P T S L N R D A I A
O P I N A I H C A L A P P A N N N B
D I S E D N A R K M E H L S I O E E
O A C A R P A T H I A N G A H V S A
P N F O E K E I Z N E K C A M O R T
E K A R A K O R U M T S I N L I N G
G I O N O L B A Y O S U D E T I C E

1. ____________________
2. ____________________
3. ____________________
4. ____________________
5. ____________________
6. ____________________
7. ____________________
8. ____________________
9. ____________________
10. ____________________
11. ____________________
12. ____________________
13. ____________________
14. ____________________
15. ____________________
16. ____________________
17. ____________________
18. ____________________
19. ____________________
20. ____________________
21. ____________________
22. ____________________
23. ____________________
24. ____________________
25. ____________________
26. ____________________
27. ____________________
28. ____________________
29. ____________________
30. ____________________
31. ____________________
32. ____________________
33. ____________________
34. ____________________
35. ____________________
36. ____________________
37. ____________________
38. ____________________
39. ____________________
40. ____________________
41. ____________________
42. ____________________
43. ____________________
44. ____________________

97. RIVERS OF THE WORLD—I

ACROSS:

2. River in south central Europe, flowing about 450 miles to the Danube River
4. The longest river in Europe, flowing 2,290 miles to the Caspian Sea
6. River in southern Spain and Portugal, flowing about 510 miles to the Gulf of Cadiz
9. River in Colombia, flowing about 1,000 miles to the Caribbean Sea
11. River in northeastern Pakistan, flowing about 480 miles to the Chenab River
13. River in central and southeastern Europe, flowing about 1,750 miles to the Black Sea
17. River in southwestern Russia, flowing 1,222 miles to the Sea of Azov
18. River in southeastern Australia, flowing 1,910 miles to the Murray River
19. River in central Europe, flowing 563 miles from the Czech Republic to the Baltic Sea
20. River in central Russia, flowing 1,042 miles to the Irtysh River
21. River in southwestern Asia, flowing from eastern Turkey about 1,700 miles to the Persian Gulf
24. The principal river of Australia, flowing 1,600 miles to the Indian Ocean
26. River in central Italy, flowing 150 miles to the Tyrrhenian Sea
28. River in southern Africa, flowing 1,300 miles to the Atlantic Ocean
32. River in northeastern France, flowing 482 miles to the English Channel
33. River in western Russia, flowing 918 miles to the Volga River
34. River in southwestern North America, passing through the Grand Canyon and flowing about 1,400 miles to the Gulf of California
37. River in southwestern Scotland, flowing 106 miles to the Irish Sea
39. The longest river in France, flowing 620 miles to the Bay of Biscay
40. River in Venezuela, flowing about 1,700 miles to the Atlantic Ocean
43. River in northern France, flowing 150 miles to the English Channel
44. The longest river in Asia, flowing 3,430 miles to the East China Sea (also called Chang)
46. River in northwestern North America, flowing 1,979 miles to the Bering Sea
47. River in the Middle East, flowing over 200 miles to the Dead Sea
49. River in northern England, flowing 70 miles to the North Sea
51. River in eastern Europe, flowing 800 miles to the Danube River
53. River in Bolivia, flowing about 1,200 miles to the Madeira River
58. River in Brazil, flowing 1,230 miles to the Amazon River
59. River in Spain and Portugal, flowing 210 miles to the Atlantic Ocean
60. River in Poland, flowing 678 miles to the Gulf of Danzig
61. River in Brazil, flowing about 1,400 miles to the Amazon River

DOWN:

1. River forming part of the boundary between China and North Korea, flowing 500 miles to the Yellow Sea
3. River in South Africa, flowing about 750 miles to the Orange River
5. River in northern India and Bangladesh, flowing about 1,560 miles to the Bay of Bengal
7. River in western Europe, flowing 810 miles to the North Sea
8. River in Spain, flowing about 500 miles to the Mediterranean Sea
10. River in southern Africa, flowing about 1,000 miles to the Indian Ocean
12. River in England, flowing 70 miles to the Irish Sea
13. River in eastern Europe, flowing 876 miles to the Black Sea
14. River in western Africa, flowing about 2,600 miles to the Gulf of Guinea
15. River in western Europe, flowing about 580 miles to the North Sea
16. River forming part of the boundary between the United States and Mexico, flowing 1,800 miles to the Gulf of Mexico
18. River in Spain and Portugal, flowing about 475 miles to the Atlantic Ocean
22. River forming part of the boundary between England and Scotland, flowing 97 miles to the North Sea
23. River in northeastern North America, the outlet of the Great Lakes system, flowing 744 miles to the Atlantic Ocean
25. River in southern Russia, flowing 1,574 miles to the Caspian Sea; considered part of the traditional boundary between Europe and Asia
27. River forming part of the boundary between the United States and Canada, flowing 75 miles to the Atlantic Ocean
29. The longest river in Africa, flowing 3,485 miles to the Mediterranean Sea
30. River in central Russia, flowing 2,364 miles to the Arctic Ocean
31. River in northeastern Siberia, flowing 1,335 miles to the East Siberian Sea
35. River in Switzerland and southeastern France, flowing 504 miles to the Mediterranean Sea
36. River in central Russia, flowing about 2,500 miles to the Kara Sea
38. River in central Europe, flowing 725 miles to the North Sea
41. River in southern Asia, flowing about 1,900 miles to the Arabian Sea
42. River in central Africa, flowing about 2,900 miles to the Atlantic Ocean (also called Congo)
43. River in France, flowing 268 miles to the Rhone River
45. River in England, flowing 30 miles to the North Sea
48. River in France, flowing 325 miles to the Seine River
50. River in southeastern Europe, flowing about 583 miles to the Danube River
52. River forming part of the boundary between China and Russia, flowing 2,700 miles to the Sea of Okhotsk
54. River in northern India and Pakistan, flowing about 475 miles to the Chenab River
55. River in eastern Russia, flowing 2,648 miles to the Laptev Sea
56. River forming part of the boundary between Poland and Russia, flowing about 500 miles to the Narew River
57. River in Germany, flowing 142 miles to the Rhine River

Name ______________________________ Date ____________________

97. Rivers of the World—I

98. RIVERS OF THE WORLD—II

The answers to the following clues are hidden in the puzzle. Circle the answer in the puzzle and then write the answer next to the correct number. Answers can be found horizontally, vertically, diagonally, and backward.

1. River in southern England, flowing 209 miles through London to the North Sea
2. River in northern Brazil, flowing about 3,300 miles to the Atlantic Ocean; carrying the largest volume of water of any river in the world
3. River in southeastern Asia, flowing 2,600 miles to the South China Sea
4. River in northwestern Brazil, the most important tributary of the Amazon River, flowing about 2,100 miles
5. River in western Canada, flowing 340 miles to Lake Winnipeg
6. River in Wales and England, flowing 210 miles to the Bristol Channel
7. River in southeastern South America, flowing 1,000 miles to the Rio de la Plata
8. River in central Brazil, flowing about 500 miles to the Amazon River
9. River in western Turkey, flowing about 240 miles to the Aegean Sea
10. River in western Canada, flowing 1,054 miles to the Slave River
11. River in central Canada, flowing 1,000 miles to Hudson Bay
12. The longest river in the United States, flowing 2,714 miles from the Rocky Mountains to the Mississippi River
13. River in the eastern United States, flowing 287 miles to Chesapeake Bay
14. River in northwestern Poland, flowing 492 miles to the Oder River
15. River in China, flowing 2,900 miles to the Gulf of Chihli (also called Hwang)
16. River in Peru and Brazil, flowing about 2,100 miles to the Amazon River
17. River in Nigeria, flowing about 800 miles to the Niger River
18. River in Afghanistan and Pakistan, flowing 320 miles to the Indus River
19. River in central Italy, flowing 251 miles to the Tyrrhenian Sea
20. River in eastern Europe, flowing 631 miles to the Don River
21. River in southern Africa, flowing about 1,650 miles to the Indian Ocean
22. River in eastern Russia, flowing 1,587 miles to the Yenisey River
23. The chief river of Ireland, flowing 224 miles to the Atlantic Ocean
24. River in eastern Siberia, flowing 1,767 miles to the Lena River
25. River in Brazil and Argentina, flowing about 2,050 miles to the Rio de la Plata
26. River forming part of the boundary between the United States and Canada, flowing 400 miles to the Bay of Fundy
27. River in northern Italy, flowing 405 miles to the Adriatic Sea
28. River in eastern Brazil, flowing 1,800 miles to the Atlantic Ocean
29. River in northwestern Canada, flowing 2,514 miles to the Beaufort Sea
30. River in eastern Europe, flowing 876 miles to the Black Sea
31. River in central South America, flowing about 1,300 miles to the Parana River
32. River forming part of the boundary between Brazil and Peru, flowing about 600 miles to the Amazon River
33. River in China and Myanmar, flowing about 1,750 miles to the Andaman Sea
34. River in northern Italy, flowing about 220 miles to the Adriatic Sea
35. River forming part of the boundary between Brazil and Bolivia, flowing about 750 miles to the Mamore River
36. River in western Colombia, flowing about 600 miles to the Magdalena River
37. River in southwestern Canada, flowing about 700 miles to the Pacific Ocean
38. River in France, Belgium, and the Netherlands, flowing 270 miles to the North Sea
39. River in central Canada, flowing 400 miles from Lake Winnipeg to Hudson Bay
40. River forming part of the boundary between Argentina and Paraguay, flowing about 700 miles to the Paraguay River
41. River in southwestern Asia, flowing about 1,150 miles to the Euphrates River
42. River in France, Luxembourg, and Germany, flowing 320 miles to the Rhine River
43. River in central Myanmar, flowing about 1,200 miles to the Bay of Bengal
44. River in southern India, flowing 475 miles to the Bay of Bengal
45. River in central France, flowing about 300 miles to the Garonne River
46. River in central Russia, flowing 1,110 miles to the Barents Sea
47. River forming the boundary between Guyana and Suriname, flowing about 450 miles to the Atlantic Ocean
48. River in northwestern Africa, flowing about 1,000 miles to the Atlantic Ocean
49. River in Spain and Portugal, flowing 566 miles to the Atlantic Ocean
50. River in the central United States, flowing about 2,330 miles to the Gulf of Mexico
51. River in eastern Europe, flowing 633 miles to the Baltic Sea
52. River in northwestern Myanmar, flowing about 500 miles to the Irrawaddy River
53. River in southern Asia, flowing about 1,800 miles to the Bay of Bengal
54. River in southeastern Europe, flowing about 230 miles to the Aegean Sea
55. River in southern Spain, flowing about 360 miles to the Gulf of Cadiz
56. River in central Germany, flowing 305 miles to the Rhine River
57. River forming part of the boundary between Colombia and Peru, flowing about 1,000 miles to the Amazon River
58. River in central Russia, flowing 1,262 miles to the Volga River
59. River in southwestern France, flowing 402 miles to the Gironde River
60. River in northwestern India, flowing about 675 miles to the Sutlej River

Name ______________________________ Date ____________________

98. Rivers of the World—II

E S E R E D N E M T H P A R A G U A Y E N C
N E S E N E G A L E R E S M C N O N D I I H
Y V C E L N Y E L L O W C W A N I V D Z W U
T E S S O M A A C U A C H W M D A A A N D R
N R O K A M M H G A A N E F O R E D W E N C
A N E I A O E O U M E H L R T N A I A K I H
R M N Z W N F N A T C P D U O K P G R C H I
U C O E A N K R D T I B E R P P A E R A C L
O N E B R A H M A P U T R A I E A B I M E L
C T T M T D W K L N I H A S G M C U U N O S
R D S A A L S E Q R C L S P A A D H G L E T
S A N Z R A I P U C X I C K A K R O O L W E
A I D I S E A O I R S S S O A J D O L R S N
L P R R E R S R V S U U S C M R O E N L A O
W U O G A S A A I N G G G H O A S S E N C D
E R O N I V T M R N U A U D L O Y E U N E B
E U A M A T D E U F S T H A M E S O U O C Z
N S T J O H N T R K I B T O Y A M U T U P A
E I N O N N A H S O K A V E R I J A Q U R L

1. ______________________
2. ______________________
3. ______________________
4. ______________________
5. ______________________
6. ______________________
7. ______________________
8. ______________________
9. ______________________
10. ______________________
11. ______________________
12. ______________________
13. ______________________
14. ______________________
15. ______________________
16. ______________________
17. ______________________
18. ______________________
19. ______________________
20. ______________________
21. ______________________
22. ______________________
23. ______________________
24. ______________________
25. ______________________
26. ______________________
27. ______________________
28. ______________________
29. ______________________
30. ______________________
31. ______________________
32. ______________________
33. ______________________
34. ______________________
35. ______________________
36. ______________________
37. ______________________
38. ______________________
39. ______________________
40. ______________________
41. ______________________
42. ______________________
43. ______________________
44. ______________________
45. ______________________
46. ______________________
47. ______________________
48. ______________________
49. ______________________
50. ______________________
51. ______________________
52. ______________________
53. ______________________
54. ______________________
55. ______________________
56. ______________________
57. ______________________
58. ______________________
59. ______________________
60. ______________________

99. POPULAR PLACES TO VISIT IN THE WORLD

The answers to the following clues are hidden in the puzzle. Circle the answer in the puzzle and then write the answer next to the correct number. Answers can be found horizontally, vertically, diagonally, and backward.

1. The temple of Athena on the Acropolis at Athens, regarded as one of the finest examples of Doric architecture
2. An iron structure in Paris, 984 feet high, designed for the Exposition of 1889
3. A famous early Gothic cathedral built in Paris
4. An independent state within Rome, created as the headquarters for the Pope
5. A monumental defensive structure in northern China, extending approximately 2,000 miles between the ancient Chinese empire and Mongolia
6. An ancient city in southern Italy, destroyed by an eruption of Mt. Vesuvius in 79 A.D.
7. Roman sports arena where games, races, and gladiatorial combats where held; the largest building of its kind in the ancient world
8. Brazil's second largest city, noted for its night life
9. The shipping route connecting the Atlantic and Pacific Oceans
10. A prehistoric structure in England, a giant arrangement of dressed stones, some with lintels
11. The world's highest uninterrupted waterfall, 3,212 feet, in southeastern Venezuela
12. The walled citadel of Moscow containing the government offices of Russia
13. Site of a Nazi extermination camp in southwestern Poland during World War II
14. The birthplace of Muhammad and holy city of Islam to which Muslims make pilgrimages
15. The largest and oldest of the United States national parks, established in 1872
16. Pacific islands owned by Ecuador, where some of the world's most unusual plant and animal life have been studied extensively by scientists
17. Port city in northeastern Italy, built on 118 islands
18. Site of history's largest amphibious attack, the Allied invasion of France on June 6, 1944, code-named D-Day
19. The oldest permanent city in the United States, founded by Spain in 1565
20. Site of the largest pyramids built in Egypt
21. The magnificent cathedral in Constantinople, the greatest monument of Byzantine Christianity
22. Resort in Monaco on the Mediterranean Sea
23. City in northeastern Italy, noted for its leaning tower
24. The official London residence of the British sovereign
25. A mausoleum of white marble, India's greatest monument
26. A huge gorge formed by the Colorado River in the southwestern United States, about one mile in depth and eighteen miles wide in some places
27. The principal place of worship in the Vatican Palace at Rome, decorated with frescoes by Michelangelo
28. An island of Chile in the South Pacific, noted for its numerous stone sculptures called monoliths
29. Resort city in southwestern Mexico on the Pacific coast
30. A colossal stone figure in Egypt with a man's head and a lion's body
31. Site of the beautiful palace of Louis XIV of France, scene of the signing of a treaty between the Allies and Germany after World War I
32. Latin American peninsula where the ruins of ancient Mayan pyramids, palaces, and carvings are located
33. A British crown colony, fortress, and naval base, called the "Key of the Mediterranean"
34. A resort city and cataract between Lake Ontario and Lake Erie in western New York
35. Capital of Israel, regarded as holy by Jews, Christians, and Muslims
36. Resort town in southeastern Switzerland
37. The magnificent temple complex at the site of the ancient capital of the Khmer empire in Cambodia
38. The former site of the chief United States immigration station
39. City in southern Peru, formerly the capital of the Inca empire
40. A British crown colony in southeastern China
41. U.S. city famous for its gambling casinos
42. Village in central Belgium, scene of Napoleon's final defeat in 1815
43. A Gothic church in London, burial place of English kings and notables
44. A huge structure comprising a monastery, church, and royal residence, built by Philip II of Spain in the 16th century
45. The coast region of southeastern France and northwestern Italy
46. Site of a U.S. naval base, bombed by the Japanese on December 7, 1941

Name ______________________________ Date ____________________

99. Popular Places to Visit in the World

S L A N A C A M A N A P A N G K O R W A T M
A N O R M A N D Y D N A L S I R E T S A E A
G I Y T I C N A C I T A V E R S A I L L E S
R L A U S C H W I T Z S C I P O R D A T N T
A S S M S A G E V S A L O H C I O S L W O O
N L P I L C P S H M V D I Z V C U S A P T N
D L J E S M A T F A E N U I Z R J T H E S E
C A B N O T A M T J X C E U E U E R A A W H
A F A P L B I I A U D R C J O R A C M R O E
N L B U C K I N G H A M P A L A C E J L L N
Y E U R G Y E S E A I H P O S A I G A H L G
O G S E G I X T E C O L O S S E U M T A E E
N N T W R I B E C A H S J N L V O A P R Y L
A A A O S T Z R I P S A F G G N E F D B N L
I S U T N C K A A U H I P R T K A N S O O I
N T G L A K O B C L C O P E P N O M I R T S
C M U E T C R B C C T I C A L I E N I C R I
E O S F A U U E E O S A N T Z C S C G E E S
L R T F C Z O Y M A R O R W C I S A E S D L
T I I I U C I R S L L A F A R A G A I N A A
A T N E Y O P G O S I G A L A P A G O S M N
M Z E P A R T H E N O N F L A I R O C S E D

1. ______________
2. ______________
3. ______________
4. ______________
5. ______________
6. ______________
7. ______________
8. ______________
9. ______________
10. ______________
11. ______________
12. ______________
13. ______________
14. ______________
15. ______________
16. ______________
17. ______________
18. ______________
19. ______________
20. ______________
21. ______________
22. ______________
23. ______________
24. ______________
25. ______________
26. ______________
27. ______________
28. ______________
29. ______________
30. ______________
31. ______________
32. ______________
33. ______________
34. ______________
35. ______________
36. ______________
37. ______________
38. ______________
39. ______________
40. ______________
41. ______________
42. ______________
43. ______________
44. ______________
45. ______________
46. ______________

Name ______________________ Date ______________

100. Flags of the Countries of the World—I

Identify the country by its flag and then write the name of the country next to the correct number.

1. ______________________
2. ______________________
3. ______________________
4. ______________________
5. ______________________
6. ______________________
7. ______________________
8. ______________________
9. ______________________
10. ______________________
11. ______________________
12. ______________________
13. ______________________
14. ______________________
15. ______________________
16. ______________________
17. ______________________
18. ______________________
19. ______________________
20. ______________________
21. ______________________
22. ______________________
23. ______________________
24. ______________________
25. ______________________
26. ______________________
27. ______________________
28. ______________________
29. ______________________
30. ______________________
31. ______________________
32. ______________________
33. ______________________
34. ______________________
35. ______________________
36. ______________________
37. ______________________
38. ______________________
39. ______________________
40. ______________________
41. ______________________
42. ______________________
43. ______________________
44. ______________________
45. ______________________
46. ______________________
47. ______________________
48. ______________________
49. ______________________
50. ______________________

100. FLAGS OF THE COUNTRIES OF THE WORLD—I

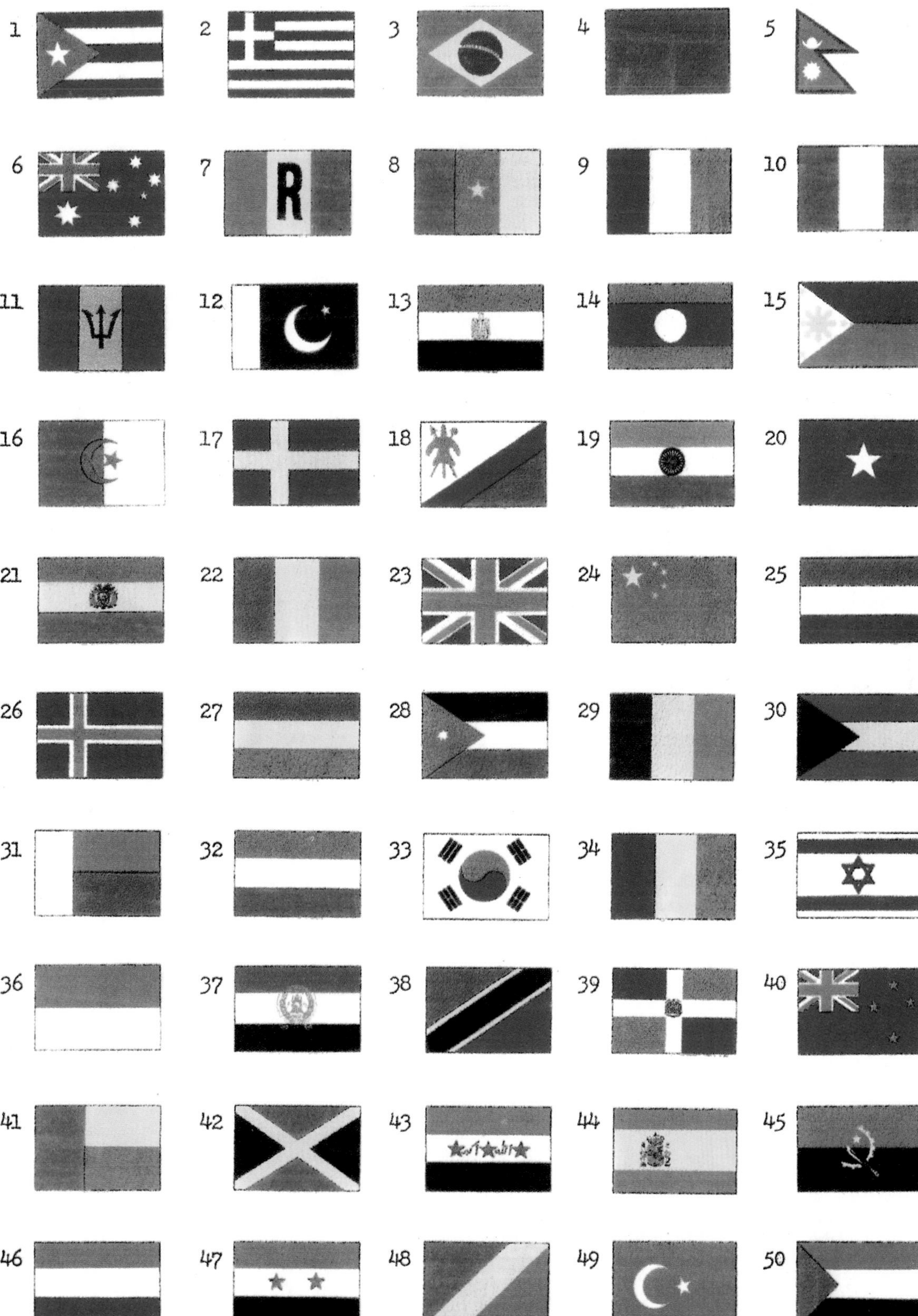

101. FLAGS OF THE COUNTRIES OF THE WORLD—II

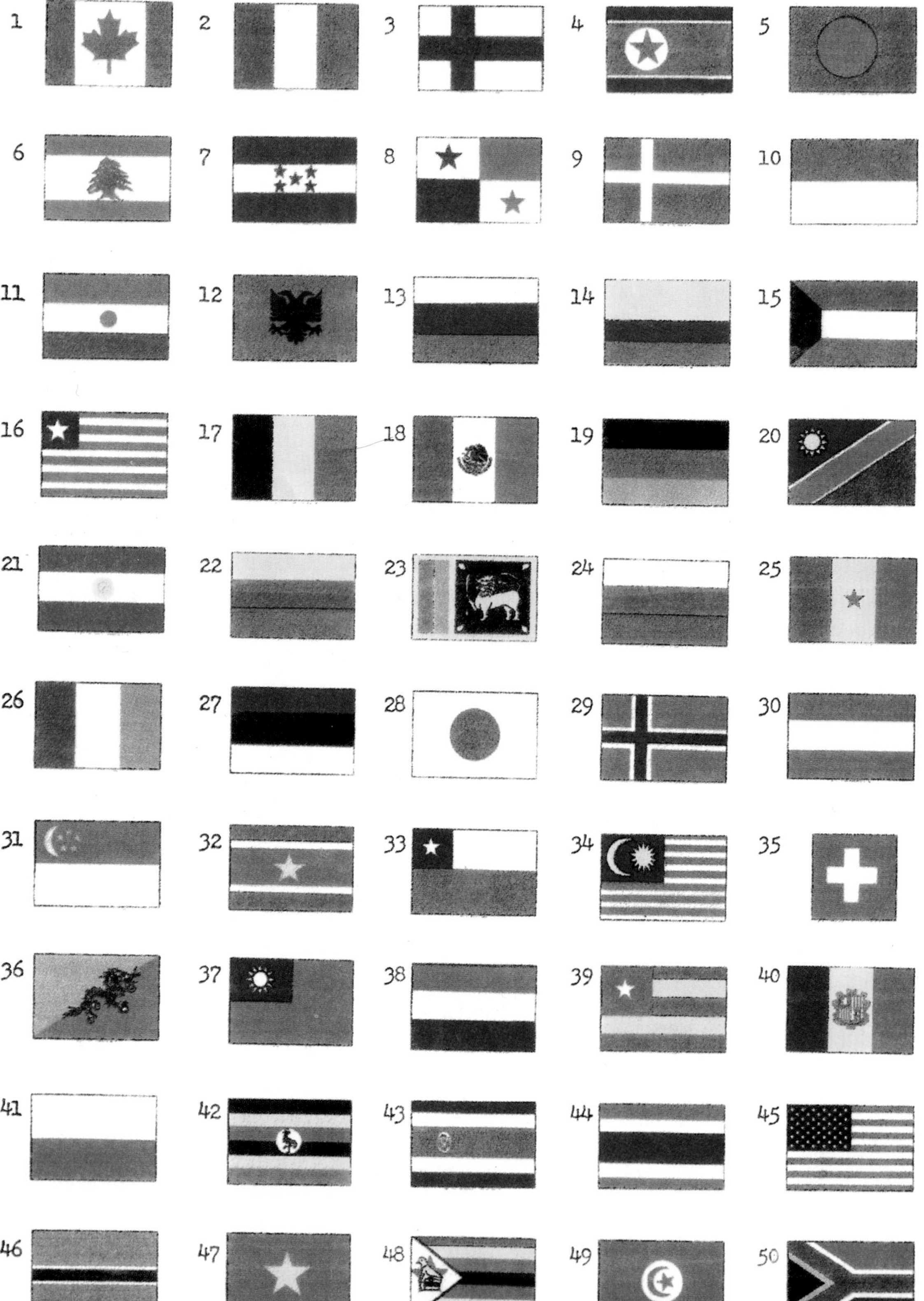

Name ______________________ Date ______________

101. Flags of the Countries of the World—II

Identify the country by its flag and then write the name of the country next to the correct number.

1. ______	26. ______
2. ______	27. ______
3. ______	28. ______
4. ______	29. ______
5. ______	30. ______
6. ______	31. ______
7. ______	32. ______
8. ______	33. ______
9. ______	34. ______
10. ______	35. ______
11. ______	36. ______
12. ______	37. ______
13. ______	38. ______
14. ______	39. ______
15. ______	40. ______
16. ______	41. ______
17. ______	42. ______
18. ______	43. ______
19. ______	44. ______
20. ______	45. ______
21. ______	46. ______
22. ______	47. ______
23. ______	48. ______
24. ______	49. ______
25. ______	50. ______

Answer Key

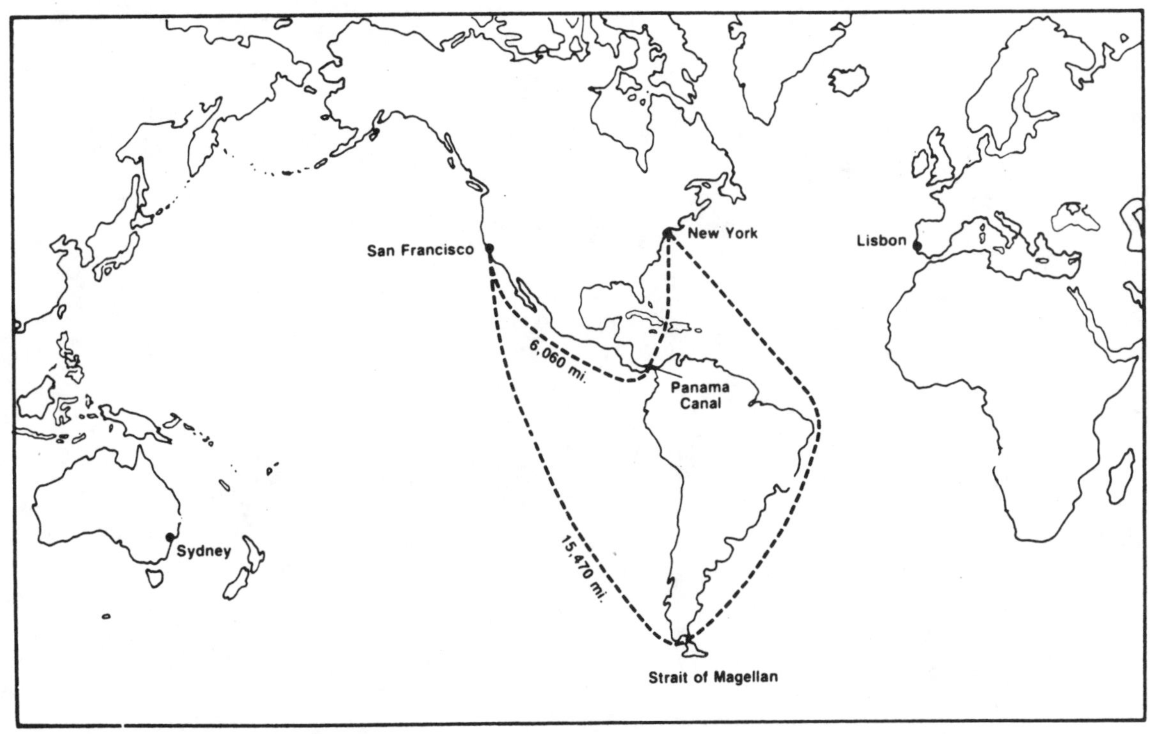

San Francisco
New York
Lisbon
6,060 mi.
Panama Canal
Sydney
15,470 mi.
Strait of Magellan

1. Prehistoric Cultures

1. HOMOSA**P**IENS
2. CA**R**BON14
3. PAL**E**OLITHIC
4. PRE**H**ISTORY
5. SOC**I**ETY
6. NEW**S**TONE
7. OLDS**T**ONE
8. D**O**GS
9. A**R**TIFACTS
10. NEOL**I**THIC
11. TE**C**HNOLOGY
12. I**C**EAGE
13. C**U**LTURE
14. ARCHAEO**L**OGISTS
15. AL**T**AMIRA
16. AGRIC**U**LTURE
17. ANTH**R**OPOLOGISTS
18. POLYTH**E**ISM
19. NOMAD**S**

2. Civilization in Southwest Asia

1. CYRUS
2. CUNEIFORM
3. COVENANT
4. TIGRIS
5. CHALDEANS
6. PERSIAN
7. ZIGGURAT
8. EUPHRATES
9. BARTER
10. ARTISAN
11. PICTOGRAM
12. ASTRONOMY
13. SCRIBES
14. PHOENICIANS
15. FERTILECRESCENT
16. PROPHET
17. HAMMURABI
18. POLYTHEISM
19. NEBUCHADNEZZAR
20. HEBREWS
21. LITERACY
22. MOSES
23. MONOTHEISM
24. ASSYRIANS
25. ZOROASTER
26. IRAQ
27. SUMERIANS

3. The Ancient Egyptians

1. CAR**T**ER
2. C**H**AMPOLLION
3. ROS**E**TTASTONE
4. CAT**A**RACTS
5. DY**N**ASTY
6. SAR**C**OPHAGUS
7. MUMMIF**I**CATION
8. HATSH**E**PSUT
9. SI**N**AI
10. VUL**T**URE
11. RAMS**E**SII
12. HIERO**G**LYPHICS
13. PAP**Y**RUS
14. **P**YRAMIDS
15. **T**HEBES
16. N**I**LE
17. COBR**A**
18. TUTA**N**KHAMON
19. O**S**IRIS

4. Ancient India and China

1. R A J **A** H S
2. S A **N** S K R I T
3. R E I N **C** A R N A T I O N
4. **I** N D U S
5. R I V **E** R O F S O R R O W S
6. G A **N** G E S
7. C A S **T** E S
8. G O B **I**
9. M O **N** S O O N
10. B U **D** D H A
11. N **I** R V A N A
12. K H Y B E R P **A** S S
13. B R **A** H M I N S
14. O R A C L E B O **N** E S
15. H I N **D** U K U S H
16. C O N F U **C** I U S
17. T **H** A R
18. H I N D U **I** S M
19. M A **N** C H U R I A
20. H I M A L **A** Y A S

5. The Mediterranean World of Greece—I

1. MINOTAUR
2. SOPHOCLES
3. CRETE
4. OLYMPIA
5. HADES
6. THUCYDIDES
7. ILIAD
8. ARISTOTLE
9. ATHENS
10. PARIS
11. SOCRATES
12. ALEXANDER
13. PELOPONNESUS
14. POSEIDON
15. PLATO
16. PARTHENON
17. DISCUSTHROWER
18. ACROPOLIS
19. SPARTA
20. HELOTS
21. ODYSSEY
22. BARBAROI
23. THEFROGS
24. AEGEAN
25. MARATHON
26. ATHENA
27. TRAGEDY
28. EPIC
29. HOMER

6. The Mediterranean World of Greece—II

1. HESTIA
2. PYTHAGORAS
3. ZEUS
4. ARCHIMEDES
5. HERA
6. PHIDEAS
7. PERICLES
8. PLATO
9. ARES
10. HERODOTUS
11. APHRODITE
12. THALES
13. PHALANX
14. LYCEUM
15. DRACO
16. MACEDONIA
17. THETROJANWOMEN
18. HIPPOCRATES
19. EURIPIDES
20. EUCLID
21. PHEIDIPPIDES
22. APOLLO
23. KNOWTHYSELF
24. ANTIGONE
25. ARCHONS
26. NIKE
27. THESPIS
28. AESCHYLUS
29. ODES

7. Ancient Rome

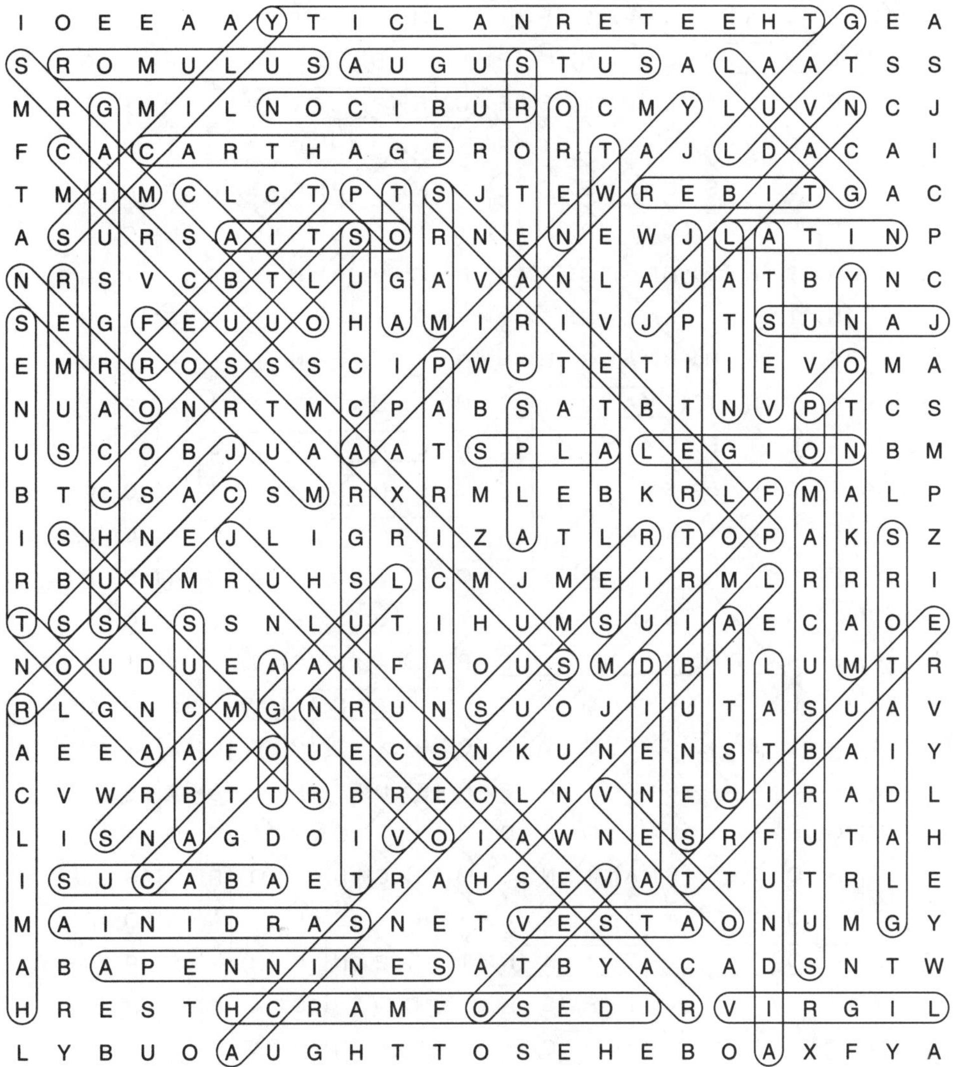

1. Romulus
2. Circus Maximus
3. toga
4. Forum
5. Carthage
6. Latin
7. Julius Caesar
8. Vesta
9. gladiators
10. Tiber
11. latifundia
12. censor
13. Julian
14. Cato
15. plebeians
16. The Eternal City
17. Sicily
18. Virgil
19. Mars
20. Apennines
21. tribunes
22. Ides of March
23. Twelve Tables
24. Ostia
25. Mark Antony
26. Sardinia
27. Hamilcar
28. Remus
29. praetors
30. Po
31. Janus
32. veto
33. Gaul
34. Tiberius Gracchus
35. Jupiter
36. Appian Way
37. Marcus Brutus
38. patricians
39. Hannibal
40. Rubicon
41. legion
42. Corsica
43. tribute
44. Aeneid
45. abacus
46. Alps
47. consuls
48. Gaius Gracchus
49. Venus
50. Nero
51. Augustus

8. The Roman Heritage

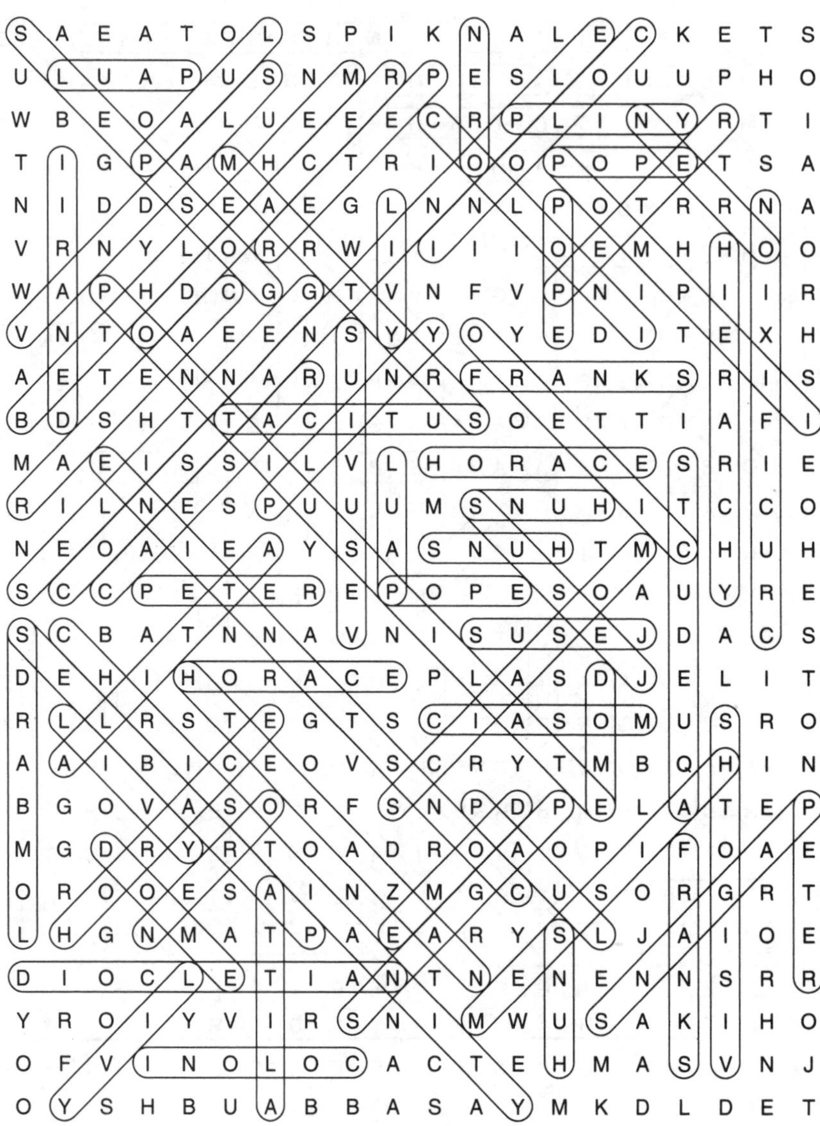

1. aqueducts	11. Huns	21. Vesuvius	31. Pontius Pilate
2. Vandals	12. Pompeii	22. Constantinople	32. pope
3. Odoacer	13. Christianity	23. Horace	33. Tacitus
4. crucifixion	14. Franks	24. parables	34. Gentiles
5. Diocletian	15. Cicero	25. Paul	35. Pliny
6. Visigoths	16. pagans	26. Bethlehem	36. martyrs
7. Constantine	17. Nazareth	27. Attila	37. Gospels
8. Nero	18. dome	28. Caesar	38. coloni
9. denarii	19. messiah	29. hierarchy	39. Livy
10. Jesus	20. Peter	30. mosaics	40. Lombards

9. The Byzantine Empire

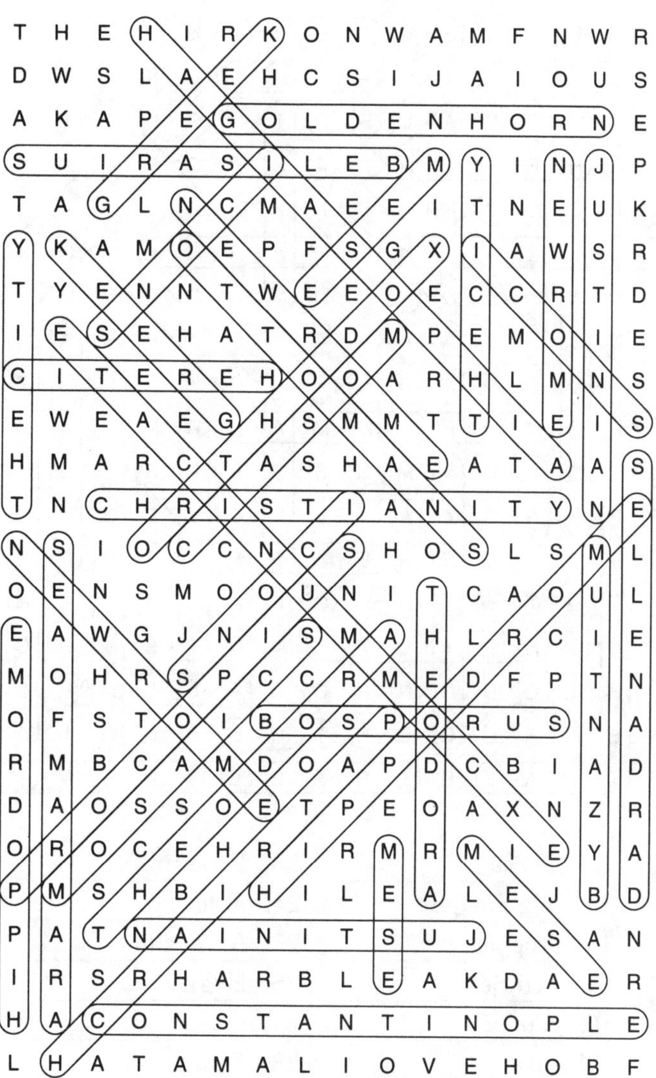

1. mosaics
2. Constantinople
3. Justinian
4. Bosporus
5. patriarch
6. Greek
7. icons
8. Ottomans
9. Sea of Marmara
10. Dardanelles
11. Golden Horn
12. New Rome
13. Byzantium
14. Procopius
15. Belisarius
16. Theodora
17. The City
18. Mese
19. Hagia Sophia
20. Hippodrome
21. heretic
22. Orthodox
23. Christianity
24. excommunicate

10. The Rise of Islam

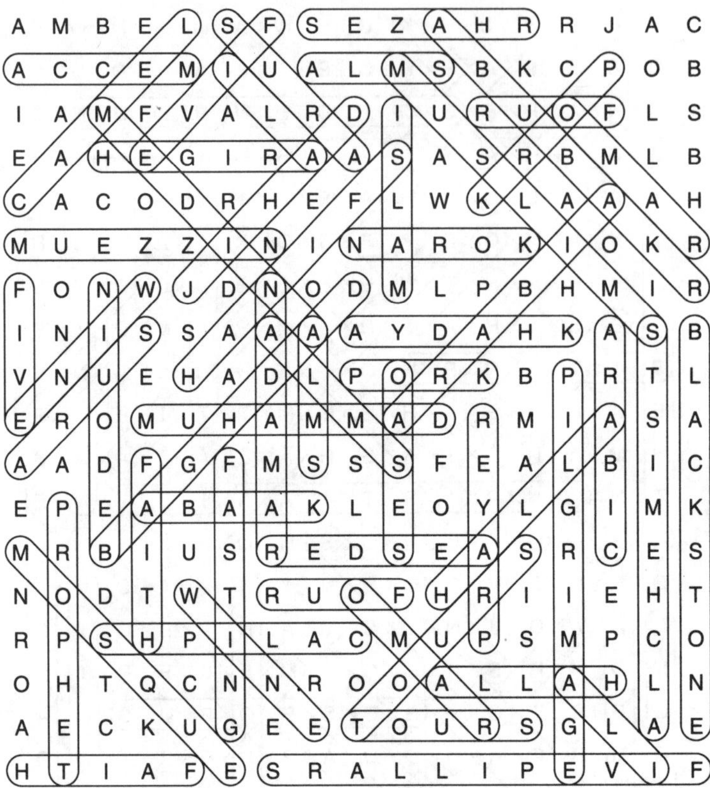

1. Arabia
2. hanifs
3. oases
4. camel
5. Allah
6. five
7. Muslims
8. Koran
9. jihad
10. Five Pillars
11. Arabic
12. Mecca
13. pilgrimage
14. prophet
15. Red Sea
16. Kaaba
17. sura
18. Muezzin
19. Ali
20. faith
21. Omar
22. Muhammad
23. Bedouin
24. alms
25. Ramadan
26. Hegira
27. wine
28. Tours
29. Rhazes
30. alchemists
31. pork
32. Islam
33. Khadya
34. mosque
35. Black Stone
36. four
37. Medina
38. fasting
39. caliphs
40. Baghdad
41. prayer
42. Abubakr

11. The Early Middle Ages

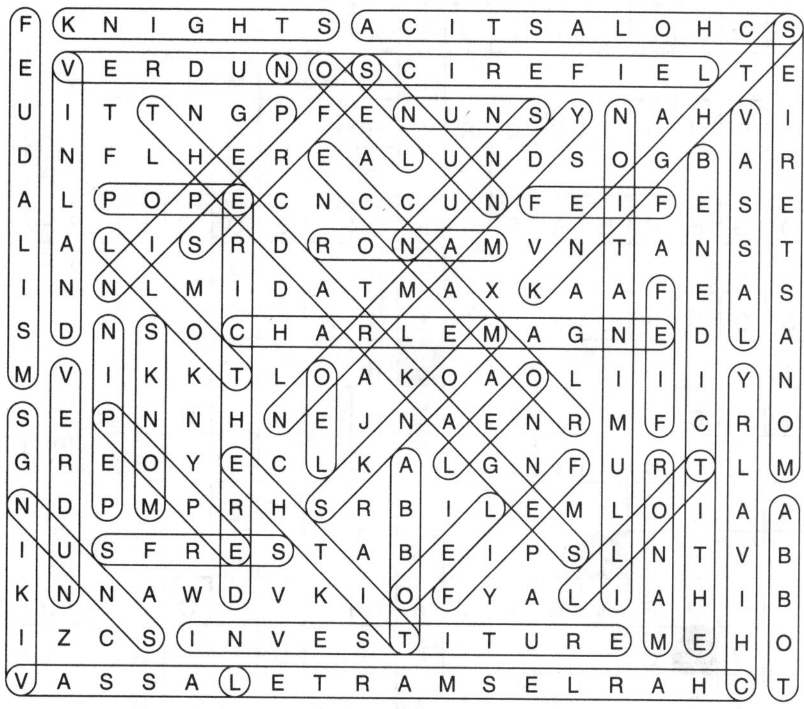

1.	The Dark Ages	11.	nuns	21.	Leo
2.	tithe	12.	Verdun	22.	Benedict
3.	knights	13.	toll	23.	serfs
4.	Charlemagne	14.	Vinland	24.	illumination
5.	investiture	15.	pope	25.	Romance
6.	abbot	16.	monasteries	26.	monks
7.	chivalry	17.	manor	27.	Leif Ericson
8.	Eric the Red	18.	Vikings	28.	vassal
9.	fief	19.	Charles Martel	29.	Scholastica
10.	Pepin	20.	feudalism	30.	Normandy

12. The High Middle Ages

Across

1. WILLIAM
4. ALCHEMISTS
8. CHAUCER
10. ROME
11. ROGERBACON
12. BEOWULF
14. SONGOFROLAND
18. GUILD
19. TROUBADOURS
22. OTTO
23. TOLL
27. JOURNEYMAN
28. RICHARD
30. THEAGEOFFAITH
33. OXFORD
34. RELIC
37. FRIARS
40. SQUIRE
44. MASTERPIECE
45. POPE
46. DAME
48. ARTISANS
49. BURGESSES
52. HANSEATIC
53. FABLES
55. HERETIC
56. MONKS
57. ELCID
59. DOMINICANS
60. KNIGHTS

Down

2. MARCOPOLO
3. ACRE
5. MANOR
6. SERFS
7. CAMBRIDGE
9. JOUSTING
13. BURGHERS
15. ABBOT
16. JUREE
17. WOOL
19. TITHE
20. BOURGEOISIE
21. USURY
24. LORD
25. ROMANESQUE
26. PARIS
29. HAROLD
30. TITHE
31. FIEF
32. THOMASAQUINAS
35. MASS
36. PAGE
38. ROME
39. SIEGFRIED
41. APPRENTICE
42. SERFS
43. NOTREDAME
47. PARIS
50. SIMONY
51. DANTE
54. URBAN
56. MOAT
58. NUNS

13. The Origin of European Nations

1. CORTES
2. RICHARD
3. HUNDREDYEARSWAR
4. JOANOFARC
5. URBAN
6. FERDINAND
7. IVANTHEGREAT
8. CALAIS
9. JOHNHUSS
10. CANNONS
11. BONIFACE
12. THEGREATSCHISM
13. RECONQUISTA
14. URAL
15. NATIONSTATE
16. PARLIAMENT
17. ISABELLA
18. THEBLACKDEATH
19. JOHN
20. MAGNACARTA
21. CZAR
22. WARSOFTHEROSES
23. JOHNWYCLIFFE
24. NATIONALISM
25. LONGBOW
26. ESTATESGENERAL

THE ORIGIN OF EUROPEAN NATIONS

14. The Golden Age of China

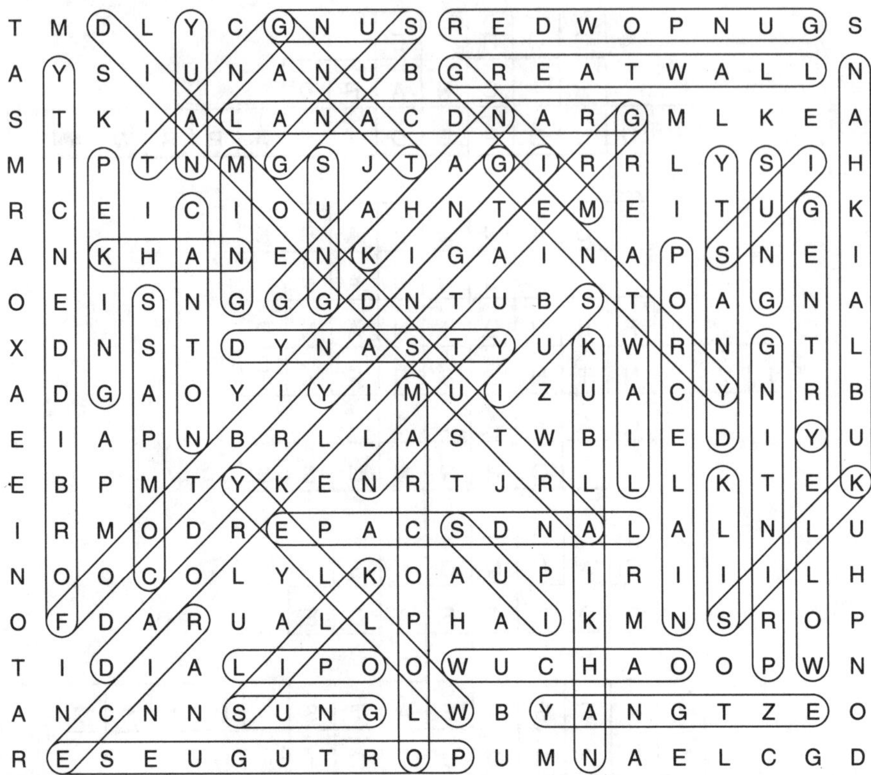

1. Great Silk Road
2. porcelain
3. Marco Polo
4. Forbidden City
5. dynasty
6. foot binding
7. Diamond Sutra
8. T'ang
9. Canton
10. Wu Chao
11. Yellow
12. printing
13. khan
14. Sung
15. landscape
16. Yang-ti
17. Kublai Khan
18. Great Wall
19. Peking
20. Sung
21. rice
22. Grand Canal
23. Yangtze
24. compass
25. gentry
26. Yuan
27. silk
28. Sui
29. gunpowder
30. Li Po
31. Portuguese
32. Ming

15. The Golden Age of India

1. SHAHJAHAN
2. ARABIAN
3. MADRAS
4. BRAHMAN
5. VISHNU
6. SULTAN
7. NURJAHAN
8. CASTE
9. HINDUKUSH
10. BABUR
11. VASCODAGAMA
12. ALLAH
13. RAJPUTS
14. TAJMAHAL
15. NALANDA
16. INDUS
17. CALICO
18. AGRA
19. AKBAR
20. POETKING
21. ELEPHANTA
22. HIMALAYAS
23. ARABIAN
24. ITIHAS
25. CEYLON
26. RASAS
27. SHIVA
28. SHAKUNTALA
29. ISLAM
30. NALANDA
31. DELHI
32. HINDUISM
33. BENGAL
34. KALIDASA
35. MAHAL / MUMTAZMAHAL
36. CHANDRAGUPTA
37. DUNGAREE
38. GOA
39. KSHATRIYA
40. MINARETS
41. SUTTEE
42. GURU
43. INDUS
44. AGRA
45. GUPTA
46. TAMERLANE
47. SRILANKA
48. PORTUGUESE
49. GANGES
50. PURDAH
51. GURU
52. ALLAH
53. MUGHAL
54. CASHMERE

16. The Golden Age of Japan

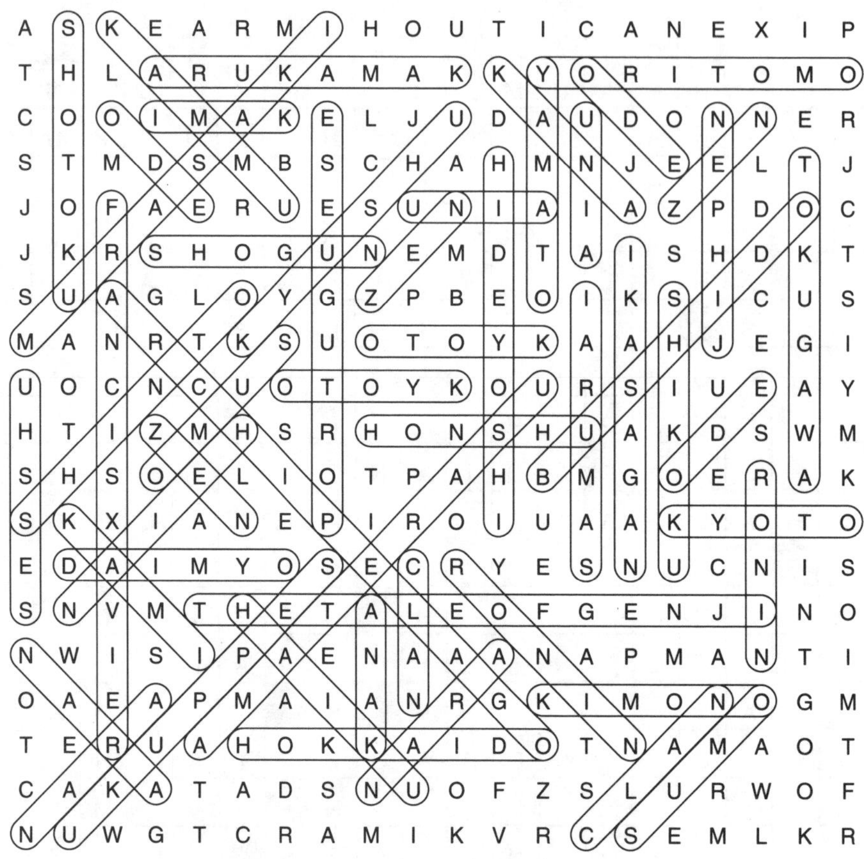

1. samurai
2. Shinto
3. shogun
4. Honshu
5. The Tale of Genji
6. Hideyoshi
7. Nagasaki
8. bushido
9. kimono
10. clan
11. Francis Xavier
12. Edo
13. Yamato
14. nampan
15. Ainu
16. Shotoku
17. Portuguese
18. Zen
19. Shikoku
20. Kamakura
21. archipelago
22. kami
23. daimyo
24. sumo
25. jih pen
26. Amaterasu
27. Ronin
28. Yoritomo
29. Hokkaido
30. Kammu
31. seppuku
32. Kyoto
33. Nara
34. Tokugawa
35. Kyushu
36. haiku
37. kana
38. Heian
39. Murasaki
40. Sesshu

17. The Golden Age of Southeast Asia

1. VIETNAM
2. SOUTHCHINASEA
3. KHMERS
4. ANGKOR
5. BAYOFBENGAL
6. MALAY
7. HINDUISM
8. MEKONG
9. HANOI
10. JAYAVARMAN
11. MONGOLS
12. BORNEO
13. CHAOPHRAYA
14. GULFOFSIAM
15. ISLAM
16. ANGKORWAT
17. KAMPUCHEA
18. STRAITOFMALACCA
19. BUDDHISM
20. RED
21. THAIS
22. SIAM
23. SUMATRA
24. IRRAWADDY
25. VISHNU
26. CHINA
27. CAMBODIA

THE GOLDEN AGE OF SOUTHEAST ASIA

18. Early African Empires

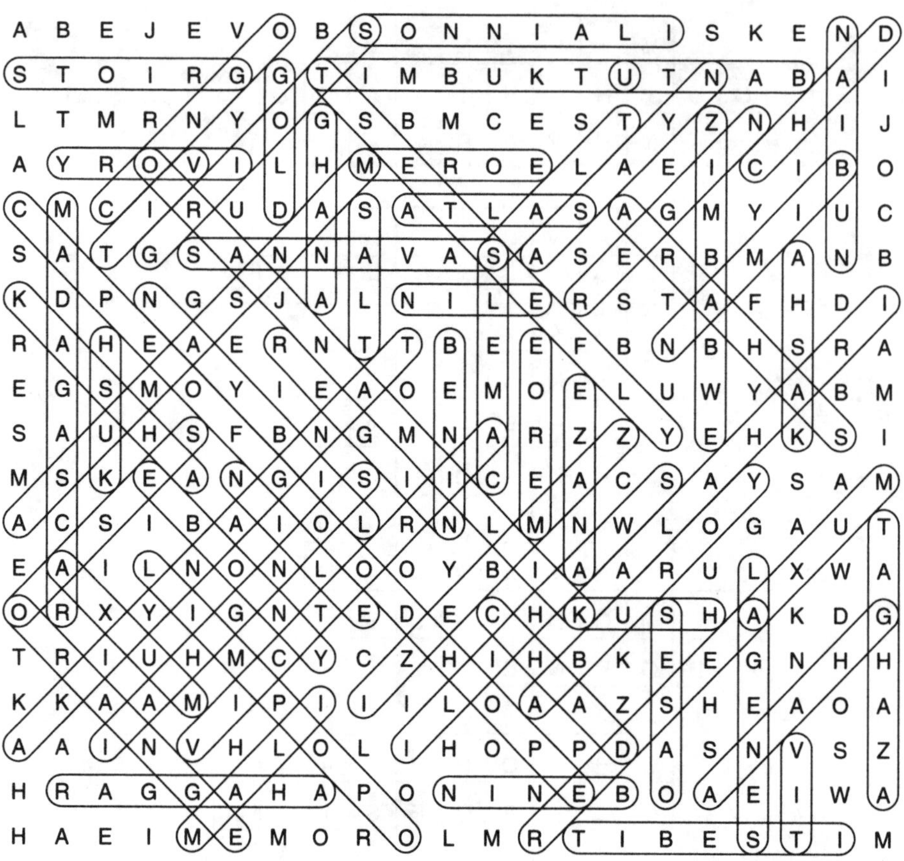

1. Timbuktu
2. Madagascar
3. oases
4. Mansa Musa
5. Congo
6. Kilimanjaro
7. Swahili
8. Kush
9. Victoria
10. griots
11. Songhai
12. Ezana
13. Zimbabwe
14. Chad
15. Tsetse fly
16. Limpopo
17. Sonni Ali
18. salt
19. Namib
20. Kasha
21. Orange
22. Mali
23. Tibesti
24. Nyasa
25. Sahara
26. ivory
27. Nile
28. Benin
29. Senegal
30. Tanganyika
31. Atlas
32. Red Sea
33. Bantu
34. camels
35. Nubian
36. Cape of Good Hope
37. gold
38. Axum
39. savannas
40. Taghaza
41. Kalahari
42. Ahaggar
43. Yoruba
44. Meroe
45. Niger
46. Tiv
47. ebony
48. Ghana
49. Zambezi
50. Libyan

19. Early American Empires

1. MONT**E**ZUMA
2. INC**A**S
3. SIER**R**AMADRES
4. QUETZA**L**COATL
5. MA**Y**AS
6. AM**A**ZON
7. OL**M**ECS
8. AZT**E**CS
9. **R**OCKIES
10. TENOCHT**I**TLAN
11. CUZ**C**O
12. YUC**A**TAN
13. CHICHE**N**ITZA
14. MAIZ**E**
15. PANA**M**A
16. HUITZILO**P**OCHTLI
17. QU**I**PU
18. SIER**R**ANEVADAS
19. TOLT**E**CS
20. ANDE**S**

20. The Renaissance

Across

5. MILAN
7. TIBER
9. MEDICI
10. MILAN
11. ROME
14. LAST SUPPER
16. GLOBE
17. ITALY
18. MACHIAVELLI
20. THE PRINCE
21. DANTE
22. PISA
24. THE DIVINE COMEDY
25. MADONNA
27. GIOTTO
29. GUTENBERG
33. RAPHAEL
34. PETRARCH
36. JULIUS
38. MONA LISA
39. FLORENCE
42. RABELAIS
43. BOCCACCIO
44. DON QUIXOTE

Down

1. DAVID
2. DA VINCI
3. REBIRTH
4. ARNO
6. VENICE
7. THE MAGNIFICENT
8. GENOA
12. RABELAIS
13. CERVANTES
15. SHAKESPEARE
18. MICHELANGELO
19. SISTINE CHAPE
23. PISA
26. DONATELLO
28. HUMANIST
30. ERASMUS
31. CHAUCER
32. BRUEGHEL
35. ROME
37. VATICAN
40. ROME
41. MORE

21. The Protestant Reformation

1. JOHANNGUTENBERG
2. ULRICHZWINGLI
3. HUGUENOTS
4. ANABAPTISTS
5. HENRY
6. JOHNKNOX
7. WITTENBERG
8. INDULGENCES
9. ERASMUS
10. MARTINLUTHER
11. JOHNCALVIN
12. KATHERINEVONBORA
13. PRESBYTERIANS
14. HERETIC
15. INDEX
16. INPRAISEOFFOLLY
17. LEO
18. PURITANS
19. EXCOMMUNICATED
20. ELIZABETH
21. PREDESTINATION
22. ANGLICAN
23. THOMASMORE
24. MARTINLUTHER

22. The Scientific Revolution

1. FRANCE
3. VESALIUS
9. ENGLAND
11. SWITZERLAND
15. HOLLAND
16. PARE
18. LEEUWENHOEK
21. NEWTON
22. ITALY
23. NEWTON
25. BRAHE
28. CELSIUS
29. DENMARK
31. GALILEO
33. POLAND
34. ENGLAND
35. HARVEY
36. VESALIUS

2. NEWTON
4. SWEDEN
5. LEEUWENHOEK
6. PARACELSUS
7. HARVEY
8. FAHRENHEIT
10. GALILEO
12. TORRICELLI
13. COPERNICUS
14. COPERNICUS
17. NEWTON
19. HOLLAND
20. KEPLER
24. GALILEO
26. GERMANY
27. HUYGENS
30. KEPLER
32. PARE

23. The Age of Exploration

	1 S				2 H				3 I	S	A	B	E	L	L	4 A	
5 L	A	T	I	T	U	D	E									Z	
	N				D						6 V			7 D		T	
	T				S						8 E	M	P	I	R	E	
	A			9 C	O	L	U	M	B	U	S			A		C	
	M				N						P			Z			
10 C	A	B	O	T	■	11 I	12 S	T	H	M	U	S			13 L		
	R				14 V		T				C				O		
15 N	I	N	A		E		R		16 C		17 C	O	L	O	N	Y	
	A			18 A	R	M	A	D	A		I				G		19 H
			20 D		R	■	I	■	B						I		I
21 E			A		22 A	S	T	R	O	L	23 A	B	24 E		T		S
N			G		Z				T		L		R		U		P
G		25 C	A	R	A	V	E	L			E		26 I	N	D	I	A
L			M		N						X		C		E		N
27 A	S	I	A		O		28 C	O	M	P	A	S	S				I
N				29 J			A				N		O		30 P		O
D		31 F		O			B				D		N		A		L
		R		32 H	E	N	R	Y			E				N		A
33 S	P	A	I	N			A		34 P	O	R	T	U	G	A	L	
		N					L								M		
35 P	A	C	I	F	I	C			36 M	A	G	E	L	L	A	N	
		E															

24. Spanish Exploration in the New World

					1 F				2 M				3 I					4 N			
	5 C	O	R	T	E	S		6 D	E	L	E	O	N			7 S		I			
					R				S				C			T		N		8 P	
	9 H		10 T		11 D	E	S	O	T	O		12 S	A	N	T	A	M	A	R	I	A
	I		E		I				I							U				Z	
	S		13 N	I	N	A		14 A	Z	T	E	C		15 M	A	G	E	L	L	A	N
	P		O	■	A	■	16 C	■	O				17 C			U				R	
	A		18 C	O	N	Q	U	I	S	T	A	D	O	R	E	S		19 P	E	R	U
	N		H	■	D		Z						L			T		H		O	
20 P	I	N	T	A			C			21 V			U			I		I			
	O		I			22 M	O	N	T	E	Z	U	M	A		N		L			
	L		T		23 I					S			B			E		I			24 B
	A		L		S					25 P	E	R	U		26 P			P			A
		27 B	A	H	A	M	A	S		U			S		A			P			L
			N		B					C					L			I			B
					E					C		28 F		29 C	O	R	O	N	A	D	O
	30 S	E	V	I	L	L	E		31 K	I	N	O			S			E			A
					L							U						S			
	32 I	N	D	I	A	N	S		33 C	H	A	R	L	E	S						

25. French Exploration in the New World

1 LOUIS
2 QUEBEC
3 ONTARIO
4 LOUISIANA
5 HURON
6 MISSISSIPPI
7 CHAMPLAIN
8 FRONTENAC
9 MARQUETTE
10 HURON
11 FURS
12 JESUITS
13 ERIE
14 NEWORLEANS
15 COUREURSDEBOIS
16 VERRAZANO
17 SUPERIOR
18 MICHIGAN
19 FURS / FRANCIS
20 LASALLE
21 CARTIER
22 JOLIET
23 BEAVER
24 VERMONT
25 MONTREAL
26 LASALLE
27 ACADIA
28 CHAMPLAIN
29 STLAWRENCE
30 CARTIER

26. English Exploration in the New World

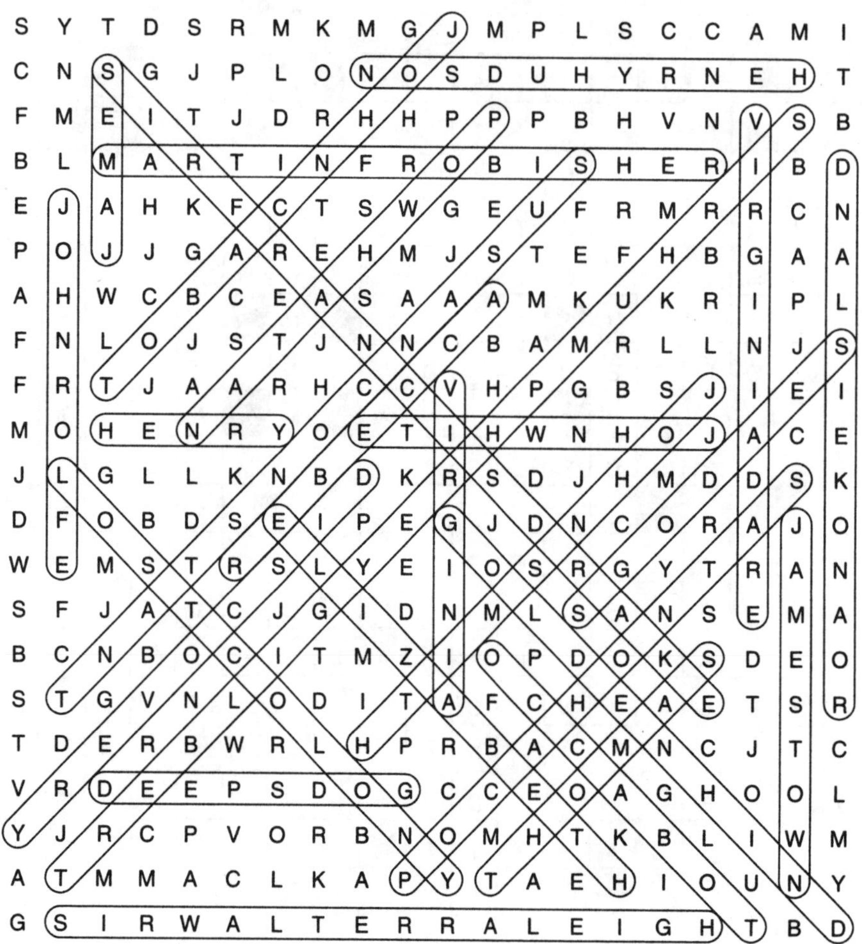

1. Sir Francis Drake
2. Godspeed
3. John White
4. Henry Hudson
5. John Smith
6. John Rolfe
7. Sir Walter Raleigh
8. Susan Constant
9. "sea dogs"
10. Powhatan
11. Elizabeth
12. Rebecca
13. John Cabot
14. tobacco
15. Virginia
16. John Cabot
17. Virginia Dare
18. James
19. Martin Frobisher
20. Thomas
21. Roanoke Island
22. John Rolfe
23. Sir Humphrey Gilbert
24. "Lost Colony"
25. Discovery
26. Henry
27. Pocahontas
28. Golden Hind
29. Jamestown
30. Sir Francis Drake

27. Shifts in European Power

1. AL**S**ACE
2. RIC**H**ELIEU
3. CATHER**I**NEDEMEDICI
4. WILLIAMO**F**ORANGE
5. AMS**T**ERDAM
6. STATE**S**GENERAL
7. FERD**I**NAND
8. HE**N**RY
9. THIRTYY**E**ARSWAR
10. REP**U**BLIC
11. THENETHE**R**LANDS
12. EDICT**O**FNANTES
13. TREATYOFWEST**P**HALIA
14. RAB**E**LAIS
15. MONT**A**IGNE
16. REMBRA**N**DT
17. CA**P**ITALISM
18. STADTH**O**LDER
19. STBARTHOLOME**W**SDAYMASSACRE
20. THENETH**E**RLANDS
21. DESCA**R**TES

28. The Elizabethan Age

1. MARYSTUART
2. WILLIAMSHAKESPEARE
3. JAMESBURBAGE
4. GOLDENHIND
5. HAMLET
6. PURITANS
7. ELIZABETH
8. THAMES
9. MACBETH
10. PROTESTANT
11. GLOBETHEATER
12. ANNEHATHAWAY
13. SEADOGS
14. SIRFRANCISDRAKE
15. STPAULS
16. VIRGINQUEEN
17. ROMEOANDJULIET

THE ELIZABETHAN AGE

29. The Stuart Kings

```
N S E B B O H S A M O H T H A M E S C O T
O L T H A J M J A T S O L E S I D A R A P
T E H G L O A A P A R L I A M U T I S I A
L O G L Y R A M R I W H O X A H O N E W R
I D I O J S G E E Y I N W L O R O N S T L
M D R R O L R S P S L A M L K M L E O J I
N J F I H A L B C E L A I A M G I W A A A
H A O O N H J E M R I C S O R R T M O M M
O M N U L W A S W L A E C Z O Y E O I E E
J E O S O B H G L M M F A T C S G D T S N
D S I R C H R I S T O P H E R W R E N R T
I T T E K L W H G E F R G L O R I L A E Y
V O I V E M O W S S O E C G E J K A N I B
I W T O D L T U I V R E A R L T C R O L G
N N E L F E O P I C A I N M E H S M I A V
E K P U S H L U H S N M A T A V L Y T V A
R M P T T Y D A I I G N I R C R I O A A S
I F A I M H R T G S E W L B V T Y L R C N
G C G O S L A R O T C E T O R P D R O L A
H B U N E A I M A S S A C H U S E T T S T
T T B S I V A S E L R A H C D A L A S C I
H S D R O L F O E S U O H R G A D Q E N R
A H C S P S E I S D A E H D N U O R R B U
T H A B E A S C O R P U S D I V I N O S P
```

1. James
2. John Milton
3. Charles
4. Puritans
5. Scotland
6. Glorious Revolution
7. Virginia
8. Sir Christopher Wren
9. James
10. Petition of Right
11. Charles
12. James
13. Parliament
14. John Locke
15. Mary
16. Cavaliers
17. Mary
18. Massachusetts
19. Tories
20. William Laud
21. Roundheads
22. habeas corpus
23. House of Commons
24. Charles
25. Thames
26. Thomas Hobbes
27. divine right
28. Whigs
29. Louis
30. Oliver Cromwell
31. Mary
32. Paradise Lost
33. Jamestown
34. Restoration
35. House of Lords
36. New Model Army
37. Catholic
38. Plymouth
39. William of Orange
40. Lord Protector

30. The Age of Absolute Monarchs

1. JEANBAPTIS**T**ECOLBERT
2. MARIAT**H**ERESA
3. FREDE**E**RICK
4. VERS**A**ILLES
5. PETERTHE**G**REAT
6. SEVENY**E**ARSWAR
7. HOHENZ**O**LLERN
8. HALLO**F**MIRRORS
9. ROM**A**NOV
10. HAPS**B**URG
11. JEANBAPTI**S**TERACINE
12. CATH**O**LIC
13. MONA**L**ISA
14. LO**U**IS
15. JEANBAP**T**ISTELULLY
16. MOLI**E**RE
17. MADAMEDE**M**AINTENON
18. PIERREC**O**RNEILLE
19. AN**N**E
20. JULESM**A**ZARIN
21. BOU**R**BON
22. FREDERI**C**KTHEGREAT
23. P**H**ILIP
24. THE**S**UNKING

31. The Enlightenment

```
T R L A C Y S U S T E V M A R M I C H E L M A R
T H E A L Y N C I N D L A R R T O P H Y L V A E
A R D E N I S D I D E R O T L E L I Z B I F A N
N A N R U A E S S U O R S E U Q C A J N A E J N
T H A F F R E I D A A R R J O N S A S N I T E A
J O H D A R N N E J A N E O T I B S B N I V E L
L Y K M A C A J U D L U C H R B A O A P O E R G
M B C A R M D N A V E R I A T L O V S H I L I D
C A I A P R S L C W A L P N O T E R T S E H A C
L R R A H R K M C O R A D N O C K E I A R N T S
T O E E Y P L O I P I E S S A J E O L C I H L U
R N D C S H H L A T N S D E E B A S L T A T O E
N D E N I I E P S S H E M B N E S T E A F T V E
N E R W O L F G A N G A M A D E U S M O Z A R T
O M F R C O F B O R L E V S R K S E E T E B A T
E O E U R S N A I V I G D T E I D R U S S A I T
Y N G O A O F R P H I S O I E I E X Q N S S O R
T T R H T P E O R W N A R A D I Z A O O I T N A
U E O N S H I Q D V E R S N I N T Y R H A I I L
L S E C R E E U S T M O A B R I A S A O L L T O
W Q G N J S L E E F E C R A S O J C B O U L H N
S U O N C I T V I R G B E C A C H N O R F E O L
N I R F F O E G E S E R E H T E I R A M C H T E
K E A S P E K E J O S E P H H A Y D N S U F I L
S U E O W I G H I S A B A R K M G K M J R F Y A
```

1. Voltaire
2. Adam Smith
3. laissez faire
4. Marie Therese Geoffrin
5. Ludwig van Beethoven
6. Baron de Montesquieu
7. salons
8. Johann Sebastian Bach
9. Jean Jacques Rousseau
10. philosophes
11. Denis Diderot
12. baroque
13. George Frederick Handel
14. Paris
15. Candide
16. Wolfgang Amadeus Mozart
17. Bastille
18. Francois Marie Arouet
19. Joseph Haydn
20. physiocrats

32. The French and Indian War

1. PIT**T**SBURGH
2. GEORGEWAS**H**INGTON
3. NEWORL**E**ANS
4. BENJAMIN**F**RANKLIN
5. GEO**R**GE
6. FORTDUQU**E**SNE
7. CA**N**ADA
8. FORTNECE**C**SSITY
9. LOUISJOSEP**H**DEMONTCALM
10. JEFFREY**A**MHERST
11. HURO**N**S
12. EDWAR**D**BRADDOCK
13. LOU**I**S
14. MO**N**TREAL
15. RE**D**COATS
16. IROQUO**I**S
17. P**A**RIS
18. JOH**N**FORBES
19. JAMES**W**OLFE
20. WILLI**A**MPITT
21. FLO**R**IDA

33. Revolution in Colonial America

```
P H I L A D E L P H I A E B I P T G E O N A V S E S
S T A M A N I L K N A R F N I M A J N E B T H O T B
O H N G I F B O S T O B L E Z W A R U S E R E A O I
V O L E E F A D A B P A T R I O T S I C E N O Y F R
C M S I E O S Y B O K R A F T F V L N S A C C W P A
F A D P I T R C E G R O F Y E L L A V C D O C P C N
I S R P A A R G U T A N W E S A R O M E T O A R N O
L J D I P T X I E N T D I S W F O I R T Y U E L B A
T E S S S M R M H K M E L N C A N I S I L R N E E M
L F X S T M R I J T C M R P V U B I L R D N E N N E
J F R I E D R I C H V O N S T E U B E N W A S I E B
E E A S N C P E L K C N L E S O E V A O R T C A D J
A R R S F G K A O D H T M N L J E N T B A S J P I A
J S M I B L T C R F J E R A H R H K B M N B M S C J
S O L M K R B O D I N S N P E O R M P A J O S A T E
M N H D E C L N N W S Q D R J O J A I M G S P M A J
A L T N J B D C O H K U A P Y C C S Z T B T H O R B
D A T I H U Y O R E Y I B A S T S I L A Y O L H N D
A O R P G A N R T E G E O R G E W A S H I N G T O N
N S L N J L N D H L G U J A H T V N C F L A L S L C
H G A N M D A C R R K T X L A M S A L D E C O N D R
O I H M S S E N O J L U A P N H O J N Y P A U W V K
J O Y O K N M E A C A S I M I R P U L A S K I Z C A
J A I F H E G S B L K R K A G M R D E L T C S L J S
```

1. Lord North
2. Benedict Arnold
3. Lexington
4. Lafayette
5. Patriots
6. Stamp Act
7. Thomas Jefferson
8. Trenton
9. George
10. Philadelphia
11. Patrick Henry
12. Lord Cornwallis
13. Concord
14. France
15. George Washington
16. minutemen
17. John Locke
18. John Jay
19. Casimir Pulaski
20. Yorktown
21. Thomas Paine
22. Paris
23. John Adams
24. thirteen
25. Friedrich von Steuben
26. Redcoats
27. Loyalists
28. Boston
29. Louis
30. Benjamin Franklin
31. Hessians
32. Baron de Montesquieu
33. Mississippi
34. boycott
35. John Paul Jones
36. Florida
37. John Hancock
38. Valley Forge
39. John Andre
40. Paul Revere

34. Revolution in France

	1 D		2 C	O	N	S	E	R	3 V	A	T	I	V	E	S			
	I								E							4 B		
	5 R	O	6 B	E	S	P	I	E	R	R	E					O		
	E		A						S						7 J	U	L	Y
	C		S				8 M		A							R		
	T		T			9 R	A	D	I	C	A	L	S			G		
10 L	O	U	I	S			R	■	L					11 D		E		
	R		L		12 G	U	I	L	L	O	13 T	I	N	E		O		
	Y		L				E	■	E	■	R			L		I		
14 P			E			15 M	A	R	S	E	I	L	L	A	I	S	E	
A							N				C			U		I		
16 R	E	I	G	N	O	F	T	E	R	R	O	R		N		E		
I							O				L			A				
S		17 J	A	C	O	B	I	N			O			Y				
							N	■	18 P	A	R	I	19 S		20 P			
21 M	O	D	E	R	A	T	E	S					E		A			
							T				22 E	M	I	G	R	E	S	
							T						N		I			
							E						E		S			

35. Napoleon Bonaparte

1. CONTINE**N**TALSYSTEM
2. TRAF**A**LGAR
3. JOSE**P**HINE
4. C**O**RSICA
5. DUKEOFWE**L**LINGTON
6. THELITTL**E**CORPORAL
7. HORATI**O**NELSON
8. NATIO**N**ALISM
9. EL**B**A
10. WATERL**O**O
11. ALEXA**N**DER
12. NOTRED**A**ME
13. JOSE**P**H
14. P**A**RIS
15. GUER**R**ILLAS
16. AUS**T**ELITZ
17. STH**E**LENA

36. The Industrial Revolution

1 A	R	2 K	W	R	I	G	H	3 T		4 W		5 V	O	L	6 T	A				7 T	
		A						U		A					A		8 D			O	
		Y			9 F			L		T		10 B	E	L	L		A			W	
					U		11 S	L	A	T	E	R			B		G			N	
	12 C		13 D		L		T					O			O		U			S	
	A		I		T		E		14 M			15 W	H	I	T	N	E	Y		H	
	R		16 C	R	O	M	P	T	O	N		N					R			E	
	T		K		N	■	H	■	R						17 M	A	R	C	O	N	I
	W		E			18 B	E	S	S	E	M	E	R		C		E			D	
	R		N				N		E						A						
19 D	I	E	S	E	L		S				20 F	A	R	A	D	A	Y				
	G						O			21 E					A						
	H		22 P			23 U	N	I	O	N		24 D	A	I	M	L	E	R			
25 S	T	R	I	K	E					G											
			C							L							26 J				
27 P	E	R	K	I	N				28 H	A	R	G	R	E	A	V	E	S			
			E							N							N				
29 W	H	I	T	N	E	Y				D		30 D	I	C	K	E	N	S			
																	E				
											31 J	A	C	Q	U	A	R	D			

37. Revolutions and Reactions

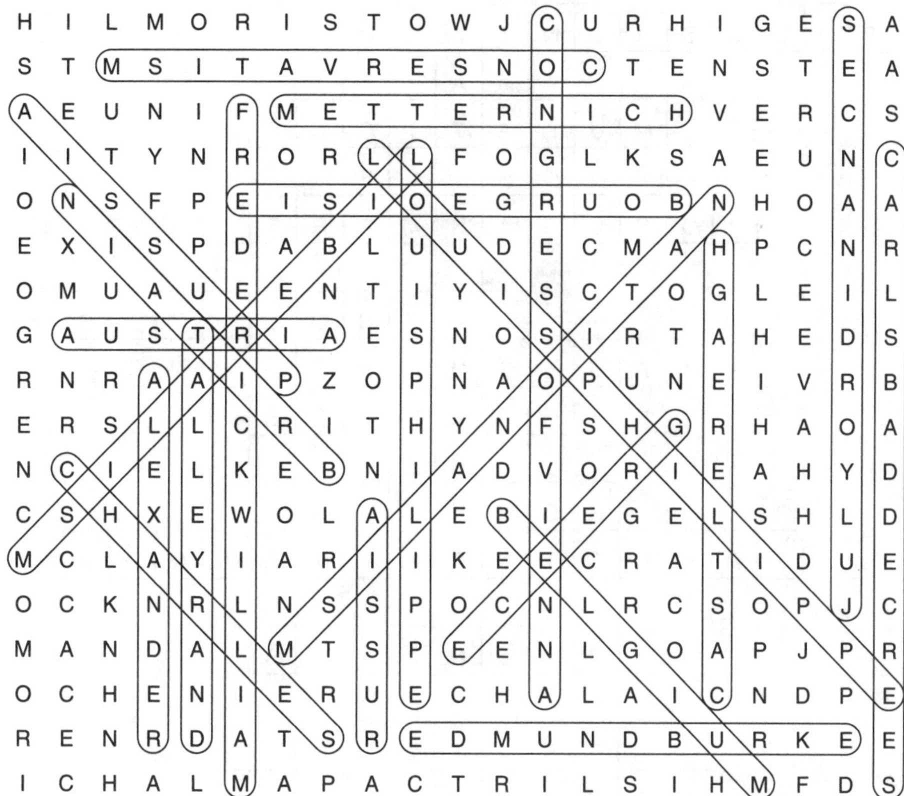

1. Congress of Vienna
2. bourgeoisie
3. Talleyrand
4. July Ordinances
5. Alexander
6. Metternich
7. liberalism
8. Austria
9. Louis Philippe
10. Greece
11. Edmund Burke
12. Carlsbad Decrees
13. Russia
14. Frederick William
15. Belgium
16. conservatism
17. Prussia
18. Castlereagh
19. Charles
20. nationalism
21. Britain
22. Louis Philippe

38. Latin American Independence

1. TOUSSAINTLOUVERTURE
2. HAITI
3. MULATTOES
4. CHILE
5. JOSESANMARTIN
6. CATHOLICISM
7. JAMESMONROE
8. CREOLES
9. BRAZIL
10. BOLIVIA
11. FRANCISCOMIRANDA
12. SPANISH
13. ARGENTINA
14. MESTIZOS
15. NATIONALISM
16. MIGUELHIDALGO
17. PORTUGUESE
18. DOMPEDRO
19. MEXICO
20. SIMONBOLIVAR
21. CAUDILLO
22. FRENCH
23. PENINSULARS
24. AYACUCHO
25. VENEZUELA

LATIN AMERICAN INDEPENDENCE

39. The Triumph of Nationalism

1. PRUSSIA
2. HOLSTEIN
3. BISMARCK
4. GARIBALDI
5. GARIBALDI
6. ALSACE
7. EMMANUEL
8. VIENNA
9. KAISER
10. ROME
11. VERSAILLES
12. VATICAN
13. LORRAINE
14. REDSHIRTS
15. CAVOUR
16. AUSTRIA
17. REICH
18. REALPOLITIK
19. ALSACE
20. WILLIAM
21. SCHLESWIG
22. VENETIA
23. JUNKERS

40. Imperialism in Africa

1 LIBYA
2 EGYPT
3 BOERS
3 BELGIUM
4 SUEZ
5 LIVINGSTONE
6 UGANDA
7 FASHODA
8 PORTUGAL
9 RINDERPEST
10 ZAIRE
11 SPAIN
12 CAILLIE
13 IMPERIALISM
14 ASSIMILATION
15 RHODES
16 ETHIOPIA
17 PROTECTORATE
18 FRANCE
19 KIMBERLEY
20 BRITAIN
21 NILE
22 LIVINGSTONE
23 STANLEY
24 GERMANY
25 ITALY
26 MALARIA
27 PATERNALISM
28 LESSEPS
29 BRITAIN
30 IFNI
31 LIBERIA
32 BERLIN
33 FRANCE
34 STANLEY
35 RED
36 SPAIN
37 KITCHENER
38 NIGERIA
39 RED

41. Imperialism in India

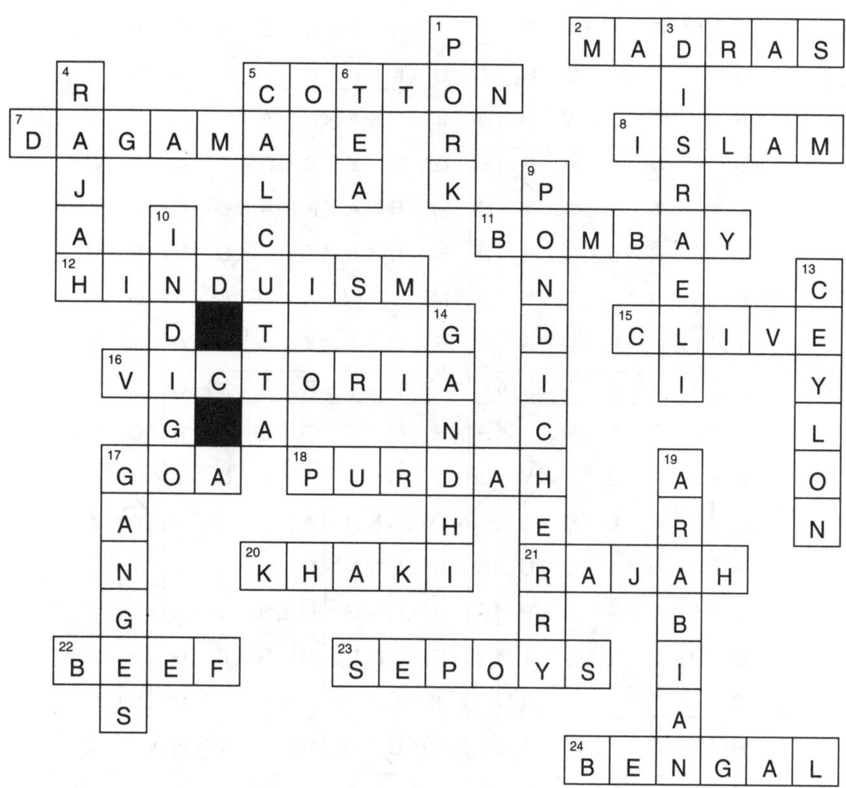

42. Imperialism in China

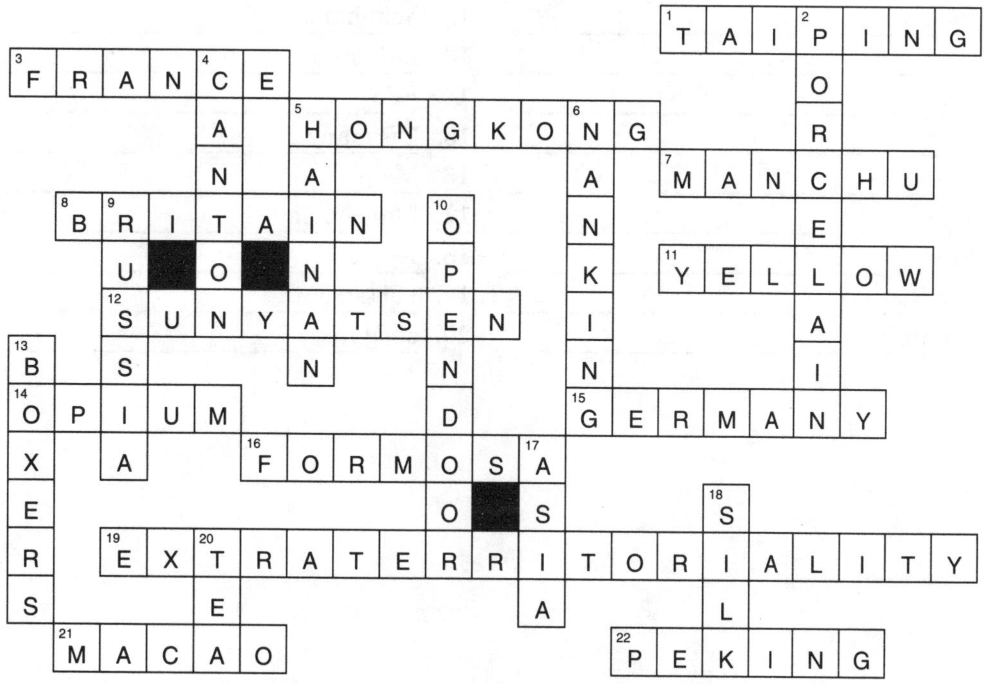

43. Imperialism in Japan

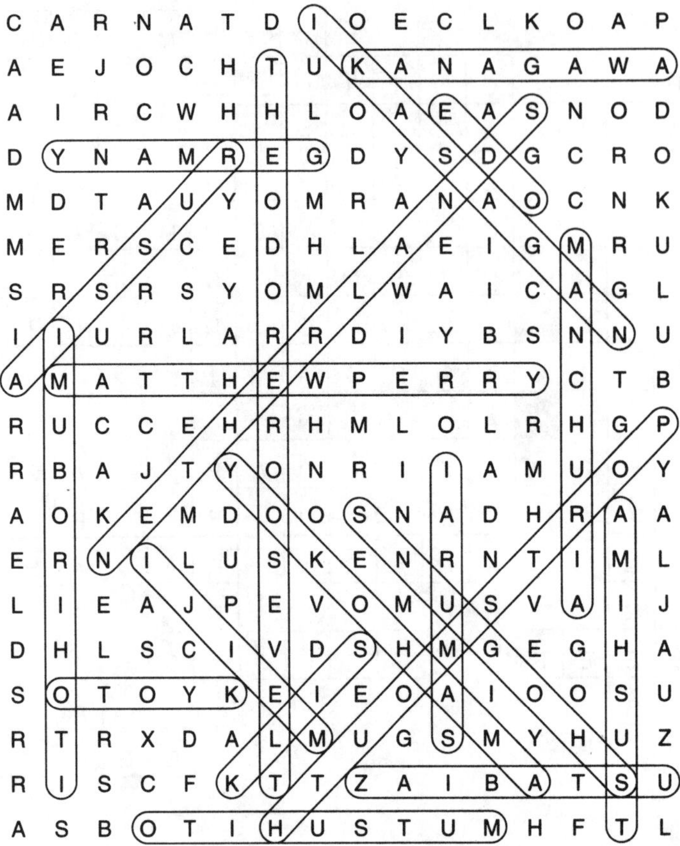

1. Nagasaki
2. Matthew Perry
3. Russia
4. Netherlands
5. Kanagawa
6. silk
7. Tsushima
8. Mutsuhito
9. Theodore Roosevelt
10. Ito Hirobumi
11. samurai
12. Yokohama
13. Zaibatsu
14. Edo
15. Germany
16. Meiji
17. Manchuria
18. Kyoto
19. Portsmouth
20. shoguns

44. Imperialism in Southeast Asia

1. NEWGU**I**NEA
2. BUR**M**A
3. SINGA**P**ORE
4. CEL**E**BES
5. BO**R**NEO
6. T**I**MOR
7. JAV**A**
8. MANI**L**A
9. O**I**L
10. **S**IAM
11. **M**EKONG
12. R**I**CE
13. RA**N**GOON
14. **S**ULU
15. C**O**FFEE
16. R**U**BBER
17. SUMA**T**RA
18. INDOC**H**INA
19. GEORG**E**DEWEY
20. SAR**A**WAK
21. **S**AIGON
22. **T**IN
23. GU**A**M
24. **S**UGAR
25. PHIL**I**PPINES
26. FR**A**NCE

45. Inventors and Reformers

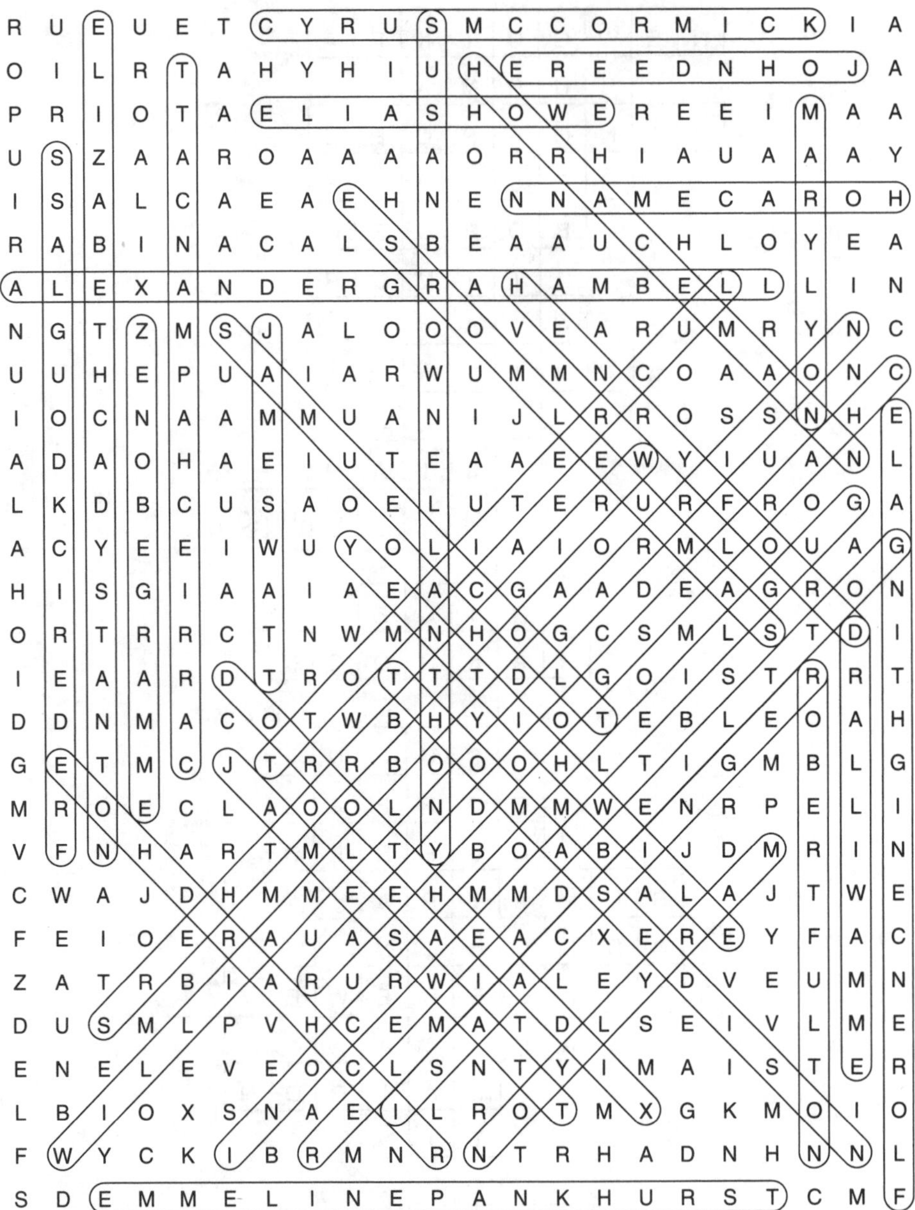

1. James Watt
2. Florence Nightingale
3. Wright Brothers
4. Alexander Graham Bell
5. Lucretia Mott
6. Zenobe Gramme
7. Guglielmo Marconi
8. Cyrus McCormick
9. Carrie Chapman Catt
10. Samuel Morse
11. Emmeline Pankhurst
12. Robert Fulton
13. Charles Goodyear
14. Mary Lyon
15. Elias Howe
16. Thomas Edison
17. Elizabeth Cady Stanton
18. Gottlieb Daimler
19. Richard Hoe
20. Horace Mann
21. Dorothea Dix
22. Isaac Singer
23. John Deere
24. Emma Willard
25. Samuel Colt
26. Frederick Douglass
27. Eli Whitney
28. Susan Brownell Anthony
29. Henry Ford
30. William Lloyd Garrison

46. Currents of Thought—I

1. PAUL**C**EZANNE
2. JOHNST**U**ARTMILL
3. LORDBY**R**ON
4. WILLIAMWO**R**DSWORTH
5. EUGENED**E**LACROIX
6. MAXPLA**N**CK
7. AUGUS**T**WEISMANN
8. JAN**S**IBELIUS
9. GUSTAVEC**O**URBET
10. JEAN**F**RANCOISMILLET
11. JOHNKEA**T**S
12. VICTOR**H**UGO
13. HON**O**REDAUMIER
14. AUG**U**STECOMTE
15. GRE**G**ORMENDEL
16. THOMAS**H**ARDY
17. JOHNDAL**T**ON

47. Currents of Thought—II

1. CHARLESDI**C**KENS
2. MARIEC**U**RIE
3. ALEXANDE**R**SCRIABIN
4. JAMESCLE**R**KMAXWELL
5. HONORED**E**BALZAC
6. LUDWIGVA**N**BEETHOVEN
7. VINCEN**T**VANGOGH
8. LOUI**S**BLANC
9. CLAUDEM**O**NET
10. ERNESTRUTHER**F**ORD
11. ROBER**T**OWEN
12. FRIEDRIC**H**ENGELS
13. GIACOM**O**PUCCINI
14. PAULGA**U**GUIN
15. WILHELMROENT**G**EN
16. MARYS**H**ELLEY
17. IGORS**T**RAVINSKY

48. Currents of Thought—III

1. PABLOPI**C**ASSO
2. FRANZSCH**U**BERT
3. KARLMA**R**X
4. MAU**R**ICERAVEL
5. GIUS**E**PPEVERDI
6. VASILYKA**N**DINSKY
7. HERBER**T**SPENCER
8. ADAM**S**MITH
9. ANTONDV**O**RAK
10. CHARLES**F**OURIER
11. ROBER**T**KOCH
12. ARNOLDSC**H**ONBERG
13. JOHNC**O**NSTABLE
14. ROBERTSCH**U**MANN
15. RICHARDWA**G**NER
16. PERCYBYSS**H**ESHELLEY
17. ALBER**T**EINSTEIN

49. Currents of Thought—IV

1 ISAA**C**ALBENIZ
2 JOSEPHT**U**RNER
3 DMITR**R**IMENDELEEV
4 DAVID**R**ICARDO
5 JOS**E**PHLISTER
6 JEREMYBE**N**THAM
7 FEODORDOS**T**OEVSKI
8 CHARLE**S**DARWIN
9 TH**O**MASMALTHUS
10 SIGMUND**F**REUD
11 LEO**T**OLSTOY
12 FRIEDRIC**H**NIETZSCHE
13 IVANPAVL**O**V
14 ALEXANDERP**U**SHKIN
15 AU**G**USTERENOIR
16 KAT**H**EKOLLWITZ
17 LOUISPAS**T**EUR

50. The Spanish-American War

Across

2. BLACKJACK
4. CUBA
5. SANTIAGO
7. REED
10. GUANTANAMO
11. PARIS
16. WEYLER
17. AGUINALDO
18. REED
19. SANJUANHILL
22. DEWEY
23. HAVANA
24. CUBA
25. MILES
27. PUERTORICO
29. DELOME
30. PULITZER
32. ROUGHRIDERS

Down

1. SANTIAGO
3. PHILIPPINES
4. CERVERA
6. GUAM
8. HAY
9. ROOSEVELT
12. SUGAR
13. PERSHING
14. SIGSBEE
15. MAINE
20. BUTCHER
21. SAMPSON
22. DELOME
23. HEARST
26. MCKINLEY
28. MILES
31. REMINGTON

51. The Panama Canal

			1 A		2 L	O	C	K				3 I	S	T	H	4 M	U	S		
5 F	R	A	N	C	E				6 C							A				
			C		S				O		7 M	C	8 C	U	L	L	O	U	9 G	H
		10 R	O	O	S	E	V	E	L	T			A			A			A	
			N		E				O				R			R			T	
		11 B			12 P	A	N	A	M	A	13 C	I	T	Y		I			U	
14 G	O	R	G	A	S				B		O		E			A			N	
O		Y					15 G	A	I	L	L	A	R	D			16 W			
R		C			17 H				A		O						I		18 T	
19 G	O	E	20 T	H	A	L	S				21 N	A	S	H	V	I	L	L	E	
A			E		Y												S		N	
S			N										22 B	A	L	B	O	A		
																	N			

52. World War I

```
N E E D H A M R O B E R T S G N I H S R E P J N H O J
A I K A V O L S O H C E Z C A L L I E D P O W E R S B
Y L F I N L A N D E G R O E G D Y O L L D I V A D T I
L U L A C E N T R A L P O W E R S S N S P S P W O M G
E S G A L M P T L E K L D C O A I U N M O O V E U S B
A I N O T A F E S O J Z N A R F D C J E L M E S G B E
G T O A S V B C N R F C A J G R A J R A A J M T H B R
U A S E L L I A S R E V L D E R P S N C N W K E B C T
E N L A F D A A S H A G R V S I E D T D D N G R O Z H
O I I D R A I V T A L M O B C J M B B A L R A N Y A A
F A W S A A E R I C H V O N L U D E N D O R F F T R K
N S W K N I J G E A I O I U E M E M Y E Z B E R N N S
A M O I Z A N E R U S R R E M A A M G A N S U O O I V
T I R V F S B O V O P R O S E R C E M C T N B N R C O
I S D E E B U A T O E A T I N N S T A O B U A T F H T
O M O H R R U S L S E G T E C E O Y N B S C X T N O I
N A O S D Y T I S A E N I N E L R I M I D A L V R L L
S I W L I E R H F E F R V U A S A I J G A B T G E A T
W L G O N V C W E O X J F O U R T E E N P O I N T S S
P L L B A R T H U R Z I M M E R M A N N T M L C S J E
E I S G N D R G E D E K S M L E H L I W R E S I A K R
B W J M D O G F I G H T S C N O M A N S L A N D E J B
S N I L E P P E Z L I T H U A N I A E N G E I P M O C
F E R D I N A N D F O C H G E R F F O J S E U Q C A J
```

1. *Lusitania*
2. Tannenberg
3. Gavrilo Princip
4. "no-man's-land"
5. Ferdinand Foch
6. Sarajevo
7. Verdun
8. Central Powers
9. George
10. Western Front
11. Arthur Zimmermann
12. "Over There"
13. Czechoslovakia
14. Czar Nicholas
15. Marne
16. *Sussex*
17. David Lloyd George
18. Estonia
19. "dogfights"
20. Yugoslavia
21. Franz Josef
22. Needham Roberts
23. "Big Bertha"
24. Latvia
25. William Sims
26. Franz Ferdinand
27. "doughboy"
28. Kaiser Wilhelm
29. Somme
30. Allied Powers
31. Brest Litovsk
32. League of Nations
33. zeppelins
34. Bolsheviks
35. John J. Pershing
36. Compiegne
37. Georges Clemenceau
38. Fourteen Points
39. Poland
40. Jacques Joffre
41. Finland
42. "U-boats"
43. Eastern Front
44. Erich von Ludendorff
45. Vittorio Orlando
46. Versailles
47. *Falaba*
48. Vladimir Lenin
49. Lithuania
50. Woodrow Wilson

53. Russia in Revolution

1. SOVIET
2. MOSCOW
3. SIBERIA
4. TROTSKY
5. COMINTERN
6. GEORGIA
7. RED SQUARE
8. BOLSHEVIKS
9. RASPUTIN
10. PETROGRAD
11. REDS
12. KRONSTADT / KULAK
13. TROTSKY
14. ALEXANDRA
15. PROLETARIAT
16. SOVIET UNION
17. PRAVDA
18. ANASTASIA / ALEXIS
19. CHEKA
20. SOVIET
21. PRAVDA
22. ALEXI
23. NICHOLAS
24. LENIN
25. DUMA
26. LENIN
27. COMMUNISTS
28. STALIN

54. Shifts in World Power

1. MOHANDA**S**GANDHI
2. REZAK**H**AN
3. CHIANGKA**I**SHEK
4. MUSTA**F**AKEMAL
5. MAHA**T**MA
6. IBN**S**AUD
7. VENUST**I**ANOCARRANZA
8. SU**N**YATSEN
9. S**W**ARAJ
10. ALVARO**O**BREGON
11. SATYAG**R**AHA
12. FRANK**L**INROOSEVELT
13. THEO**D**OREHERZL
14. EMILIANOZA**P**ATA
15. ZI**O**NISTS
16. JA**W**AHARLALNEHRU
17. VICENT**E**GOMEZ
18. ATATU**R**K

55. The Years between the Wars

	H	O	O	V	E	R						C		J	A	Z	Z					
	U						D	O	L	E		U		O						P		
	G		B		P					L		L		Y						I		
	H	A	R	D	I	N	G			I		L	O	C	A	R	N	O		L		
	E		E	■	C					O		E		E						S		
	S		C	H	A	R	L	E	S	T	O	N			D	O	L	L	F	U	S	S
			H	■	S			A						D				I		D		
	P	I	T	T	S	B	U	R	G	H		C	H	A	P	L	I	N		S		
					O			H	■	O				W				D		K		
							W	A	L	L	S	T	R	E	E	T		B		I		
								R		L				S		A		E				
R	O	O	S	E	V	E	L	T		Y						L		R		P		
	K									W	O	O	L	F		K		G		A		
	I			D						O						I		H		L		
	E			A	R	M	S	T	R	O	N	G				E				M		
	S			D						D			R	E	D	S	C	A	R	E		
		F	L	A	P	P	E	R	S											R		

56. The Rise of Totalitarian States

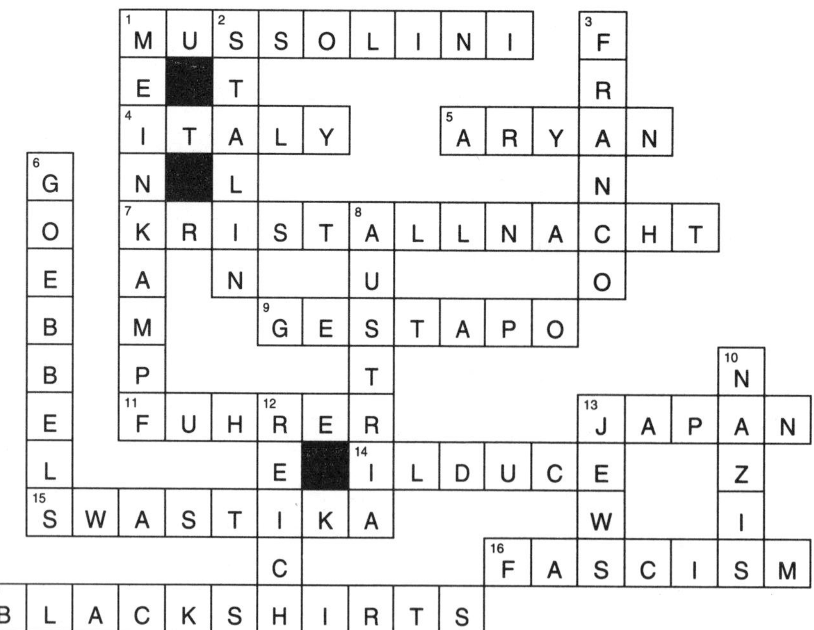

57. World War II

```
A U S C H W I T Z L L I H C R U H C I T S
I R U O S S I M S M N E I S E N H O W E R
R G P Y Z H U K O V L I C A S H M M O L U
O I Z N A P I Y A L T A L I D I O P J A H
M J N M A L L I E S S I X A D R N I I L T
E P O T U A T L P R A A R W T O T E M A R
J M T T X S F A E P B G A H V S G G A M A
T O L I Y E S L A H N Y A D D H O N T E C
N L S O T I H O R I H E U N A I M E S I A
E U E G U A D A L C A N A L Z M E L U N M
Z F C V F E K A H I K G S N R A R L A M R
A T P F E R T Y A I N E A E T C Y U C J E
K W I E O S H J R E Y I L B U A W A O C R
I A L M T C O K B L I T Z K R I E G L K A
M F E T I A S O O M I L E M M O R E O J A
A F D V O N I L R H O K I N A W A D H F H
K E A B M J G N T H G I R W N I A W L B P
D Y A M A M O T O M W C J S N A M U R T S
```

1. Pearl Harbor
2. Hitler
3. blitzkrieg
4. Mussolini
5. Stalin
6. Allies
7. Truman
8. Okinawa
9. MacArthur
10. Auschwitz
11. Nimitz
12. Hirohito
13. Compiegne
14. Holocaust
15. Axis
16. Hiroshima
17. Wainwright
18. Midway
19. Rome
20. *Missouri*
21. Stalingrad
22. Rommel
23. kamikaze
24. Roosevelt
25. Yamamoto
26. Dunkirk
27. Montgomery
28. Guadalcanal
29. Petain
30. Halsey
31. El Alamein
32. Churchill
33. Vichy
34. Anzio
35. Tojo
36. Zhukov
37. Patton
38. D-Day
39. De Gaulle
40. Yalta
41. Iwo Jima
42. Eisenhower
43. Nagasaki
44. Luftwaffe

58. Post-World War II

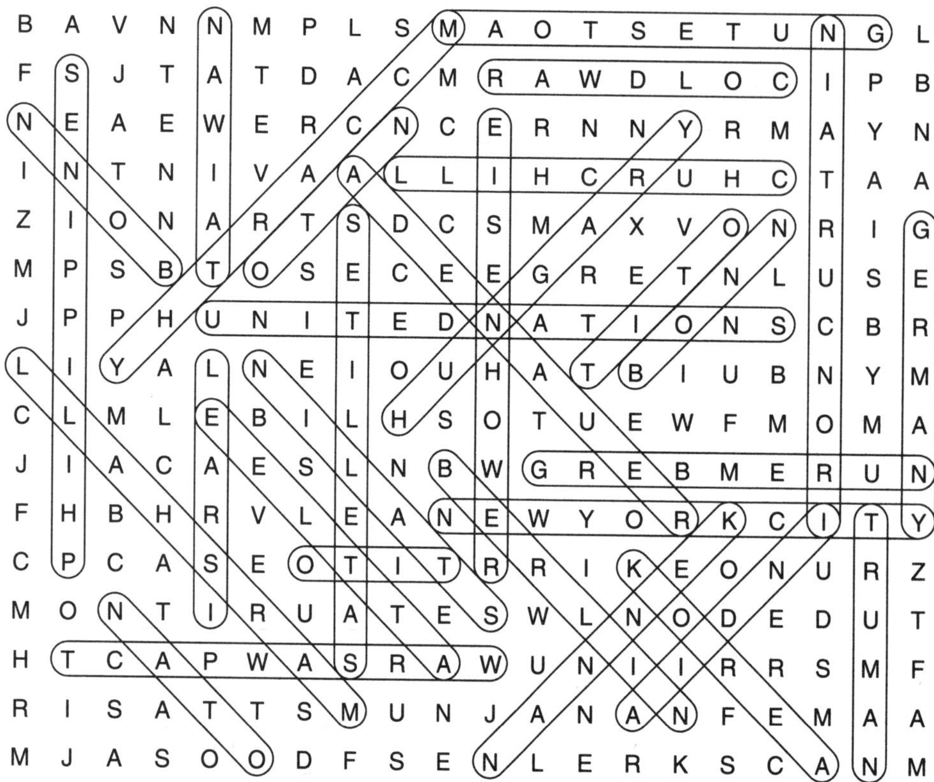

1. United Nations
2. Germany
3. NATO
4. Cold War
5. Kennan
6. Warsaw Pact
7. Truman
8. Israel
9. Mao Tse-tung
10. Marshall
11. Bonn
12. satellites
13. Stalin
14. Hungary
15. Nuremberg
16. iron curtain
17. Berlin
18. Philippines
19. Adenauer
20. Churchill
21. Attlee
22. Taiwan
23. India
24. Eisenhower
25. New York City
26. Korea
27. Tito
28. McCarthy

59. The Cold War Turns Hot

1. HARRY**T**RUMAN
2. DEANAC**H**ESON
3. CHOU**E**NLAI

4. DOUGLASMA**C**ARTHUR
5. LANDOFTHEM**O**RNINGCALM
6. YA**L**U
7. MATTHEWRI**D**GWAY

8. YELLO**W**SEA
9. W**A**KE
10. SYNGMAN**R**HEE

11. THIR**T**YEIGHTH
12. SEO**U**L
13. A**R**MISTICE
14. PYO**N**GYANG
15. KIMIL**S**UNG

16. INC**H**ON
17. SEA**O**FJAPAN
18. DWIGH**T**EISENHOWER

60. Nationalism in Africa

<table>
<tr><td></td><td></td><td>1 N</td><td></td><td>2 N</td><td></td><td></td><td></td><td></td><td>3 T</td><td></td><td></td><td></td><td></td><td></td><td></td><td></td><td></td></tr>
<tr><td></td><td>4 M</td><td>A</td><td>L</td><td>I</td><td></td><td></td><td></td><td>5 B</td><td>U</td><td>R</td><td>U</td><td>N</td><td>D</td><td>I</td><td></td><td></td><td></td></tr>
<tr><td></td><td></td><td>M</td><td>■</td><td>G</td><td></td><td>6 T</td><td></td><td></td><td>T</td><td></td><td></td><td></td><td></td><td></td><td></td><td>7 C</td><td></td></tr>
<tr><td>8 Z</td><td>A</td><td>I</td><td>R</td><td>E</td><td></td><td>U</td><td></td><td>9 S</td><td>U</td><td>D</td><td>A</td><td>10 N</td><td></td><td>11 C</td><td>H</td><td>A</td><td>D</td></tr>
<tr><td>A</td><td></td><td>B</td><td></td><td>R</td><td></td><td>N</td><td></td><td>E</td><td></td><td></td><td></td><td>I</td><td></td><td></td><td></td><td>B</td><td></td></tr>
<tr><td>M</td><td></td><td>I</td><td></td><td></td><td></td><td>I</td><td></td><td>L</td><td></td><td></td><td></td><td>12 G</td><td>A</td><td>13 M</td><td>B</td><td>I</td><td>A</td></tr>
<tr><td>B</td><td></td><td>A</td><td></td><td></td><td>14 A</td><td>S</td><td>W</td><td>A</td><td>N</td><td></td><td></td><td>E</td><td></td><td>A</td><td></td><td>N</td><td></td></tr>
<tr><td>I</td><td></td><td></td><td></td><td></td><td></td><td>I</td><td></td><td>S</td><td>■</td><td>15 M</td><td></td><td>R</td><td></td><td>L</td><td></td><td>D</td><td></td></tr>
<tr><td>16 A</td><td>L</td><td>17 G</td><td>E</td><td>18 R</td><td>I</td><td>A</td><td></td><td>19 S</td><td>W</td><td>A</td><td>H</td><td>I</td><td>L</td><td>I</td><td></td><td>A</td><td></td></tr>
<tr><td></td><td></td><td>H</td><td>■</td><td>W</td><td></td><td></td><td></td><td>I</td><td>■</td><td>N</td><td></td><td>A</td><td></td><td></td><td></td><td></td><td></td></tr>
<tr><td></td><td></td><td>20 A</td><td>P</td><td>A</td><td>R</td><td>T</td><td>H</td><td>E</td><td>I</td><td>D</td><td></td><td></td><td>21 N</td><td></td><td></td><td>22 G</td><td></td></tr>
<tr><td></td><td></td><td>N</td><td>■</td><td>N</td><td></td><td></td><td></td><td></td><td></td><td>E</td><td></td><td>23 L</td><td>I</td><td>B</td><td>Y</td><td>A</td><td></td></tr>
<tr><td>24 U</td><td>25 G</td><td>A</td><td>N</td><td>D</td><td>A</td><td></td><td></td><td>26 N</td><td></td><td>L</td><td></td><td></td><td>L</td><td></td><td></td><td>B</td><td></td></tr>
<tr><td></td><td>U</td><td></td><td></td><td>A</td><td></td><td></td><td>27 H</td><td>A</td><td>R</td><td>A</td><td>M</td><td>28 B</td><td>E</td><td>E</td><td></td><td>O</td><td></td></tr>
<tr><td></td><td>I</td><td></td><td></td><td></td><td></td><td></td><td></td><td>S</td><td></td><td></td><td></td><td>E</td><td></td><td></td><td></td><td>N</td><td></td></tr>
<tr><td>29 A</td><td>N</td><td>G</td><td>O</td><td>L</td><td>A</td><td></td><td></td><td>S</td><td></td><td>30 K</td><td>E</td><td>N</td><td>Y</td><td>A</td><td></td><td></td><td></td></tr>
<tr><td></td><td>E</td><td></td><td></td><td></td><td></td><td></td><td></td><td>E</td><td></td><td></td><td></td><td>I</td><td></td><td></td><td></td><td></td><td></td></tr>
<tr><td>31 Q</td><td>A</td><td>D</td><td>D</td><td>A</td><td>F</td><td>I</td><td></td><td>R</td><td></td><td>32 T</td><td>A</td><td>N</td><td>Z</td><td>A</td><td>N</td><td>I</td><td>A</td></tr>
</table>

61. Developments in the Middle East

T	O	B	R	I	E	M	A	D	L	O	G	E	O	R
A	N	E	L	I	Z	A	Y	E	A	B	L	A	R	O
D	J	I	M	M	Y	C	A	R	T	E	R	P	H	A
A	N	R	U	T	O	L	T	N	A	U	Y	O	S	N
S	T	U	A	C	E	P	O	V	S	T	R	W	I	O
R	H	T	R	A	L	N	L	P	I	R	A	I	M	N
A	M	A	R	S	A	X	L	N	X	N	S	H	E	A
W	S	S	U	B	A	O	A	Y	D	L	I	Z	L	B
N	I	G	E	B	M	I	H	C	A	N	E	M	A	E
A	A	L	I	M	T	D	K	M	Y	O	M	A	S	L
J	D	S	U	S	T	G	H	I	W	M	A	L	U	A
S	U	F	I	E	R	N	O	W	A	J	L	O	R	C
D	J	R	H	N	A	A	M	P	R	N	S	R	E	F
R	H	R	M	W	A	M	E	L	E	I	I	P	J	W
C	A	Q	S	B	K	I	I	L	N	C	O	S	C	H
N	S	A	B	D	E	L	N	A	S	S	E	R	L	O
T	A	F	A	R	A	R	I	S	A	Y	A	G	M	B

1. Islam
2. Tehran
3. Abdel Nasser
4. Lebanon
5. Six-Day War
6. Jimmy Carter
7. Jerusalem
8. Anwar Sadat
9. OPEC
10. Israel
11. Ayatollah Khomeini
12. Aswan
13. Menachim Begin
14. PLO
15. Judaism
16. Golda Meir
17. Sinai
18. Beirut
19. Yasir Arafat
20. Christianity

62. Change and Conflict in Asia

1. VIET**C**ONG
2. HIRO**H**ITO
3. INDIR**A**GANDHI
4. RICHARD**N**IXON
5. BAN**G**LADESH
6. MAOZ**E**DONG
7. OS**A**KA
8. INDO**N**ESIA
9. IN**D**IA
10. DOUGLASMA**C**ARTHUR
11. SAIG**O**N
12. CHI**N**A
13. A**F**GHANISTAN
14. JAWAHAR**L**ALNEHRU
15. BE**I**JING
16. KAMPU**C**HEA
17. PAKIS**T**AN
18. HOCH**I**MINH
19. FERDINA**N**DMARCOS
20. MOHANDA**S**GANDHI —
21. MALAY**S**IA
22. PHIL**I**PPINES
23. SING**A**PORE

63. The World in Change

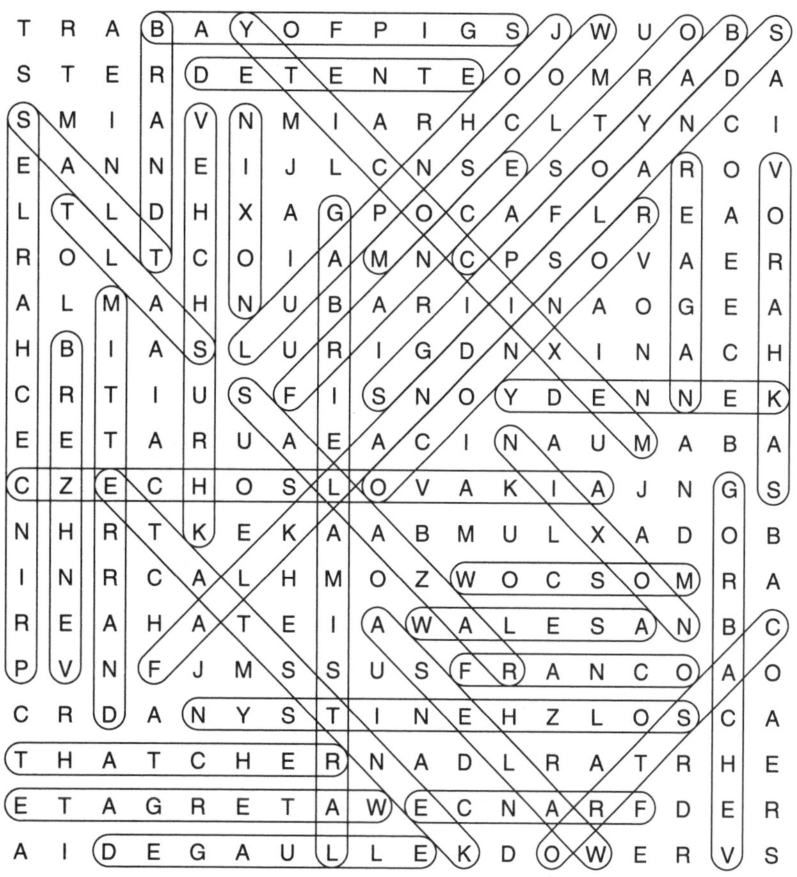

1. Thatcher
2. Kent State
3. Solzhenitsyn
4. Castro
5. Walesa
6. SALT
7. Mitterrand
8. Prince Charles
9. Bay of Pigs
10. De Gaulle
11. Mexico City
12. Nixon
13. Czechoslovakia
14. O'Connor
15. Khrushchev
16. John Paul
17. detente
18. Gorbachev
19. Franco
20. Watergate
21. Gabriela Mistral
22. Moscow
23. Salazar
24. Brezhnev
25. Falkland Islands
26. Kennedy
27. Sakharov
28. France
29. Brandt
30. Reagan

64. A New Age of Exploration

1. DISCOVERY
2. SKYLAB
3. GARN; GEMINI
4. MCAULIFFE
5. MOJAVE
6. SOYUZ
7. HOUSTON
8. SPUTNIK
9. YEAGER
10. GAGARIN
11. GLENN
12. RIDE
13. CRIPPEN; CHALLENGER
14. ARMSTRONG
15. EAGLE
16. CAPE CANAVERAL
17. COLUMBIA
18. EXPLORER
19. VIKING; VOYAGER
20. GLENN
21. NASA
22. APOLLO
23. MERCURY
24. EDWARDS
25. ALDRIN
26. YOUNG
27. BLUFORD
28. SHEPARD
29. RUTAN
30. GARN

65. Famous Quotations in World History

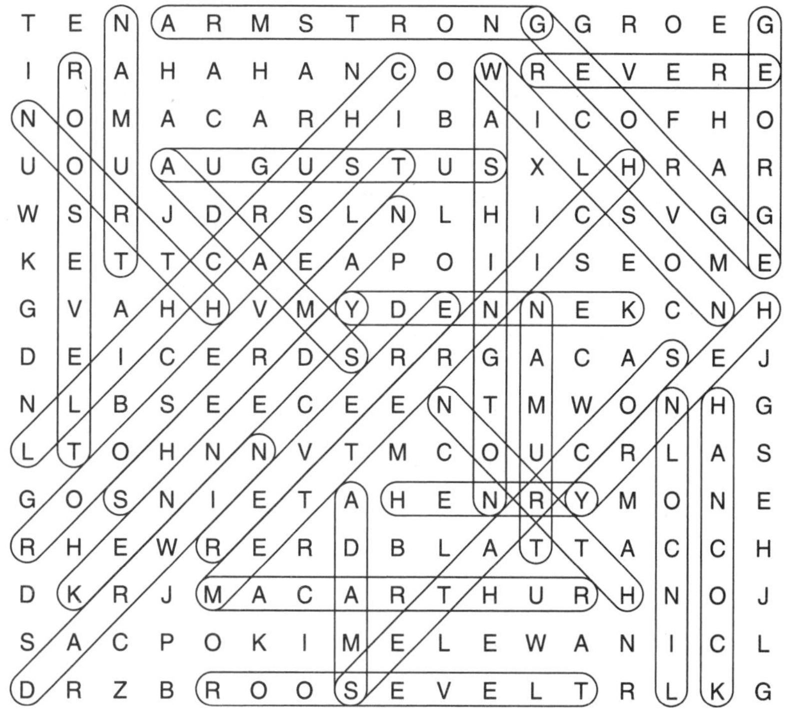

1. Metternich
2. Wilson
3. Augustus
4. Hancock
5. Sherman
6. Armstrong
7. Truman
8. Churchill
9. Henry
10. Darwin
11. Roosevelt
12. Socrates
13. Lincoln
14. MacArthur
15. George
16. Adams
17. Revere
18. Roosevelt
19. North
20. Kennedy
21. Roosevelt
22. Washington

66. World History Nicknames

1 **W**ILLIAM
2 MUSS**O**LINI
3 E**R**IC
4 BO**L**IVAR
5 ME**D**ICI
6 **H**ENRY
7 ATT**I**LA
8 LOUI**S**
9 PE**T**ER
10 MESOP**O**TAMIA
11 GE**R**MANY
12 HENR**Y**
13 CONSTANTI**N**OPLE — CONSTA**N**TINOPLE
14 H**I**TLER
15 BISMAR**C**K
16 BAL**K**ANS
17 ALEXA**N**DER
18 IV**A**N
19 ROM**M**EL
20 K**E**MAL
21 JAME**S**

67. World History Potpourri—I

																		1 K
			2 W	3 A	T	T		4 V		5 M						6 L	E	O
	7 C			O				8 E	D	I	S	O	N		9 M			R
	10 H	Y	D	R	O	G	E	N		N				11 M	E	C	C	A
	E			T				U		O		12 G			R			N
13 G	E	R	14 M	A	N	15 Y		S		16 A	D	A	M		C		17 A	
	T	■	A			E				N		B		18 B	U	R	M	A
	19 A	R	G	O	N	A	U	T	S			R			R		U	
	H		E			G				20 F	R	I	D	21 A	Y		N	
			L		22 J	E	N	23 N	E	R		E		G			D	
	24 S	A	L	K		R	■	E	■	E		L		R			S	
	I	■	A				25 A	R	G	U	S		26 H	A	27 L	L	E	Y
28 B	A	R	N	A	R	D		O		D					E	■	N	
	M										29 V	I	R	G	I	L		

68. World History Potpourri—II

Across

4. NEBUCHADNEZZAR
8. ALI
9. SHEPARD
10. GUTENBERG
12. BISMARCK
14. SOCRATES
17. CHINA
18. POLAND
20. MING
21. POLAND
22. SHAKESPEARE
24. ELLIS
25. FLEMING
26. HAMLET
30. VESPUCCI
31. SWIFT
32. ITALY
35. CONFUCIUS
37. KARMA
38. JACQUESCARTIER
40. FIVE
41. METEORITE
42. WESTMINSTER
43. SIDDHARTHAGAUTAMA

Down

1. BENJAMINFRANKLIN
2. METEOR
3. LINDBERGH
5. DINGO
6. VERSAILLES
7. DAGAMA
10. GOA
11. MEDUSA
13. KAMIKAZE
15. ACROPOLIS
16. FOSSILS
17. COPERNICUS
19. DIET
23. DARWIN
27. LUFTWAFFE
28. IVAN
29. BAROQUE
33. MEDICI
34. HOMER
36. FORD
38. JAMES
39. SMITH

69. World History Potpourri—III

70. World History Potpourri—IV

71. World History Potpourri—V

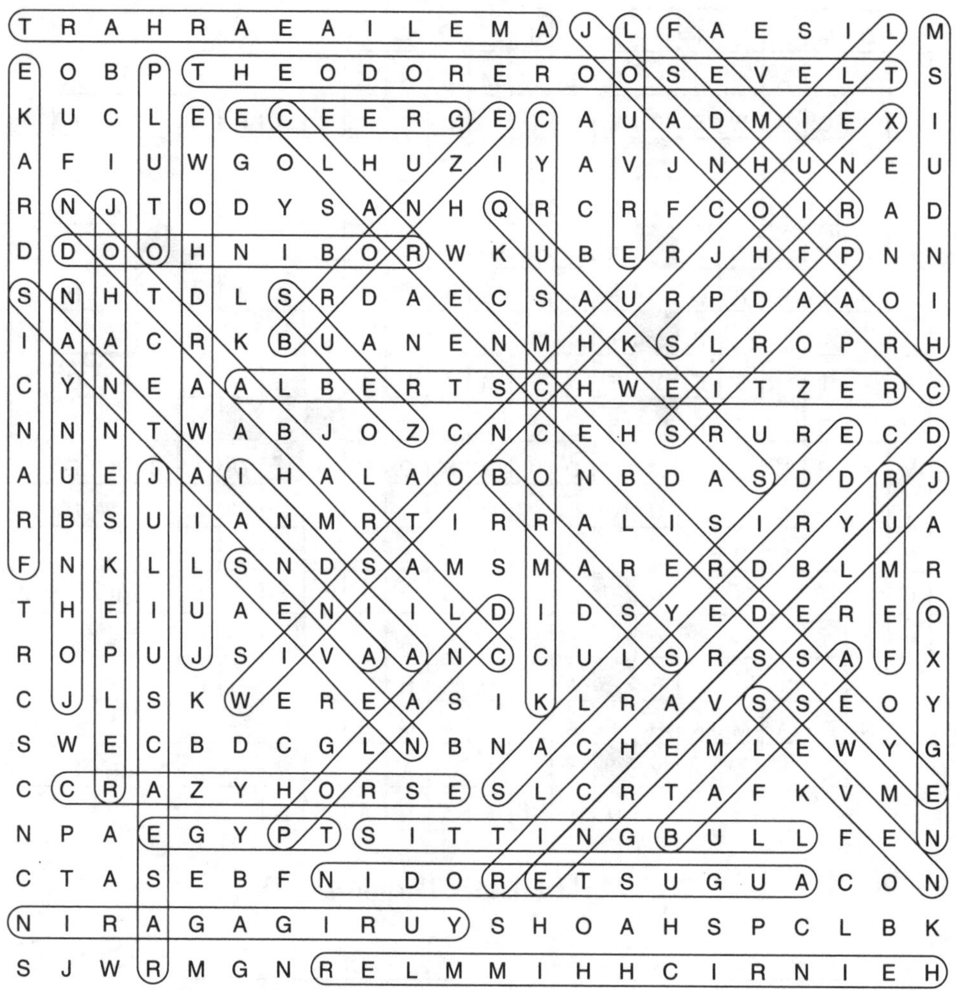

1. Yuri Gagarin
2. Joan of Arc
3. Poland
4. Robin Hood
5. Jules Verne
6. Louvre
7. Amelia Earhart
8. balsa
9. Cyrus McCormick
10. Suez
11. Auguste Rodin
12. Quakers
13. Julia Ward Howe
14. brass
15. Crazy Horse
16. Paris
17. Hinduism
18. John Bunyan
19. bronze
20. Clara Barton
21. Albert Schweitzer
22. Pluto
23. Richard Byrd
24. Francis Drake
25. oxygen
26. Winston Churchill
27. Theodore Roosevelt
28. Greece
29. Johannes Kepler
30. seven
31. Egypt
32. Clarence Birdseye
33. Sitting Bull
34. femur
35. India
36. Heinrich Himmler
37. Sphinx
38. Julius Caesar
39. Sally Ride
40. Santa Anna

72. World History Potpourri—VI

1. MILKY**W**AY
2. ARTHURC**O**NANDOYLE
3. THEODORE**R**OOSEVELT
4. ENG**L**AND
5. COLERI**D**GE
6. ADOLF**H**ITLER
7. GLAC**I**ER
8. KNE**S**SET
9. FA**T**IMA
10. EC**O**LOGY
11. JOHN**R**OLFE
12. BAB**Y**LONIA
13. RA**P**HAEL
14. TRIGON**O**METRY
15. MON**T**ESQUIEU
16. KRU**P**P
17. OXF**O**RD
18. BAYOFF**U**NDY
19. PANC**R**EAS
20. JE**R**ICHO
21. GE**I**GER

73. World History Potpourri—VII

1. SINCLAIRLE**W**IS
2. R**O**USSEAU
3. HE**R**OD
4. QUETZA**L**COATL
5. CAMBRI**D**GE
6. EIG**H**T
7. LA**I**KA
8. ROSHHA**S**HANAH
9. GEOME**T**RY
10. TH**O**R
11. CE**R**ES
12. OMARKHA**Y**YAM
13. ETHIO**P**IA
14. WILLIAMB**O**OTH
15. VINCEN**T**VANGOGH
16. JOSE**P**HSTALIN
17. ER**O**S
18. OCEAN**U**SHOPKINS
19. HE**R**MES
20. WATE**R**LOO
21. CUB**I**T

74. Women in World History

1. LYON
2. WUCHAO
3. CATHERINE
3. CURIE
4. RIDE
5. BROOKS
6. MARY
7. MARY
8. ANTHONY
9. NIGHTINGALE
10. ROSS
11. OCONNOR
12. ANASTASIA
13. TUBMAN
14. SANGER
15. MEAD
16. POCAHONTAS
17. SACAGAWEA
18. ANNE
19. ALEXANDRA
20. ELIZABETH
21. BRONTE
22. GANDHI
23. PAVLOVA
24. JOANOFARC
25. VICTORIA
26. LILIUOKALANI
27. STOWE
28. CATHERINE
29. HATSHEPSUT
30. REMARQUE
31. BUCK
32. CLEOPATRA
33. DARE
34. KELLER
35. PANKHURST
36. MARIEANTOINETTE
37. EARHART
38. MEIR
38. MARY
39. HELEN
40. ISABELLA
41. SHELLEY
42. AQUINO
43. ADAMS
44. BARTON

75. Biblical Names in World History

1. LUKE
2. AHAB
3. RUTH
4. MATTHEW
5. EVE
6. PAUL
7. NOAH
8. SALOME
9. ESTHER
10. THOMAS
11. SAMUEL
12. SIMON
13. RAPHAEL
14. NOAH
15. GABRIEL
16. JOSHUA
17. SOLOMON
18. SAMSON
19. JOB
20. GOLIATH
21. ISHMAEL
22. JAMES
23. MOSES
24. SARAH
25. DAVID
26. ADAM
27. BENJAMIN
28. JEZEBEL
29. MICHAEL
30. AARON
31. SAUL
32. LAZARUS
33. HAGAR
34. ZECHARIAH
35. AHAB
36. PETER
37. JEREMIAH
38. ABEL
39. ABRAHAM
40. CAIN
41. ESAU
42. DANIEL
43. URIEL
44. PHILIP
45. EZEKIEL
46. JONAH / JOHN
47. ISAIAH
48. ISAIAH
49. JOSH
50. ELIJAH
51. JOSEPH
52. DELILAH
53. HAGAR
54. MARK
55. ADAM
56. JACOB
57. REBEKAH
58. MARY

76. Mythological Names in World History—I

1. APOLLO
2. PLUTO
3. FLORA
4. LAIUS
5. PYGMALION
6. ZEUS
7. CLYTEMNESTRA
8. ORPHEUS
9. CALLIOPE
9. CERES
10. PARIS
11. OEDIPUS
12. PRIAM
13. PAN
14. DEMETER
15. CHARYBDIS
16. DIDO
17. MIDAS
18. AGAMEMNON
19. ATHENA
20. HEPHAESTUS
21. ENDYMION
22. WILLIAMTELL
23. AENEAS
24. THOR
25. ELECTRA
26. AJAX
26. AESCULAPIUS
27. ARTEMIS
28. HERCULES
29. NIKE
30. FRIGGA
31. PROMETHEUS
32. ASCLEPIUS
33. HECTOR
33. HECUBA
34. MARS
35. FLYINGDUTCHMAN
35. FLORA
36. MERCURY
37. ARES
38. EUROPA
39. FAUST
40. JANUS
41. BOREAS
42. ADONIS
43. GALATEA
43. GAIA
44. MINERVA
45. THESEUS
46. JUNO
47. CUPID
48. ROMULUS
48. ROMULUS
49. ODIN
50. HYMEN
51. EURYDICE
51. EURYDICE
52. HERMAPHRODITUS
52. HERA
53. SATURN
54. NIOBE
54. NIOBE
55. ATLAS
55. ATLAS
56. NEPTUNE
56. NEPTUNE
57. EROS
58. NIKE
59. LEDA
60. MENELAUS
61. VENUS
62. POLYPHEMUS
63. MEDEA

77. Mythological Names in World History—II

```
J E F E R J U P I T E R N S O L C I N
Z D A H A L A G M O R O I T E W J O A
E H N O S C O C A S S A N D R A S A R
P O S E I D O N P A U M A H R I E T C
H T R Y I D O O J D N E I E E L L S I
Y A S V P T S O R I O P S C Y L L A S
R N A P I E T I D O R H P A T I I C S
U T U R A N U S S N C I V I S B H O U
S I T R G N U A I Y I S S U N S C J S
I G A D B N D L C S E T L O L O A C R
N O F L A I R O A U Y O K C R C R L U
H N S E M E P E R S E P H O N E A A A
I E C P M P D H U A S H H E M P N N T
A O R U H T R A S A S E A U P O E C O
W F A M K I T O L E P L S I S E M E N
A S L H E L N T T U P E G A S U S L I
T O E O A S A X O E S S J R T M U O M
H R T S R P A U L B U N Y A N H A T J
A E S U L A T N A T O S E S S Y L U F
```

1. Achilles
2. Minotaur
3. Arthur
4. Pandora
5. Jupiter
6. Aesop
7. Pegasus
8. Sphinx
9. Pecos Bill
10. Ulysses
11. Cronus
12. Lancelot
13. Zephyrus
14. Godiva
15. Scylla
16. Merlin
17. Hermes
18. Nemesis
19. Icarus
20. Oceanus
21. Tantalus
22. Vulcan
23. Atlas
24. Eros
25. Leda
26. Poseidon
27. Helios
28. Paul Bunyan
29. Antigone
30. Uranus
31. Proteus
32. Galahad
33. Narcissus
34. Aeolus
35. Cassandra
36. Mephistopheles
37. Jason
38. Hiawatha
39. Flora
40. Dionysus
41. Remus
42. Aphrodite
43. Triton
44. Daedalus
45. Midas
46. Persephone
47. Hera
48. Sisyphus
49. Jocasta
50. Ares

78. Popular Names in World History

										1 J												
								2 G	E	O	R	G	E									
3 P	I	4 U	S							H						5 P						
H		R		6 G			7 B			8 N	I	C	H	O	L	A	S					
I		B		R			O		9 B							U						
L		10 A	L	E	X	A	N	D	E	R			11 P	H	I	L	12 I	P				
I		N		G			I	■	N								N					
P				O			13 F	R	E	D	E	14 R	I	15 C	K		N		16 W			
	17 H	18 E	N	R	Y		A		D			I		H		19 L	O	U	I	S		
		D		Y			C		I			C		A			C		L			
		W					E		20 C	A	T	H	E	R	I	N	E		L		21 H	
	22 J	A	M	E	S				T			A		L			N		I		E	
		R					23 L					R		E			T		A		N	
		D					24 E	D	W	A	R	D		S					25 M	A	R	Y
							O														Y	

79. Foreign Words and Phrases—I

1. SEMPER**F**IDELIS
2. AL**O**HA
3. ALTE**R**IDEM
4. SEMP**E**RPARATUS
5. EPLUR**I**BUSUNUM
6. BOUR**G**EOISIE
7. AUCO**N**TRAIRE
8. LEBENS**W**ELT
9. SAY**O**NARA
10. CHESA**R**ASARA
11. ARRIVE**D**ERCI
12. EXCEL**S**IOR
13. DIT**A**TDEUS
14. WU**N**DERBAR
15. GESUN**D**HEIT
16. BONAP**P**ETIT
17. MA**H**ALO
18. EU**R**EKA
19. FAUXP**A**S
20. HABEA**S**CORPUS
21. SEHABLA**E**SPANOL
22. STATU**S**QUO

80. Foreign Words and Phrases—II

1. LAISSEZ**F**AIRE
2. BONJ**O**UR
3. SICSEMPE**R**TYRANNIS
4. ANTEB**E**LLUM
5. AD**I**OS
6. BUON**G**IORNO
7. DETE**N**TE
8. NICHT**W**AHR
9. SUBP**O**ENA
10. DI**R**IGO
11. COUP**D**ETAT
12. BON**S**OIR
13. HASTAL**A**VISTA
14. RE**N**DEZVOUS
15. HORS**D**OEUVRE
16. ENTRE**P**RENEUR
17. MANSPRIC**H**TDEUTSCH
18. ADASTRAPE**R**ASPERA
19. ENG**A**RDE
20. AVOTRE**S**ANTE
21. CRESCIT**E**UNDO
22. SILVOU**S**PLAIT

81. Vocabulary Words in World History

```
N O I T A L F N I C A P I T A L I S M
A R T I S A N C I L B U P E R I T I S
P A T R I A R C H C E L A T E T H E I
P Y A A W G H Y A M Y T R N A E E D L
R Y R A N E C R E M T I M E C R O I A
E H C U R B A O C M S M I D U A C E D
N E O E S V M T R H A A S I S C R H U
T W T R E U A S A B N T T S U Y A T E
I I U L E R M I A B Y U I S R S C R F
C J A D I P E H P B D M C I Y T Y A S
E A C F O R A E P M I I E D C T R P S
T Y F E U P B R E L R A C I R O Y A O
E A G T P R O P A G A N D A E B T U C
S T L O T M A T S T R E M Y T H R A I
C U A D L Y I A E L I T I T H E A I A
C I F D T O R T M Y L O P O N O M L L
E E T F N L C A E A G E N O C I D E I
M D B E R A I E N T S F L S E E C E S
W A I S R A M W T T S I H C R A N A M
H I T C E E G O S T R A C I S M A S O
E H T I T N H E O N O I T I L A O C W
```

1. mercenary
2. monopoly
3. apprentice
4. dynasty
5. abdicate
6. republic
7. tariff
8. coalition
9. socialism
10. inflation
11. apartheid
12. mandate
13. armistice
14. usury
15. heretic
16. artisan
17. reparations
18. martyr
19. caravel
20. genocide
21. propaganda
22. feudalism
23. ultimatum
24. patriarch
25. edict
26. theocracy
27. anarchist
28. prehistory
29. autocrat
30. capitalism
31. appeasement
32. tyrant
33. literacy
34. tithe
35. suffrage
36. culture
37. ostracism
38. ecology
39. assimilation
40. dissident

82. Important Years in World History—B.C.

					[1] 5					[2] 2	7	
[3] 1		[4] 1	[5] 4	7	8		[6] 1	[7] 5	0	0	■	[8] 3
[9] 3	0	■	0	■	6			5	■	[10] 9	[11] 3	1
0		[12] 2	4	[13] 1	■	[14] 3	5	0	0	■	0	
		7		[15] 5	5	1				[16] 1	■	[17] 2
[18] 5	6	3		0	■	0		[19] 2		[20] 7	7	6
0			[21] 1	0	0	0		1		0		0
[22] 9	0	0					[23] 2	8	0	0		0

83. Important Years in World History—0–1500

84. Important Years in World History—1500–1800

				[1] 1	7	[2] 1	5		[3] 1	6	[4] 1	8		[5] 1	7	[6] 1	2
						5					6					6	
		[7] 1		[8] 1	5	7	9		[9] 1	5	8	8		[10] 1	5	0	2
	[11] 1	6	0	7		6			5	■	9			7	■	3	
		0	■	8			[12] 1	7	7	6		[13] 1	6	5	2		
	[14] 1	5	[15] 1	9			5	■	7			6	■	4			[16] 1
	5	■	5		[17] 1	6	2	0		[18] 1	6	6	5	■	[19] 1		7
[20] 1	6	8	2		6	■	2			5	■	4		[21] 1	7	8	8
	5		[22] 1	5	4	3		[23] 1	5	3	3				9		9
					9					4		[24] 1	7	8	3		

85. Important Years in World History—1800–1900

			[1] 1		[2] 1	8	3	6		[3] 1		[4] 1	
		[5] 1	8	4	8				[6] 1	8	4	8	
			5	■	[7] 1	8	6	[8] 1		6	■	5	
[9] 1		[10] 1	8	1	2			8		[11] 1	8	4	5
8		8				[12] 1	8	4	6				
[13] 1	8	0	3			8	■	4		[14] 1	8	[15] 1	5
4		4		[16] 1	8	9	8			8		8	
				8	■	8	■	[17] 1		7		2	
[18] 1		[19] 1	8	6	5	■	[20] 1	8	6	6		1	
8		8	■	9	■	[21] 1	■	6			[22] 1	■	[23] 1
[24] 1	8	5	1		[25] 1	8	5	7		[26] 1	8	4	8
5		9				1					7		2
			[27] 1	8	5	4		[28] 1	8	7	1		9

86. Important Years in World History—1900–1990

87. Countries of the World—Latin America

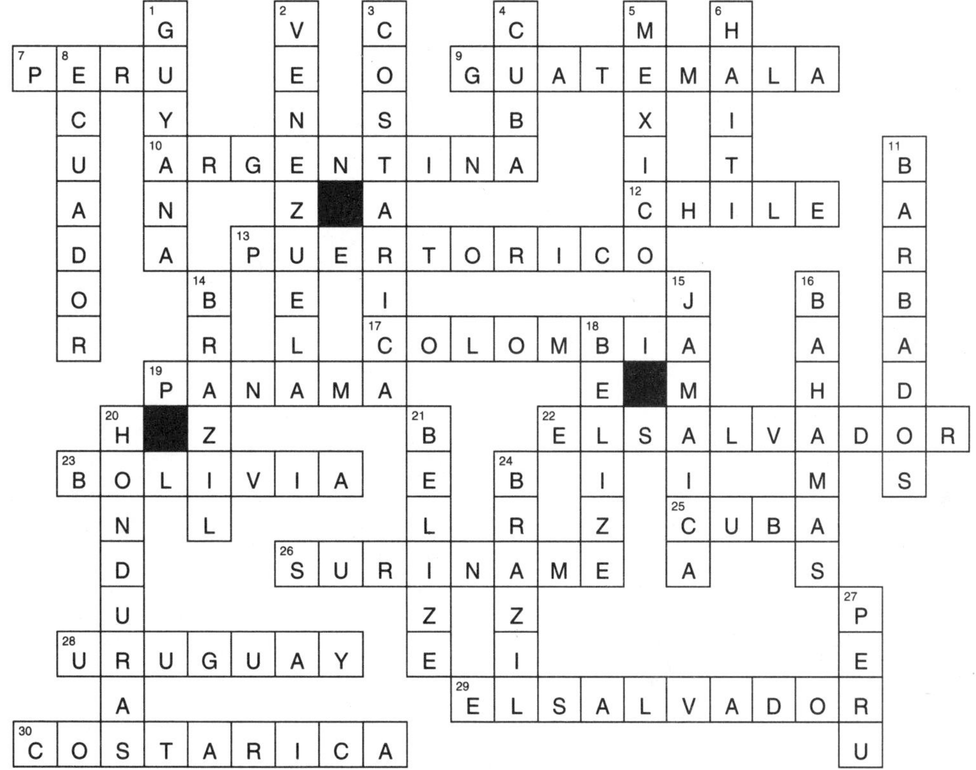

88. Countries of the World—Europe

L O N R O M D V A T I C A N C I T Y R

U D E N M A R K O N I R A M N A S G A

B D N A L L O H N E R E D O S D S E F

S N O R W A Y D E O N T B C N O P R H

E A R R O D N A D A E G E A A M A M P

A S T Y O A B N E G C A L B A N I A E

V I H Z L A A U W E E R G A C M N N A

L I E E W A I A S C E T I E N S W Y A

P R R I T A T R S H R S U S P D M D L

T I N C P J L I T A G E M A P E N X O

A L I E C H T E N S T E I N E A G I M

R Y R L D G N A S L U N F K L F I D E

L A E A N E I Y D O P A T R M R N N D

A W L N A M W N L V A N E A A A L I N

G R A D L D A S H A R Z L M L N A N A

U O N L N L E L U K T T E N I C C G L

T N D A E S C L T I A I I E W E R E T

R A L C E S E S W A O F L D O E R T O

O O I B R W E S G R U O B M E X U L C

P H U N G A R Y G T J I O C A N O M S

F U S L L A G U T R O P E P O L A N D

1. Iceland
2. Austria
3. Greece
4. Liechtenstein
5. France
6. Ireland
7. Poland
8. Sweden
9. Netherlands
10. Vatican City
11. Scotland
12. Spain
13. Hungary
14. Denmark
15. Andorra
16. Germany
17. Holland
18. Iceland
19. Portugal
20. Italy
21. Norway
22. Belgium
23. Slovakia
24. Spain
25. Switzerland
26. Northern Ireland
27. Malta
28. France
29. Denmark
30. Greece
31. Portugal
32. Wales
33. Albania
34. Greece
35. Norway
36. France
37. San Marino
38. Greenland
39. Poland
40. Luxembourg
41. Finland
42. Monaco
43. England
44. Sweden

89. Countries of the World—Africa

1 MALI
2 ALGERIA
3 ETHIOPIA
4 MOROCCO
5 LIBYA
6 ZAIRE
7 TOGO
8 LESOTHO
9 LIBERIA
10 NIGERIA
11 LIBYA
12 MOROCCO
13 ZIMBABWE
14 BENIN
15 GHANA
16 EGYPT
17 MALI
18 NIGERIA
19 GABON
20 NAMIBIA
21 MALAWI
22 NIGERIA
23 ETHIOPIA
24 BOTSWANA
25 KENYA
26 TANZANIA
27 ZAMBIA
28 EGYPT
29 ZAMBIA / ZAIRE
30 TANZANIA / TUNISIA
31 LESOTHO
32 SUDAN
33 TANZANIA
34 SUDAN
35 GABON
36 GHANA
37 NIGER
38 NAMIBIA
39 CHAD
40 GABON
41 ZAIRE
42 SOMALIA

90. Countries of the World—The Orient

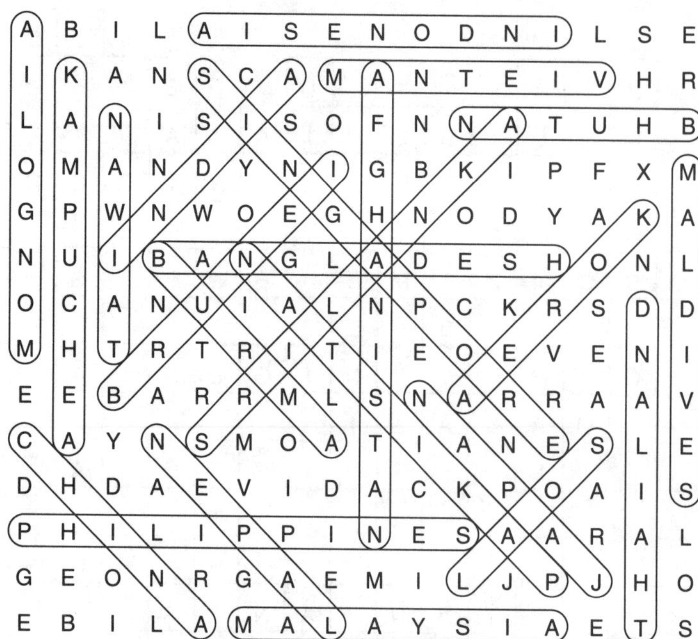

1. Japan
2. Thailand
3. Pakistan
4. China
5. Vietnam
6. Philippines
7. Korea
8. Sri Lanka
9. Kampuchea
10. Indonesia
11. China
12. Laos
13. India
14. Thailand
15. Singapore
16. Japan
17. Bhutan
18. Bangladesh
19. Mongolia
20. Indonesia
21. China
22. Philippines
23. Afghanistan
24. Singapore
25. Thailand
26. India
27. Thailand
28. Indonesia
29. Malaysia
30. Laos
31. China
32. Brunei
33. Bangladesh
34. Philippines
35. Japan
36. Indonesia
37. Nepal
38. China
39. Afghanistan
40. Thailand
41. Maldives
42. India
43. Kampuchea
44. Singapore
45. Philippines
46. China
47. Malaysia
48. Burma
49. Indonesia
50. Taiwan

91. Capital Cities of the World—Latin America

```
T A S K O E D I V E T N O M E S L I M B
O B E I S M Y A P A R A M A R I B O L C
A U N N S A N J O S E A Z I M L N E J E
L E N G M I N R R O P O G A I T N A S J
T N E S U P V S T L B E L M P B N O P M
E O Y T I C A L A M E T A U G A J K O S
Y S A O A B E G U L R C H J S N L A R N
T A C N E U I E P B V A A S A C T I T W
I I N Q A C G E R X V A A S R O F L O O
C R K A U J Y A I A H U D Z G E L I F T
O E C G V I O G N I M O D O T N A S S E
C S E A J A T A C A F S B S R J B A P G
I T M E R I H O E N M A A P O V N R A D
X Y T I C A M A N A P N L T W J E B I I
E C A S U N C I O N J J I A U A D Y N R
M B A P M E D A W O E U N A P O M L E B
S E G R O E G T S C Q A N N I A T I F A
M T G E O R G E T O W N C A K I Z O L S
```

1.	Guatemala City	Guatemala	16.	Port of Spain	Trinidad and Tobago
2.	Montevideo	Uruguay	17.	Cayenne	French Guiana
3.	Belmopan	Belize	18.	Santo Domingo	Dominican Republic
4.	La Paz	Bolivia	19.	Managua	Nicaragua
5.	Mexico City	Mexico	20.	San Juan	Puerto Rico
6.	Georgetown	Guyana	21.	Buenos Aires	Argentina
7.	Santiago	Chile	22.	San Salvador	El Salvador
8.	Panama City	Panama	23.	San Jose	Costa Rica
9.	Lima	Peru	24.	Caracas	Venezuela
10.	Port-au-Prince	Haiti	25.	Tegucigalpa	Honduras
11.	Brasilia	Brazil	26.	Asuncion	Paraguay
12.	Havana	Cuba	27.	Nassau	Bahamas
13.	Quito	Ecuador	28.	Bogota	Colombia
14.	Kingston	Jamaica	29.	Paramaribo	Suriname
15.	St. Georges	Grenada	30.	Bridgetown	Barbados

92. Capital Cities of the World—Europe

1 STOCKHOLM
2 OSLO
3 MADRID
4 PARIS
5 AMSTERDAM
6 BELFAST
7 REYKJAVIK
8 VALLETTA
9 LISBON
10 DUBLIN
11 BUCHAREST
12 VIENNA
13 HELSINKI
14 BERN
15 BUCHAREST
16 LUXEMBOURG
17 ROME
18 MOSCOW
19 BERN
20 EDINBURGH
21 AMSTERDAM
22 TIRANA
23 AMSTERDAM
24 LONDON
25 SOFIA
26 BUDAPEST
27 SOFIA
28 LISBON
29 PRAGUE
30 PARIS
31 DUBLIN
32 WARSAW
33 ATHENS
34 BERLIN
35 ROME
36 BERN
37 BRUSSELS
38 COPENHAGEN
39 VIENNA

93. Capital Cities of the World—Africa

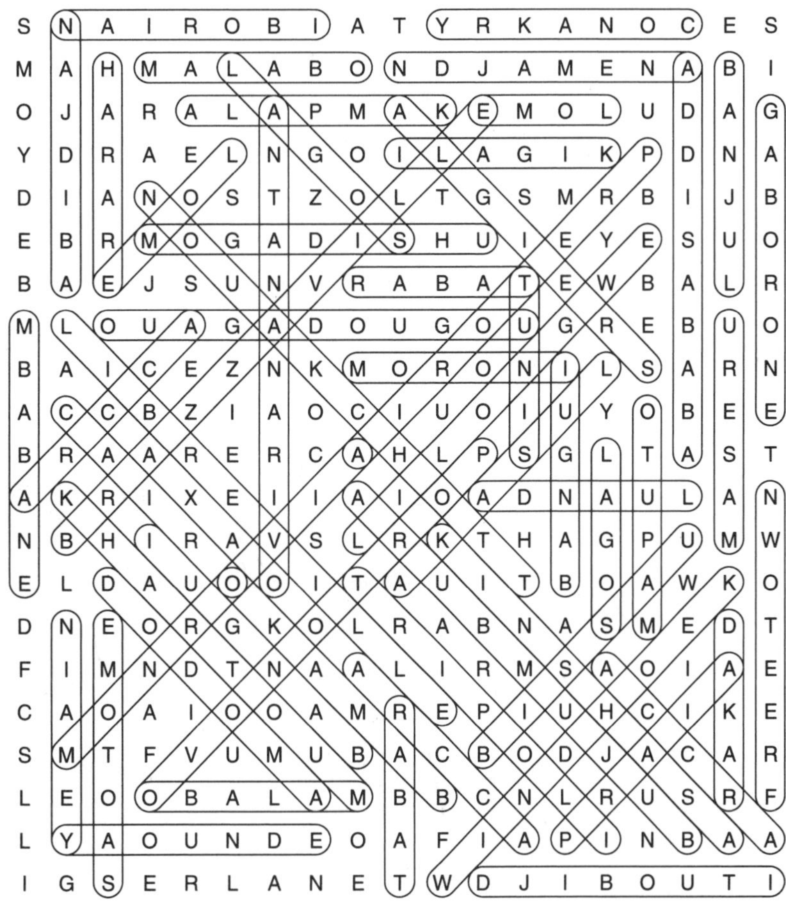

1. Monrovia — Liberia
2. Bamako — Mali
3. Libreville — Gabon
4. Algiers — Algeria
5. Accra — Ghana
6. Kinshasa — Zaire
7. Banjul — Gambia
8. Lagos — Nigeria
9. Brazzaville — Congo
10. Cairo — Egypt
11. Niamey — Niger
12. Porto-Novo — Benin
13. Kampala — Uganda
14. Rabat — Morocco
15. Nairobi — Kenya
16. N'Djamena — Chad
17. Conakry — Guinea
18. Lilongwe — Malawi
19. Tripoli — Libya
20. Lusaka — Zambia
21. Lome — Togo
22. Khartoum — Sudan
23. Kigali — Rwanda
24. Dakar — Senegal
25. Tunis — Tunisia
26. Freetown — Sierra Leone
27. Maputo — Mozambique
28. Bujumbura — Burundi
29. Gaborone — Botswana
30. Nouakchott — Mauritania
31. Ouagadougou — Burkina Faso
32. Harare — Zimbabwe
33. Dodoma — Tanzania
34. Malabo — Equatorial Guinea
35. Mogadishu — Somalia
36. Abidjan — Cote D'Ivoire
37. Windhoek — Namibia
38. Praia — Cape Verde Islands
39. Bissau — Guinea-Bissau
40. Addis Ababa — Ethiopia
41. Mbabane — Swaziland
42. Maseru — Lesotho
43. Moroni — Comoro Islands
44. Yaounde — Cameroon
45. Luanda — Angola
46. Djibouti — Djibouti
47. Antananarivo — Madagascar
48. Pretoria — South Africa
49. Sao Tome — Sao Tome and Principe
50. Bangui — Central African Republic

94. Capital Cities of the World—The Orient

1. DACCA
2. KABUL
3. SINGAPORE
4. HANOI
5. KATMANDU
6. RANGOON
7. KUALA LUMPUR
8. COLOMBO
9. TAIPEI
10. VIENTIANE
11. THIMPHU
12. BEIJING
13. ISLAMABAD
14. ULANBATOR
15. PHNOM PENH
16. NEW DELHI
17. PYONGYANG
18. DJAKARTA
19. MANILA
20. SEOUL
21. BANGKOK
22. TOKYO

CAPITAL CITIES — THE ORIENT

95. Mountains of the World—I

1 FUJI
2 RUSHMORE
3 MATTERHORN
4 WAIALEALE
5 VESUVIUS
6 ARARAT
7 MONTBLANC
8 MAYON
9 COOK
10 APO
11 KILIMANJARO
12 MITCHELL
13 ETNA
14 KOSCIUSKO
15 SNOWDON
16 PICODEANETO
17 LOGAN
18 EVEREST
19 FUJI
20 KOSCIUSKO
21 OLYMPUS
22 MONTBLANC
23 APO
24 MCKINLEY
25 ARARAT
26 SINAI
27 COOK
28 MAUNALOA
29 FUJI
30 LOGAN
31 WRANGELL
32 ELBERT
33 MAYON
34 MULHACEN
35 APO
36 ROBSON
37 STHELENS

96. Mountains of the World—II

Z A G R O S A M Y L O K J O L E N E
N P O N T I C A V A K S A L P S I K
A E S U I S U D N I P U E L E A S U
I N A I R B M A C L O R N G T P Y S
R N H S E A D V A A D U S L L A N K
B I I O L R L E I A U O A A U S I O
A N M R B S R N M T V C Y T E N R K
T E A G U A D A R R A M A E H E A W
N S L A R O R R M N H U N S S R P I
A G A Z Z R R R D O R E D E U O E N
C R Y L E T E E J U R A E J K S N K
R A A I T R S I S Y A E S U U T N E
H M S K O A O S P T S L N R D A I A
O P I N A I H C A L A P P A N N N B
D I S E D N A R K M E H L S I O E E
O A C A R P A T H I A N G A H V S A
P N F O E K E I Z N E K C A M O R T
E K A R A K O R U M T S I N L I N G
G I O N O L B A Y O S U D E T I C E

1. Apennines
2. Caucasus
3. Andes
4. Kjolen
5. Ural
6. Hindu Kush
7. Yablonoi
8. Sierra Madre
9. Cantabrian
10. Zagros
11. Atlas
12. Pennines
13. Carpathian
14. Elburz
15. Grampian
16. Alps
17. Kushokwin
18. Sierra Morena
19. Mackenzie
20. Rockies
21. Guadarrama
22. Vosges
23. Himalayas
24. Pyrenees
25. Appalachian
26. Kunlun
27. Sierra Nevada
28. Cambrian
29. Taebaek
30. Sudetic
31. Ghats
32. Kolyma
33. Ore
34. Sayan
35. Pindus
36. Rhodope
37. Tsinling
38. Altai
39. Pontic
40. Stanovoi
41. Karakorum
42. Arakan
43. Jura
44. Taurus

97. Rivers of the World—I

1. YALU
2. DRAVA
3. VAAL
4. VOLGA
5. GANGES
6. GUADIANA
7. RHINE
8. EBRO
9. MAGDALENA
10. LIMPOPO
11. JHELUM
12. MERSEY
13. DANUBE / DNIEPER
14. NIGER
15. MEUSE
16. RIOGRANDE
17. DON
18. DARLING / DOURO
19. ODER
20. TOBOL
21. EUPHRATES
22. TWEED
23. STLAWRENCE
24. MURRAY
25. URAL
26. ARNO
27. STCROIX
28. ORANGE
29. NILE
30. YENISEY
31. KOLYMA
32. SEINE
33. OKA
34. COLORADO
35. RHONE
36. OB
37. CLYDE
38. ELBE
39. LOIRE
40. ORINOCO
41. INDUS
42. ZAIRE
43. SOMME / SAONE
44. YANGTZE
45. TYNE
46. YUKON
47. JORDAN
48. MARNE
49. TEES
50. SAVA
51. TISZA
52. AMU
53. MAMORE
54. RAVI
55. LENA
56. BUG
57. RUHR
58. XINGU
59. MINO
60. VISTULA
61. RIONEGRO

98. Rivers of the World—II

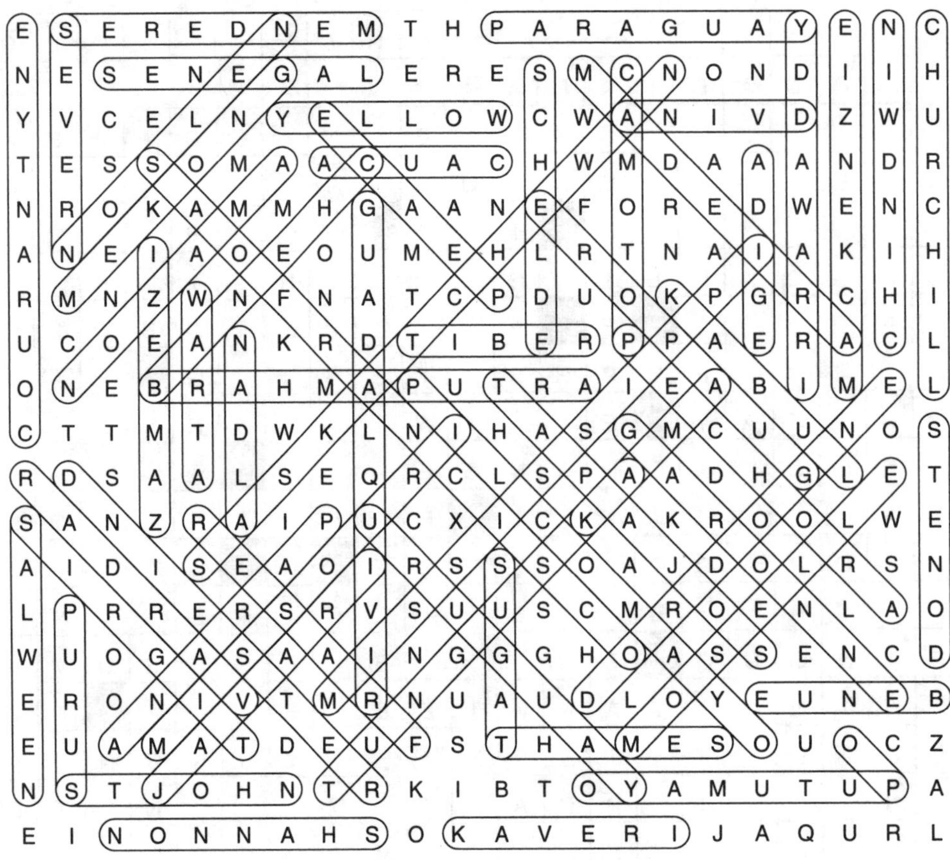

1. Thames
2. Amazon
3. Mekong
4. Madeira
5. Saskatchewan
6. Severn
7. Uruguay
8. Tapajos
9. Menderes
10. Peace
11. Churchill
12. Missouri
13. Potomac
14. Warta
15. Yellow
16. Purus
17. Benue
18. Kabul
19. Tiber
20. Donets
21. Zambezi
22. Tunguska
23. Shannon
24. Aldan
25. Parana
26. St. John
27. Po
28. Sao Francisco
29. Mackenzie
30. Dniester
31. Paraguay
32. Javari
33. Salween
34. Adige
35. Guapore
36. Cauca
37. Fraser
38. Schelde
39. Nelson
40. Pilcomayo
41. Tigris
42. Moselle
43. Irrawaddy
44. Kaveri
45. Dordogne
46. Pechora
47. Courantyne
48. Senegal
49. Tagus
50. Mississippi
51. Dvina
52. Chindwin
53. Brahmaputra
54. Vardar
55. Guadalquivir
56. Main
57. Putumayo
58. Kama
59. Garonne
60. Chenab

99. Popular Places to Visit in the World

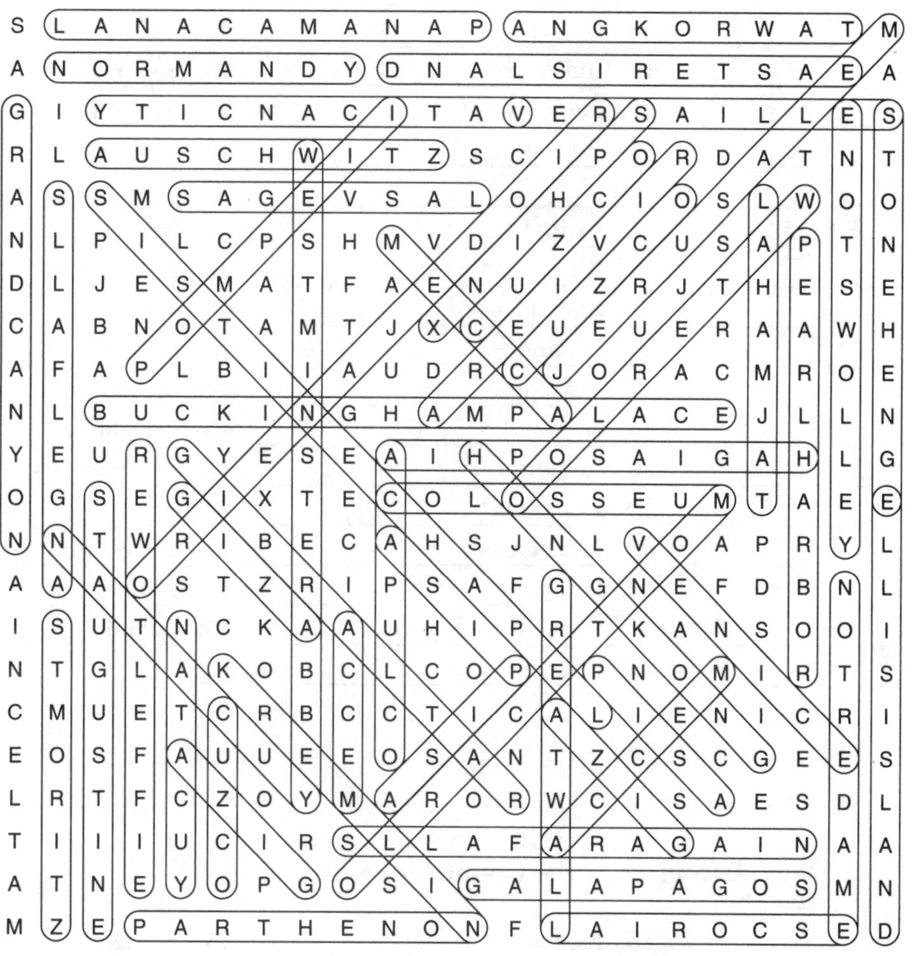

1. Parthenon
2. Eiffel Tower
3. Notre Dame
4. Vatican City
5. Great Wall
6. Pompeii
7. Colosseum
8. Rio de Janeiro
9. Panama Canal
10. Stonehenge
11. Angel Falls
12. Kremlin
13. Auschwitz
14. Mecca
15. Yellowstone
16. Galapagos
17. Venice
18. Normandy
19. St. Augustine
20. Giza
21. Hagia Sophia
22. Monte Carlo
23. Pisa
24. Buckingham Palace
25. Taj Mahal
26. Grand Canyon
27. Sistine Chapel
28. Easter Island
29. Acapulco
30. Sphinx
31. Versailles
32. Yucatan
33. Gibraltar
34. Niagara Falls
35. Jerusalem
36. St. Moritz
37. Angkor Wat
38. Ellis Island
39. Cuzco
40. Hong Kong
41. Las Vegas
42. Waterloo
43. Westminster Abbey
44. Escorial
45. Riviera
46. Pearl Harbor

100. Flags of the Countries of the World—I

1. Cuba
2. Greece
3. Brazil
4. Libya
5. Nepal
6. Australia
7. Rwanda
8. Cameroon
9. France
10. Nigeria
11. Barbados
12. Pakistan
13. Egypt
14. Laos
15. Philippines
16. Algeria
17. Sweden
18. Lesotho
19. India
20. Somalia
21. Bolivia
22. Mali
23. United Kingdom
24. China
25. Sierra Leone
26. Iceland
27. Ethiopia
28. Jordan
29. Romania
30. Bahamas
31. Madagascar
32. Hungary
33. South Korea
34. Chad
35. Israel
36. Monaco
37. Afghanistan
38. Tanzania
39. Dominican Republic
40. New Zealand
41. Benin
42. Jamaica
43. Iraq
44. Spain
45. Angola
46. Luxembourg
47. Syria
48. Congo
49. Turkey
50. Sudan

101. Flags of the Countries of the World—II

1. Canada
2. Italy
3. Finland
4. North Korea
5. Bangladesh
6. Lebanon
7. Honduras
8. Panama
9. Denmark
10. Indonesia
11. Niger
12. Albania
13. Russia
14. Colombia
15. Kuwait
16. Liberia
17. Belgium
18. Mexico
19. Germany
20. Namibia
21. Argentina
22. Lithuania
23. Sri Lanka
24. Bulgaria
25. Senegal
26. Ireland
27. Estonia
28. Japan
29. Norway
30. Austria
31. Singapore
32. Suriname
33. Chile
34. Malaysia
35. Switzerland
36. Bhutan
37. Taiwan
38. Netherlands
39. Togo
40. Andorra
41. Poland
42. Uganda
43. Costa Rica
44. Thailand
45. United States
46. Botswana
47. Vietnam
48. Zimbabwe
49. Tunisia
50. South Africa